Implementing 802.1X Security Solutions for Wired and Wireless Networks

Implementing 802.1X Security Solutions for Wired and Wireless Networks

Jim Geier

Wiley Publishing, Inc.

Implementing 802.1X Security Solutions for Wired and Wireless Networks

Published by
Wiley Publishing, Inc.
10475 Crosspoint Boulevard
Indianapolis, IN 46256
www.wiley.com

Copyright © 2008 by Wireless-Nets, Ltd.

Published by Wiley Publishing, Inc., Indianapolis, Indiana

Published simultaneously in Canada

ISBN: 978-0-470-16860-8

Manufactured in the United States of America

10 9 8 7 6 5 4 3 2 1

*I dedicate this book to Brian and Denise,
my son and daughter-in-law.*

About the Author

Jim Geier is the founder of Wireless-Nets, Ltd., and the company's principal consultant. His 25 years of experience includes the analysis, design, software development, installation, and support of numerous secure wireless network-based systems for municipalities, enterprises, airports, homes, retail stores, manufacturing facilities, warehouses, and hospitals worldwide. Jim is the author of several books, including *Deploying Voice over Wireless LANs* (Cisco Press), *Wireless LANs* (SAMS), *Wireless Networks — First Step* (Cisco Press), *Wireless Networking Handbook* (Macmillan), and *Network Reengineering* (McGraw-Hill). He is the author of numerous tutorials for www.Wi-FiPlanet.com and other publications. Jim has been active within the Wi-Fi Alliance, responsible for certifying interoperability of 802.11 (Wi-Fi) wireless LANs. He has also been an active member of the IEEE 802.11 Working Group, responsible for developing international standards for wireless LANs. He served as Chairman of the IEEE Computer Society, Dayton Section, and Chairman of the IEEE International Conference on Wireless LAN Implementation. He is an advisory board member of several leading wireless LAN companies. Jim's education includes a bachelor's and master's degree in electrical engineering and a master's degree in business administration.

Contact Jim Geier at jimgeier@wireless-nets.com.

Credits

Executive Editor
Carol Long

Senior Development Editor
Tom Dinse

Production Editor
William A. Barton

Copy Editor
Luann Rouff

Editorial Manager
Mary Beth Wakefield

Production Manager
Tim Tate

**Vice President
and Executive Group Publisher**
Richard Swadley

Vice President and Publisher
Joseph B. Wikert

Compositor
Laurie Stewart,
Happenstance Type-O-Rama

Proofreader
Jennifer Larsen, Word One

Indexer
Robert Swanson

Project Coordinator, Cover
Lynsey Stanford

Contents

Introduction

When deploying a wireless or wired network, you must ensure that proper security safeguards are put in place. An enterprise, for example, often has valuable resources stored inside databases that are attached to the network. Using passwords to access specific applications is usually not good enough to keep hackers from accessing the resources in an unauthorized and sometimes crippling manner. In order to adequately protect your network from intruders, you must have mechanisms that utilize proven authentication methods that control access to the network.

The overall framework for providing access control for networks is what's referred to as a *port-based authentication system*, which some people refer to as 802.1X. The main concept of this sort of system is fairly straightforward: You simply verify that the credentials a user provides indicate that the user is authorized to use the network. If so, then you let them have access to the network. If they are not authorized, then you don't let them have access to the network. Conceptually, this isn't any different from how a security guard operates when controlling access to an important facility. Seems like simple stuff, right?

Actually, the control of access to a network involves a host of protocols and standards that are anything but simple. 802.1X is an important component, but several other standards and specifications, written by different organizations, form a complete 802.1X port-based authentication system. As examples, the IEEE standard that applies to port-based authentication is 802.1X, which addresses EAPOL, and the IETC provides RFCs for EAP, EAP-Methods, and RADIUS. All of these standards and specifications are needed to make a port-based authentication system operate. Some people mistakenly think that 802.1X does it all, but actually no single integrated standard specifies all of the components needed to implement a complete port-based authentication system. What makes matters worse is that the port-based authentication components, such as supplicants, authenticator, and authentication servers, have many different configuration settings that must be just right in order for the system to work effectively. The point is that port-based authentication is much more difficult to implement than the definition of simple authentication implies.

How This Book Is Organized

If you're planning to implement 802.1X or a complete port-based authentication system, this book will teach you how everything works and fits together, including how to configure the system and fix problems when they occur. The following important topics covered in this book will save you countless hours:

- Chapter 1, "Network Architecture Concepts": If you're a bit rusty or new to computer network concepts, then you need to read this chapter. It lays the foundation for implementing port-based authentication and will prepare you for getting the most out of this book.

- Chapter 2, "Port-Based Authentication Concepts": This is where it all begins. You'll be amazed by how many components, standards, and specifications play a role in guarding access to a network. This chapter provides a comprehensive but simple explanation of the fairly complex port-based authentication system, paving the way for you to understand the details of the individual elements covered in later chapters.

- Chapter 3, "EAPOL Protocol": Understand the details of how the EAPOL protocol, defined by 802.1X, operates between supplicants and authenticators. EAPOL is the protocol that you must understand in order to ensure proper communications between client devices and network components, such as switches and access points.

- Chapter 4, "RADIUS Protocols": Become knowledgeable about how RADIUS protocols work between authenticators and authentication servers. This is necessary to set up and troubleshoot communications with RADIUS servers.

- Chapter 5, "EAP-Methods Protocol": Learn about the different EAP-Methods, such as EAP-TLS and EAP-TTLS, which provide the communications between supplicants and authentication servers. The EAP-Methods implement specific authentication mechanisms; therefore, you must be able to differentiate them in order to choose the right one to satisfy your requirements.

- Chapter 6, "Configuring Supplicants": Avoid trial and error when configuring your port-based authentication system. This chapter, as well as the other configuration chapters that follow, offers tips based on real-world experiences setting up and maintaining port-based authentication systems. In this chapter, learn how to configure the appropriate supplicants, which operate on client devices, to make the system operate effectively.

- Chapter 7, "Configuring Authenticators": Authenticators, such as access points and switches, provide a function similar to a security gate that controls access to an important facility. This chapter explains how to best configure authenticators to optimize the operation of the port-based authentication system.

- Chapter 8, "Configuring RADIUS": RADIUS is the primary authentication server used in port-based authentication systems. Learn how to configure a RADIUS server to best satisfy your requirements.

- Chapter 9, "Troubleshooting": Because a port-based authentication system is somewhat complex, this chapter will help you avoid common pitfalls when implementing your system.

Who Should Read this Book

This book is perfect for system administrators and network engineers involved with implementing secure information systems. The in-depth explanations of authentication protocols, and the numerous tips spread throughout the book, offer significant value when implementing and supporting 802.1X-based systems. In addition, programmers, students, and instructors gain significant value by reading this book. The simple, systematic descriptions of the relatively difficult 802.1X port-based authentication protocols provide a natural flow for teaching classes and studying the various topics.

If you're new to network architecture and authentication concepts, then you should read the entire book, starting with Chapter 1 and reading all chapters in sequence. If you have a good understanding of network architecture, then you can skip Chapter 1. Those of you who already have a general knowledge of 802.1X port-based authentication can probably get by without reading Chapter 2. If you have any doubt, however, then read the entire book from cover-to-cover.

Summary

802.1X port-based authentication is much more difficult to understand and implement than is commonly thought. In fact, the majority of administrators and engineers have difficulty making these systems work properly. A lack of understanding and experience with 802.1X solutions is primarily why these troubles exist. This book, however, pulls together all of the pertinent standards and specifications, providing the concepts, methods, and tips you need to avoid common pitfalls, saving you a great deal of time and frustration.

Part

I

Concepts

In This Part

Network Architecture Concepts

To fully appreciate the operation of IEEE 802.1X–based solutions, you must have a good understanding of network architecture concepts. It's important to know the component hardware that comprises a network, the layering process used by networking protocols, various IEEE 802 standards, and wireless network issues. This chapter provides an introduction to these basic concepts, which makes the process of learning 802.1X in later chapters much easier. Unless you're a seasoned network professional, you should read this chapter. If it's been awhile since you've covered networking concepts, then spend some time skimming through the chapter, and refresh yourself with the details that you might have forgotten.

Computer Network Defined

A *computer network* enables communications between computer-based client devices, servers, and peripherals to support various applications. Figure 1-1 illustrates a computer network. In terms of the client devices, the network appears as a cloud that provides the interconnection among client devices and servers. In realty, the cloud consists of a network infrastructure that provides routing of data, voice, and video from one point to another.

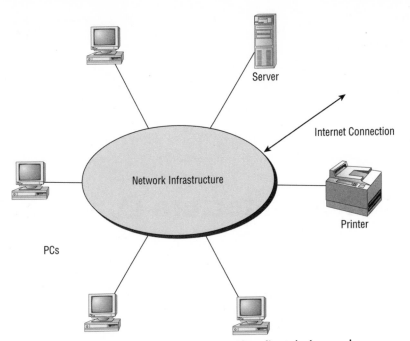

Figure 1-1: Computer network interconnecting client devices and servers

The most common network applications include e-mail, website browsing, file transfer, corporate applications, Internet Protocol (IP) telephony, and video-based security. We're all very familiar with e-mail and browsing the Web. With the use of File Transfer Protocol (FTP) software, you can also move files from one computer to another computer attached to the network. Of course many websites incorporate file-download capabilities for allowing users to download music, application software, and hardware firmware and software upgrades. Many enterprises also use networks to transport voice through the use of voice-over-IP (VoIP). In some cases, companies are making use of the network to interconnect security cameras and other video sources. As this book will explain in detail, IEEE 802.1X port-based security controls access to these applications, which can sometimes be mission-critical.

Network Components

Several basic components make up a computer network. These components include the following:

- Client devices
- Servers
- Network hardware

- Media
- Communications protocols

Client Devices

There are many different network client devices. Most users are familiar with using PCs, laptops, and printers on their network, but IP phones, cameras, game machines, and audio equipment are also becoming more common as client devices for networks. Figure 1-2 includes several examples of network client devices. IEEE 802.1X port-based authentication focuses on either allowing or not allowing client devices to have access to the network.

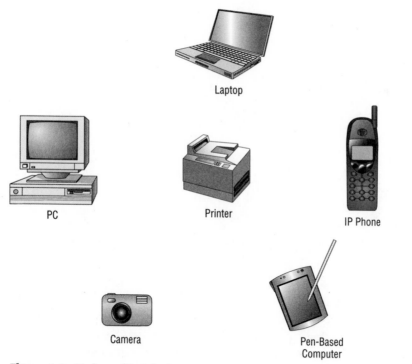

Figure 1-2: Various client devices

Servers

Network servers host application software and databases that users can access on the network. For example, an enterprise may have a warehouse management system that warehouse clerks and managers can access in order to perform inventories, check stock levels, and execute shipping of warehouse items.

In addition, as you'll see in Chapter 2, an authentication server will run *RADIUS* in order to process client devices that are authenticating with the network. A server is a centralized and shared component of the network (see Figure 1-3). As a result, sometimes the network may include multiple servers offering the same functionality in a redundant manner to increase availability by avoiding a single point of failure.

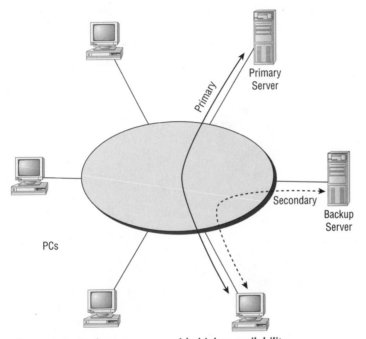

Figure 1-3: Backup servers provide higher availability.

The servers on the network consist of a hardware platform, which can be a PC running an operating system, such as Windows or Linux. The hardware platform includes a processor, memory, and interfaces that meet the performance requirements of the application that the server is supporting. The server hosts the actual application software, which an administrator installs and manages.

NOTE In addition to implementing IEEE 802.1X port-based authentication, administrators should be certain to lock down all administrative ports on servers and deactivate any un-needed utilities that the installation of application software spawns. This prevents a hacker, who is accessing the network servers from an authorized account, from manipulating the system and exploiting the network resources.

Network Hardware

The network hardware comprises the physical network infrastructure. All client devices and servers connect to the network infrastructure. Network hardware includes the following:

- Switches and hubs
- Routers
- Gateways
- Access points
- Network interface cards

Switches and Hubs

Switches and hubs provide wired interconnection points throughout the network infrastructure for the client devices. A switch or hub has multiple ports and implements the IEEE 802.3 standard (Ethernet) and IEEE 802.1 bridge protocols. Each port has a connector for attaching an Ethernet cable that connects to a client device (or other network hardware).

Figure 1-4(a) illustrates the function of a switch, which is slightly different than a hub. A switch, which implements what's referred to as *switched Ethernet*, connects a device on one port directly with another device on a different port. This connection doesn't preclude devices connected to other ports from communicating with the switch and forming connections with other devices. After the connection between two devices is made inside the switch, other devices can contend for connections.

A switch offers much faster performance than a hub, as Figure 1-4(b) depicts. When a device connected to a port on a hub connects a device connected to a different port on the same hub, the devices connected to the other ports on the hub can't communicate with the hub and form other connections. All devices interfacing with the ports on a hub, except the two already connected with each other, are blocked. As a result, most enterprises use switches.

In general, switches are relatively simple devices. They forward data, including multicast packets, throughout the network based on the Media Access Control (MAC) address that each packet is carrying. The MAC address is the actual physical address that the network devices respond to, similar to the number and street address of your home or office.

NOTE Some servers and applications periodically transmit broadcast packets, and switches forward these packets through, which can sometimes cause unnecessary traffic on the network.

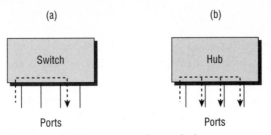

Figure 1-4: Ethernet switch vs. a hub

Routers

A router is a bit more sophisticated than a switch or hub. Routers actually route packets through a network infrastructure, as Figure 1-5 illustrates, based on the IP address carried within each packet. The IP address corresponds to the addressing that many applications respond to. As packets flow into one particular port, the router will make a decision on which outbound port to use—that is, the one that will move the packet closest to the intended destination. A *routing protocol* keeps track of which outbound ports provide optimum routing and maintains this information in a routing table. The router simply looks at the destination IP addresses the packet is carrying and looks up this destination in the routing table. The routing table contains an outbound port entry for each possible destination.

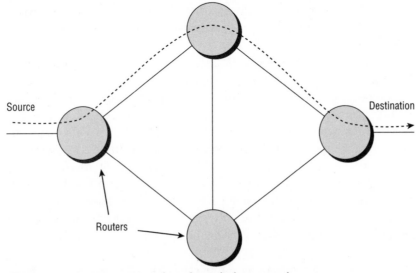

Figure 1-5: Routers route packets through the network.

An enterprise network infrastructure will generally consist of switches at the edge of the network, interfacing client devices to the network, and routers that interconnect groups of switches into separate subnets. This organization increases performance and eases management of the system.

Access Points

Wireless networks use access points to create a radio cell where wireless client devices can associate with the access point, which enables the wireless client devices to send and receive data over the wireless network. An enterprise or city will often have dozens, hundreds, or even thousands of access points installed at locations so that the radio cells of adjacent access points overlap slightly. The multiple overlapping radio cells create continuous signal coverage so that wireless client devices can roam from an area covered by one access point to an area covered by a different access point.

With access points, the flow of traffic between one wireless client and another wireless client associated with the same access point must flow through the access point, as shown in Figure 1-6. Traffic flowing from a wireless client and another network device connected to the network infrastructure flows through the access point as well. As with switches and hubs, access points implement the IEEE 802.1 bridge protocols.

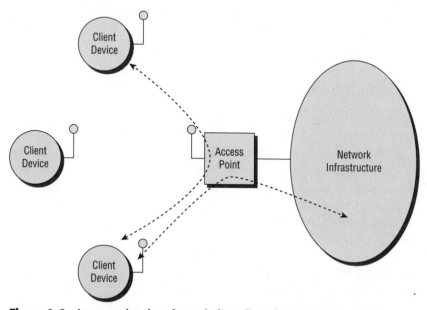

Figure 1-6: Access points interface wireless client devices to the network.

Access points are similar to hubs, except that the connections made with the client devices are wireless. Thus, an access point translates between wireless network protocols and wired network protocols. With IEEE 802.11 access points, multiple client devices can associate with a single access point at the same time, but, similar to the hub, only a single client device (or the access point) can transmit at any given time.

A switch or hub interconnects multiple access points to form a wireless network infrastructure. Each access point connects to a different wired port on the switch or hub. In most cases, the port provides Power over Ethernet (PoE) for supplying electrical power to the access point. Electrical wiring does not need to be installed at each access point location—all that's necessary is an Ethernet cable that connects the access points, limited to approximately 300 feet.

Some access points also include routing functions, and are commonly referred to as wireless routers. A wireless router is suited for home or small office applications where it's beneficial to have a wireless local area network (LAN) provided by a single device that connects to the Internet via a digital subscriber line (DSL) or cable modem. The wireless router performs the functions of an access point and also includes Dynamic Host Configuration Protocol (DHCP) and Network Address Translation (NAT). This enables the wireless network to use a single official IP address provided by the Internet service provider (ISP) for multiple client devices.

NOTE To maximize interoperability throughout an 802.1X system, be sure to keep the firmware up-to-date on all network hardware.

Network Interface Cards

Network interface cards (NICs), also referred to as client cards or network adapters, interface the client device (and other network devices) to the network. For example, you can interface a laptop to a wireless network by installing an 802.11 PC Card in the laptop. The NIC is the actual network connection, addressable by a MAC address. The following sections describe each of the various NIC form factors, which defines the physical interface between the network card and the computer.

ISA

The Industry Standard Architecture (ISA) bus is the most common bus interface in the desktop PC world. ISA has been around since the early '80s for use in the IBM PC/XT and PC/AT. Because of this, the proliferation of the ISA has been significant. Despite its lack of speed (2 Mbps), nearly all PCs manufactured up until several years ago had at least one ISA bus. The ISA bus has failed, however, to advance at the pace of the rest of the computer world, and other higher speed alternatives are now available. ISA doesn't impose too much of a performance impact on IEEE 802.11b wireless LANs, but it's not advisable to purchase new ISA cards because they may become obsolete.

PCI

The Peripheral Component Interconnect (PCI) bus is the most popular bus interface for PCs today and boasts a throughput rate of 264 Mbps. Intel originally developed and released PCI in 1993, and it satisfies the needs of most recent generations of PCs for multimedia, graphics, and networking cards.

PCI cards were the first to popularize Plug and Play (PnP) technology. PCI circuitry recognizes compatible PCI cards and then works with the computer's operating system to set the resource allocations for each card. This helps save time and prevents installation headaches.

PC Card

Developed in the early '90s by the Personal Computer Memory Card International Association (PCMCIA), the PC Card is a peripheral device (about the size of a credit card) that can provide extended memory, modems, connectivity to external devices, and, of course, wireless LAN capabilities to laptops. PC Cards are the most widely available cards for portable devices, such as laptops. In fact, they are more popular than ISA or PCI cards because of a growing usage of laptops.

If you want to share a PC Card with your desktop PC, consider using an adaptor that converts a PC Card into a PCI card. This allows you to purchase one card for use in both types of computers. You can take the PC Card on your business trips or home from work and use the same card when you're back in your office on a PC.

Mini-PCI

A Mini-PCI card is a small version of a standard desktop PCI card. It has all the same features and functionality of a normal PCI card, but it's about one quarter the size. Mini-PCI cards are integrated within laptops as an option to buyers, with antennas that are often integrated within the monitor's case or even next to the LCD screen. A strong advantage of this form of radio NIC is that it frees up the PC Card slot for other devices. In addition, manufacturers can provide Mini-PCI–based wireless connectivity at lower costs.

CF

SanDisk Corporation first introduced CompactFlash (CF) in 1994, but wireless LAN radio cards were not available in CF form until recently. A CF card is very small—it weighs half an ounce and is less than half the thickness and one quarter the volume of a PC Card radio card. The CF cards also draw very little power, which enables batteries to last longer than on devices that use PC Cards. Some PDAs (Personal Digital Assistants) come with direct CF interfaces, which results in a very lightweight and compact wireless PDA. A CF radio card is definitely the way to go, especially for compact computing devices.

NOTE Consider using a CF-to-PC Card adapter to operate the CF card in a laptop via a PC Card slot. This enables you to take advantage of the miniature radio card in the PDA and not have to purchase another card for your laptop.

Media

The media in a network interconnects all of the network components. Networks use the following types of media:

- Wire
- Optical fiber
- Air

Metallic Wire

The use of metallic wires is the most common method for interconnecting components. When computer networks first came into existence, most network wiring was coaxial cable, which was bulky and difficult to install. Conventional network wiring today consists of *twisted pair cabling*, with the most common being Category 5 twisted pair. Digital data, video, and voice signals in the form of electrical current run through the wires. Twisted pair cabling can support data rates into the Gigabit per second (Gbps) range. IEEE 802.3 (Ethernet) specifies the use of twisted pair wiring.

The flow of electrical current through metallic wires, such as Category 5 twisted pair cabling, creates an electromagnetic field around the wire. With sensitive listening equipment, a hacker could sense this field from several feet away from the wiring and possibly decode the applicable data. However, this would generally require the hacker to gain access to the facility—eavesdropping on a wired network from outside the building would be difficult, if not impossible.

Nearly all businesses have Category 5 cabling running throughout facilities, with end points (network taps) located in most offices. The cables run from each office to one of several wiring closets located in a facility. The wiring closets house the switches. The range of Category 5 cabling is limited to less than approximately 300 feet. The wiring closets are where the company places switches and other network equipment. Generally, a higher-speed backbone interconnects the switches located in the wiring closets as shown in Figure 1-7.

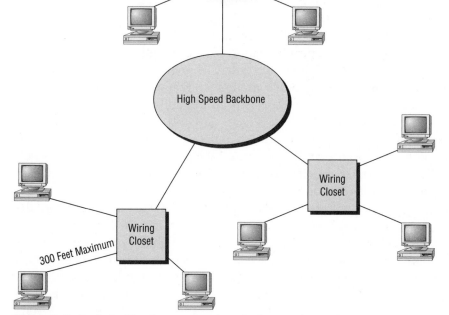

Figure 1-7: Typical wiring in an enterprise wired network

Optical Fiber

Optical fiber cabling consists of strands of glass that conduct light efficiently from one end to the other. The advantage of optical fiber as compared to metallic wiring is that fiber supports much higher data rates (up to tera bits per second), doesn't emit electromagnetic fields, and operates over a relatively long range. Thus, optical fiber makes the system more secure and supports higher-speed delivery of information. In addition, optical fiber is practical for providing high-speed connections between buildings throughout cities. An issue with optical fiber, though, is that is relatively expensive to install for each client device inside a company. In some cases, however, especially where client devices are beyond the 300-feet range from a wiring closet, optical fiber may be the only way to connect the clients.

Air

Air is the medium for wireless systems, which make use of radio waves or infrared light for transporting data, video, and voice signals. Radio waves, generally in the 2.4-GHz or higher frequencies, are the most common signaling for wireless networks. Most of the IEEE 802 standards (such as 802.11a, 802.11b, 802.11g, 802.11n, 802.15, and 802.16) use radio waves. There is an infrared version of 802.11, but there are very few, if any, implementations.

An issue with using air as a medium is that obstacles get in the way. A building will certainly have walls between wireless client devices and access points. In outdoor environments, trees and buildings fall in the path of radio and light signals. Radio waves can travel through most materials, with varying attenuation. Infrared light doesn't penetrate most obstacles it encounters. Thus, when installing wireless systems, you must carefully analyze the environment, and design the system to accommodate attenuation that occurs between the client devices and the access points. This can be difficult to accomplish, because obstacles may change position.

Electromagnetic signal sources, such as microwave ovens, other wireless systems, and even sunspot activity can impact the performance of a wireless network. These sources of interference can be sporadic and unpredictable, which may affect the network's ability to meet specified service levels. As a result, client-device connectivity may be interrupted from time to time and disrupt the data flow and protocol operation between the clients and the network.

Infrared light can't be seen by humans in most lighting conditions, but it's free from electromagnetic interference and can operate at relatively high data rates over a range of one to two miles. Cities will often implement a point-to-point infrared system to interconnect buildings, rather than undertake an expensive cable installation.

Network Types

There are several different types of computer networks, categorized primarily by the size of the area that the network operates. The following sections explain each type of network.

Personal Area Networks

A *personal area network* (PAN) connects computer devices within a relatively small area, such as in the immediate vicinity of a person's body. Figure 1-8 illustrates a PAN. A PAN may require wires for connecting the devices, or connectivity may be wireless. For example, a wired PAN may consist of a smart phone connected to a laptop via a USB cable, and headphones wired to the audio output jack on the laptop. A wireless PAN, however, may connect a phone, laptop, and headphones wirelessly. Both wired and wireless PANs allow users to listen to music streaming from a laptop or use a contact manager on the laptop to place telephone calls. Or, a person may use a PAN to connect their smart phone to a PC to synchronize contacts, schedules, and tasks.

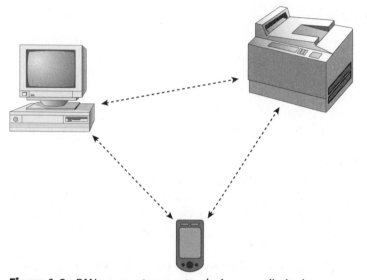

Figure 1-8: PANs connect computer devices over limited areas.

REDUCING CABLES AND IMPROVING CONVENIENCE WITH A WIRELESS PAN

Ralph purchases a new smart phone that includes a Bluetooth radio. After synchronizing the phone with a PC in his office a few times, he finds that the cable is too cumbersome. In order to make the synchronization process go smoother, he creates a wireless PAN.

Ralph purchases a Bluetooth dongle that attaches to the USB port on the PC. This allows the smart phone to synchronize with the PC without connecting a cable. In fact, he sets the phone to automatically synchronize every few minutes. With this configuration, Ralph doesn't have to remember to attach a cable and synchronize his phone before leaving his office. The phone keeps up-to-date wirelessly while sitting on the desk or holster. After Ralph gets this working, he discovers that he can add a wireless ear pod to his wireless PAN in order to listen to music streaming from his PC or phone. He uses this setup for hands-free operation of his phone while driving a car.

Most PAN networking technologies, such as IEEE 802.15 (Bluetooth wireless PAN) and other proprietary technologies, provide point-to-point network connectivity. In fact, many of the Bluetooth wireless dongles attach to a USB port on a PC or laptop and interface two devices, such as a PC and smart phone, via a serial port. In this manner, the wireless dongle is merely replacing the serial cable with a wireless connection.

Local Area Networks

A *local area network* (LAN) connects computer devices that span the size of a building or college campus. An enterprise facility or hospital will likely have a LAN that connects PCs and corporate servers. A warehouse clerk, for example, may use a PC connected to a LAN to find the status of received goods or set up a shipping transaction. In addition, a LAN will generally connect to the Internet, allowing users of the LAN to browse websites and send e-mail to users who are not connected to the LAN.

Figure 1-7 depicts a wired LAN. Nearly all companies and organizations have wired LANs, which are generally based on IEEE 802.3 (Ethernet) technologies. With Ethernet, users' computer devices connect to the network via an Ethernet cable. Ethernet is very common because it's been in existence for over 20 years. You'll find wired Ethernet LANs in nearly all facilities, such as enterprises, hospitals, and universities.

One issue with wired LANs is that they require users to operate their computers from stationary locations. This isn't much of a problem with most PCs, mainly because of their size. You simply plug a PC in to the Ethernet network and don't move it unless you're moving from one office to another. PCs don't usually need the benefits of mobility that wireless connectivity offers, except for some unique and relatively uncommon applications. For example, in an elementary school that has limited funding and can only purchase one PC for multiple classrooms, the PC can be placed on a rolling cart and be wirelessly interfaced to the network—enabling teachers to easily move the PC from classroom to classroom for effective sharing.

IEEE 802.11 wireless LANs are beginning to become more commonplace in businesses and homes. For facilities that already have wired LANs, adding wireless connectivity through a wireless LAN extends networking to areas not covered by the wired LAN (such as warehouses) and offers mobility for users (see Figure 1-9). In addition, some facility owners and managers elect to install a wireless LAN instead of wired Ethernet as the primary network for the entire facility. This isn't too common, however.

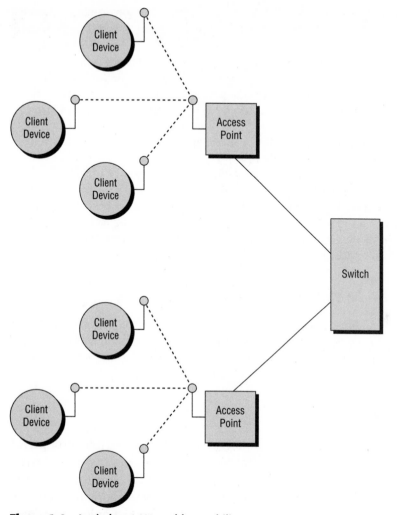

Figure 1-9: A wireless LAN enables mobility.

NOTE Wi-Fi, which stands for *Wireless Fidelity*, was created by the Wi-Fi Alliance based on IEEE 802.11 standards. The Wi-Fi Alliance requires that products undergo interoperability testing with other vendor products in order to bear the Wi-Fi logo.

**ADDING WIRELESS CONNECTIVITY TO AN EXISTING WIRED LAN
TO SUPPORT WIRELESS IP PHONES**

A major hospital in the Midwestern United States already has a wired Ethernet
network with a LAN that supports hundreds of PCs throughout the hospital.
The existing system does a great job of supporting e-mail and remote access to
applications, but doctors, nurses, and administrative staff can benefit by having
mobile phones. Dependence on wired phones often causes significant delays in
coordinating patient care as a result of the "telephone tag" that happens when
staff are only sporadically near a phone.

As a result, the hospital deployed a wireless LAN throughout its facilities to
support wireless IP phones. This was a much less costly alternative to paying
for cellular service within the hospital. With mobile phones, the hospital is able
to react much faster to patient emergencies. In addition, the deployment of the
wireless LAN puts the hospital in a position to use other wireless applications,
such as electronic patient records.

Metropolitan Area Networks

A *metropolitan area network* (MAN) provides network connectivity over the area
of an entire city or metropolitan area. For cities such as Houston and Los Angeles, a MAN can span hundreds of square miles. In other places, such as smaller
cities, a MAN may cover only a few square miles.

Optical Fiber Infrastructure

Many local governments have optical fiber installed under streets throughout
most of their downtown areas. This fiber infrastructure is in place to provide
reliable high-speed connections between various buildings throughout the
city. Fiber taps are available in many locations to facilitate interfacing network
equipment that may operate at a particular location. For example, some cities
connect wireless access points or mesh nodes to the fiber taps and make use of
the existing fiber infrastructure to provide network connectivity. Or, the fiber
infrastructure may carry network traffic from inside a building, such as city
hall, to a centralized data center for connection to the Internet.

Wi-Fi Mesh

Many municipalities are installing *Wi-Fi mesh* networks to provide wireless
connectivity for mobile Wi-Fi–equipped client devices. For example, a city may
deploy a mesh network to support wireless public-safety applications or wireless work-order processing. In addition, a municipal Wi-Fi network can provide public Internet access throughout the city.

Figure 1-10 illustrates the physical architecture of a Wi-Fi mesh network. A mesh node is similar to a wireless access point—it offers a Wi-Fi interface to client devices based on the IEEE 802.11 protocol. However, unlike access points, mesh nodes don't require a cable that connects the node to a switch. Instead, each mesh node is capable of receiving packets from a wireless client device and forwarding the packets to another mesh node. The mesh nodes implement a routing mechanism that moves packets toward a mesh node with a link back to a central connection point. Some of the mesh nodes are also gateways, which generally use a point-to-point radio link (called *backhaul*) that connects the gateway to the central point. For client devices connecting to a mesh node (not a gateway), a data packet hops from one mesh node to another mesh node until the packet arrives at a gateway, which then sends the packet directly to the central point.

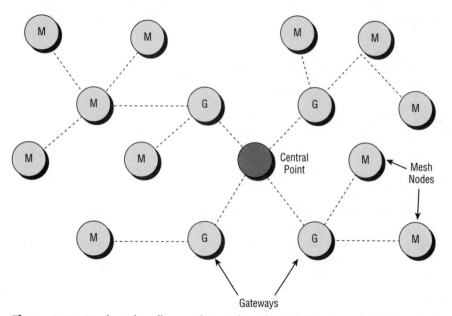

Figure 1-10: Mesh nodes allow packets to hop through the network without wires.

WiMAX

WiMAX (which stands for *Worldwide Interoperability for Microwave Access*) is a relatively new specification issued by the WiMAX Forum for providing wireless network connectivity within metropolitan areas. WiMAX is based on the IEEE 802.16 standard. The most current version of the standard, IEEE 802.16-2005, addresses both fixed and mobile wireless connectivity. Many of the WiMAX deployments to-date use licensed frequency spectrum. For example, Sprint Nextel is in the process of deploying mobile WiMAX in many major U.S. cities. Some cities that deploy Wi-Fi mesh networks make use of fixed WiMAX for connecting mesh nodes (gateways) to central points in the system. As more and more client devices become equipped with WiMAX, it may eventually replace Wi-Fi as the technology of choice for wireless MANs.

Wide Area Networks

Wide area networks (WANs) cover very large areas, sometime the entire globe. Companies with offices spread throughout a nation or the entire world can make use of a WAN to interconnect the individual networks in offices. The Internet is actually a WAN that many companies depend on every day for supporting e-mail, file transfer, and access to remote applications. In some cases, a company may create a private WAN. For example, a retail company may link all of its stores to a central data center. Every night, each of the stores can upload sales data and download changes, such as price updates. WANs make use of long-haul leased terrestrial or satellite links.

Logical Network Architecture

As discussed earlier in this chapter, a computer network consists of various hardware components, including client devices such as PCs, laptops, servers, switches, routers, and media. Up until now, this chapter addressed the network as a physical entity. In order to fully understand how the protocols work and interoperate, it's advantageous to examine a network based on its logical architecture. This view of the network is based on the classic seven-layer *Open Systems Interconnection (OSI) reference model* shown in Figure 1-11.

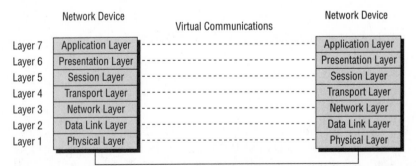

Figure 1-11: The OSI reference model offers seven layers of functionality.

Each layer of the model represents specific functions. A network may not implement all of the possible functions, but the model covers most of them. Each layer of the model does work for the layer above and doesn't care what happened at lower layers. In fact, each layer has no idea that lower layers are doing anything. In some cases, standards (such as IEEE 802.3 and IEEE 802.11) will subdivide layers of the OSI model into multiple sublayers as well.

The following explains the purpose of each layer:

- **Layer 7, Application Layer**: The application layer provides basic user applications, such as e-mail and file transfer. Simple Mail Transfer Protocol (SMTP) and File Transfer Protocol (FTP) are examples of Application Layer protocols.

- **Layer 6, Presentation Layer**: The Presentation Layer provides syntax for network entities to communicate.

- **Layer 5, Session Layer**: The Session Layer manages the flow of data between network entities.

- **Layer 4, Transport Layer**: The Transport Layer establishes and maintains end-to-end connections between network entities. Transmission Control Protocol (TCP) is an example of a Transport Layer protocol.

- **Layer 3, Network Layer**: The Network Layer provides routing throughout the network for data packets going from one network entity to another. The Internet Protocol (IP) is an example of a Network Layer protocol.

- **Layer 2, Data Link Layer**: The Data Link Layer establishes and maintains link-level connections between network devices, such as the link between an Ethernet card and an Ethernet switch. The IEEE 802 standards (such as 802.3 and 802.11) implement Data Link Layer functions.

- **Layer 1, Physical Layer**: The Physical Layer defines the electrical and mechanical specifications of the interface between network devices. For example, IEEE 802.11g is a Physical Layer standard that specifies the use of radio waves at 2.4 GHz.

NOTE The IEEE 802.1X and related standards apply to only Layer 2, the Data Link Layer.

Each specific OSI layer provides communications, relevant to its specific functions, between network entities. However, this is virtual rather than direct communication—the lower layers encapsulate data from layers above and deliver the encapsulated data to the opposite network entity. Chapter 2 explains this encapsulation process as it applies to 802.1X.

IEEE 802 Standards

The IEEE 802 standards play a big role in 802.1X port-based authentication systems. 802.1X is certainly part of the 802 standards. In addition, 802.3 and 802.11 are very important because they carry the authentication traffic.

Figure 1-12 illustrates the logical network model for the 802 standards. In general, 802.1, which includes 802.1X, provides overall network architecture for LANs, network management, internetworking between 802 LANs, and overall 802 security. 802.2, Logical Link Control (LLC), provides functionality similar to Layer 2, the Data Link Layer, of the OSI reference model. The Medium Access Control (MAC) enables multiple client devices to share a common medium, such as twisted pair cabling or a radio signal through the air. The 802.3 (Ethernet) and 802.11 (Wi-Fi) standards both define a MAC Layer. The Physical Layer (PHY) performs the actual transmission and reception of data. 802.3 100Base-T and 802.11g are PHY standards.

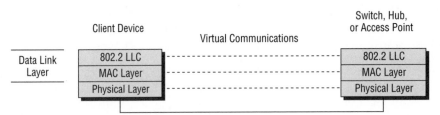

Figure 1-12: IEEE 802 logical architecture

There are several 802.3 PHY standards, which include various implementations of twisted pair wiring (10Base-T, 100Base-T, 1000Base-T) and fiber cabling. The 802.11 PHY standards include the following:

- **802.11a**: 5-GHz frequency band with data rates up to 54 Mbps; not compatible with 802.11b or 802.11g.

- **802.11b**: 2.4-GHz frequency band with data rates up to 11Mbps.

- **802.11g**: 2.4-GHz frequency band with data rates up to 54Mbps; backward compatible with 802.11b.

- **802.11n**: 2.4-GHz frequency band with data rates up to 100 Mbps; backward compatible with 802.11b and 802.11g.

Wireless Impairments

You should be familiar with the following wireless impairments when deploying 802.1X port-based authentication systems:

- Roaming delays
- Coverage holes
- Radio frequency (RF) interference

Roaming Delays

Wireless networks provide mobility that requires client devices to roam from one access point to another access point as the user moves about a facility or city. The Wi-Fi NIC in a client device periodically scans the immediate area for access points. When certain conditions are met, such as when the currently associated access point has relatively low signal strength and there are excessive data frame retransmissions, the client device NIC will initiate roaming from the currently associated access point to an access point with stronger signal strength. The client device re-associates with the new access point, and all corresponding data traffic is redirected through the new access point. Figure 1-13 illustrates the roaming process.

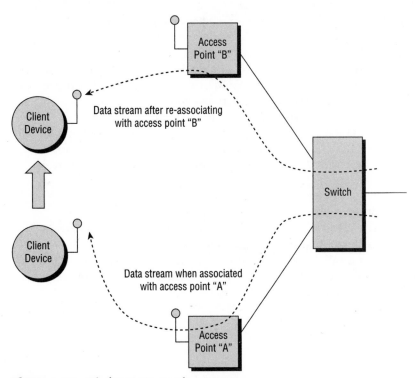

Figure 1-13: Wireless LAN roaming process

Ideally, this doesn't impede the flow of data between the client device and the network. The problem, however, is that some wireless NICs incorporate rather lengthy delays when roaming. This can wreak havoc on port-based authentication because some systems require the client device to re-authenticate at every newly associated access point. The roaming delays caused by the client device NIC may interrupt and even disrupt 802.1X authentication protocols, unless 802.1X configurations compensate for the delays.

REAL-WORLD ROAMING ON WIRELESS LANS

An extremely beneficial aspect of Wi-Fi networks is mobility. For example, a person can walk through a facility while carrying on a conversation over a Wi-Fi phone or when downloading a large file from a server. Ideally, the Wi-Fi radio inside the user device automatically roams from one access point to another as needed to provide seamless connectivity. But is this what really happens?

In the past, I've experienced issues with roaming, so I decided to perform some testing. I was especially curious about how fast roaming actually works and whether or not it's disruptive to wireless applications.

My test configuration included two access points: one access point (AP-1) set to channel 1, and the other access point (AP-2) set to channel 6. Other settings were default values, such as a beacon interval of 100 milliseconds, RTS/CTS disabled, and so on. The access points were installed in a typical office facility in a manner that provided a minimum of 25dB signal-to-noise ratio throughout each access point's radio cell, with about 20-percent overlap between cells. This is somewhat the industry standard for wireless voice applications. The roaming client in my case, though, was a laptop equipped with an internal Centrino Wi-Fi radio (Intel PRO/Wireless 2915ABG).

While standing with the wireless client within a few feet of AP-1, I used an AirMagnet Laptop Analyzer (via another Wi-Fi card inserted into the laptop's PCMCIA slot) to ensure that that I was associated with AP-1. I then kicked off an FTP transfer of a large file from the server to the laptop and started measuring the 802.11 packet trace using the AirMagnet Laptop Analyzer. With the file downloading throughout the entire test, I walked toward AP-2 until I was directly next to it. With the packet trace, I was able to view the exchange of 802.11 frames, calculate the roaming delay, and see if there was any significant disruption to the FTP stream.

After the client radio decided to re-associate, it issued several 802.11 disassociation frames to AP-1 to initiate the re-association process. The radio then broadcasted an 802.11 probe request to get responses from access points within range of the wireless client. This is likely done to ensure that the client radio has up-to-date information (beacon signal strength) of candidate access points prior to deciding which one to re-associate with.

AP-2 responded with an 802.11 probe response. Because the only response was from AP-2, the client radio card decided to associate with AP-2. As expected, the association process with AP-2 consisted of the exchange of 802.11 authentication and association frames (based on 802.11 open system authentication).

The re-association process took 68 milliseconds, which is the time between the client radio issuing the first dissociation frame to AP-1 and the client receiving the final association frame (response) from AP-2. This is quite good, and I've found similar values with other vendor access points.

The entire roaming process, however, will interrupt wireless applications for a much longer period of time. For example, based on my tests, the FTP process halts an average of five seconds prior to the radio card initiating the re-association process (issuing the first disassociation frame to AP-1). I measured 802.11 packet traces, indicating that the client radio card re-retransmits data frames many times to AP-1 (due to weak signal levels) before giving up and initiating the re-association with AP-2. This substantial number of retransmissions disrupted the file download process, which makes the practical roaming delay in my tests an average of five seconds. The Centrino radio card I tested is notorious for this problem, but I've found this to be the case with most other radio cards as well.

Vendors are likely having the radio cards hold off re-associations to avoid premature and excessive re-associations (access point hopping). Unfortunately, this disrupts some wireless applications. If you plan to deploy mobile wireless applications, then be sure to test how the roaming impacts the applications.

Every model radio card will behave differently when roaming due to proprietary mechanisms, and some cards will do better than others. Just keep in mind that roaming may take much longer than expected, so take this into account when deploying wireless LAN applications—especially wireless voice, which is not tolerant of roaming delays that exceed 100 milliseconds.

Coverage Holes

Changes made inside the facility after the initial wireless LAN is installed may alter radio frequency (RF) signal propagation. For example, a company may construct a wall, which offers significant attenuation that wasn't there before. Or, a thorough site survey may not have been done prior to installing the network. These situations often result in areas of the facility having limited or no RF signal coverage, which decreases the performance and disrupts the operation of wireless applications. In addition, the coverage holes, similar to roaming delays, may disrupt 802.1X port-based authentication system protocols, which can lead to some pesky issues. Figure 1-14 illustrates coverage holes.

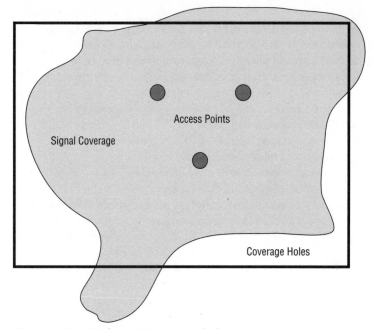

Figure 1-14: Wireless LAN coverage holes

Indications of a coverage hole include low signal-level (less than –75 dBm) and high retry rates (greater than 10 percent), regardless of noise levels. The signal in this situation is so low that the receiver in the radio card has difficulties recovering the data, which triggers retransmissions, excessive overhead, and low throughput. For example, a user will likely experience a 75 percent drop in throughput when operating from an area that has low signal levels.

To counter coverage holes, you need to improve the signal strength in the affected areas. Try increasing the transmit power, replacing the antennas with ones that have higher gain, or moving access points around to better cover the area. Keep coverage holes from popping up unexpectedly in the future by performing a periodic RF site survey, possibly every few months.

In a wireless LAN, a wireless client connects to an access point, and communication takes place between the client and the access point as the user browses the Internet, sends and receives e-mail, and/or talks to someone on a wireless IP phone. This communication includes an uplink path from the client to the access point and a downlink path from the access point to the client. For example, when a user opens their browser, the client device sends a URL page request through the uplink path to the access point. Then, the web pages are sent through the access point to the client over the downlink path. Another example is when a person—let's call her Mary—is talking on a wireless IP phone to another person—we'll call him Bob. In this case, Mary's voice packets flow over the uplink path from her IP phone to the access point, and Bob's voice packets eventually travel over the downlink path from the access point to Mary's phone. At least this is what we hope occurs—otherwise, none of these applications will work properly.

Access points periodically send beacons, which travel over the downlink path from the access to the client devices. Most Wi-Fi site survey tools receive these beacons and display the signal strength and signal-to-noise ratio (SNR) associated with the beacon signals. A person performing an RF site survey determines the optimum installation location for access points by using the beacon signal strength to determine where adequate coverage is provided. For example, you might define the target range boundary to be 20dB SNR. You then use a test tool to ensure that there is at least 20dB or better SNR throughout the covered area. Keep in mind, however, that this is only in relation to the downlink path. It doesn't take into consideration the uplink signals from the client devices.

Something to consider is that most access points have a significantly higher transmit power compared to wireless clients. Access points, for example, are typically set to their highest transmit power, which may be 100mW. This is done to seemingly maximize the signal propagation and coverage from each access point in order to minimize the number and costs of access points. Wireless clients, though, tend to have a much lower effective transmit power to conserve battery power. In this situation, the downlink signal strength will be relatively high, and the uplink signals will be much weaker. This means that the effective range between the access point and the client device is governed by the uplink signal strength. As a result, the use of only access point beacons (downlink signals) for determining coverage will indicate much better coverage than what will actually be available when the clients interact with the access point. The downlink communications will be fine, but weaker uplink signals will limit the effective range and likely disrupt communications when client devices move into areas where uplink signal strength is not good enough to support communications. Figure 1-15 illustrates the uplink and downlink paths. If the client device had a higher transmit power, then the client device could go farther away from the access point and still maintain communications with the access point.

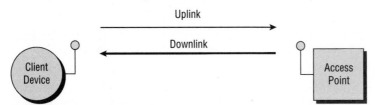

Figure 1-15: Downlink transmit power is generally greater than the uplink transmit power of client devices.

You can avoid falling into this trap with the following safeguard measures:

- **Base range measurements on the weaker uplink signal.** If the effective transmit power of the client device is lower than the access point that you plan to use in the deployment, or the signal strength of the client device at the access point (viewed by logging into the access point) is lower than the signal strength of the access point beacons at the client device (measured by the client device or signal measurement tool located next to the client device), you'll need to take the uplink signal into consideration when performing signal coverage testing. Be sure to use the weaker wireless client if the network will support multiple client devices.

- **Perform signal testing by measuring the uplink signals.** To do this, you measure a client's uplink signal strength as you walk with the device throughout the covered area. Of course you'll need to login to the access point, probably with a wireless laptop (through a web browser), to view the signal values. In addition, you'll need to periodically have the client device send something to the access point and refresh the access point display to see signal updates as you move the client device about the facility. In some cases, the weaker client device and the laptop will be the same device.

- **Consider turning down the transmit power of the access points.** If you want to maximize performance, then consider adjusting the transmit power of the access point to balance the uplink and downlink signal strengths. You can do this by turning the transmit power down to a value that makes the downlink equal to the uplink signal strength. This will increase the density of access points and increase costs due to a larger number of access points required to cover an area—but it may improve performance because of higher capacity. Fewer users will associate with each access point.

RF Interference

RF interference occupies the air medium, which delays the transmission and receipt of data and causes collisions and resulting retransmissions. These network delays may impact the operation of an 802.1X port-based authentication system. In some cases, you might need to adjust 802.1X system configuration parameters, such as timeouts, in order to compensate for impacts of RF interference (as well as other impairments).

The combination of high noise levels and high retry rates generally indicate that RF interference is impacting your wireless LAN. You can use tools such as an AirMagnet Laptop Analyzer or NetStumbler to measure noise. Also, AirMagnet has tools for testing retry rates, and most access points store retry statistics that you can view through the Admininstration Console.

If the noise level is above -85 dBm in the band where your users are operating, then RF interference has the potential for causing poor performance. In this case, the retry rates of users will be above 10 percent, which is when users start feeling the effects. This can occur, for example, when wireless users are in the same room as a microwave oven that is operating.

If you find significant RF interference is present, then find out where it's coming from and alleviate the problem. If the symptoms occur only when the microwave oven or cordless phone is operating, then try setting the access point to a different channel. That sometimes eliminates the interference.

Also, use a tool such as NetStumbler to take a quick scan of other wireless LANs that are operating in your area. If you see that others are set to the same channel as yours, then change your network to non-conflicting channels. Keep in mind that there are only three channels (1, 6, and 11) in the 2.4 GHz band which don't conflict with each other. Most homes and small offices will have their access point set to channel 6, because that's the most common factory default channel—so you may need to avoid using channel 6 with the access points near the perimeter of your enterprise.

NOTE In some cases, the root cause of poor performance may be an access point that has failed. Check applicable access points for broken antennas, status lights indicating fault conditions, and insufficient electrical power. Try rebooting the access points, which often resolves firmware lockups. Make sure that the firmware is up-to-date to minimize lockups in the future.

Addressing

There are two primary levels of addressing on a computer network: IP Addressing and MAC addressing. IP addresses enable routers and the Internet to forward data packets from one point to another on the network. The use of TCP/IP-based applications requires all network devices to have an IP address. In order to go through the Internet, official and unique IP addresses must be used. For flexibility, an enterprise can use just about any IP addresses that they want to within the enterprise's network, assuming connections to the Internet are made with official IP addresses assigned to the enterprise (generally through an ISP). In order to support the assignment of unique IP addresses to all client devices, most enterprises implement DHCP, which automatically assigns and manages the IP addresses.

IP addresses correspond at Layer 3, the Network Layer, of the OSI reference model. At Layer 2, the Data Link Layer, MAC addresses must be used. The MAC address is the physical address of the NIC and is what the NIC will respond to. Every NIC has a unique MAC address assigned during manufacturing. The manufacturer's name is coded in the MAC address. In fact, most packet sniffers will display the manufacturer's name found in the MAC address of packets.

When communicating with network devices, the various IEEE 802 standards, such as IEEE 802.3 and 802.11, have protocols that send frames based on individual MAC addresses, referred to as *unicast*, or multiple MAC addresses, referred to as *multicast*. A special case of multicast is *broadcast*, where the frame is sent to all network devices.

IEEE 802.11 Multicasting

IEEE 802.1X makes use of multicast addressing, and IEEE 802.11 wireless LANs handle multicast frames in sort of an odd way that may impact performance of an 802.1X system. As a result, it's important to understand how 802.11 multicasting works. When any single wireless client associated with an access point has the 802.11 power-save mode enabled, the access point buffers all multicast frames and sends them only after the next Delivery Traffic Indication Message (DTIM) beacon, which may be every one, two, or three beacons (referred to as the *DTIM interval*). The DTIM interval can be set in the access point configuration. The 802.11 power-save mode is optionally set by the user on the wireless client device, generally via the wireless client card's configuration utility.

The use of DTIM intervals was put in the IEEE 802.11 standard to enable sleeping stations that implement the power-save function to know when to wake up and receive multicast traffic (after every DTIM beacon), and to allow flexible configuration of the network (DTIM interval) that offers a trade-off between battery life and performance. If none of the 802.11 radios associated with the access point has the power-save mode enabled, then the access point will send multicast traffic immediately and will not wait until after the next DTIM beacon.

Setting the DTIM Interval

If you haven't considered multicasting in the past, then the DTIM interval on your access points is probably set to the default value, which is likely one, two, or three. If set to one, the access point will deliver multicast frames after every beacon. Don't forget, the significance of the DTIM interval only applies if at least one wireless client associated with the access point has the 802.11

power-save mode enabled. A DTIM interval of one, two, or three is good for performance, but it will likely hurt battery life.

I've found through testing that some wireless clients with power-save enabled will receive the last multicast frame sent by the access point and then continue staying awake until after the next beacon. In other words, the client radio stays awake for the entire beacon interval. If the beacon interval is set to 100 milliseconds (the common default value) and multicast traffic is occurring within each 100 millisecond interval (typical for many multicast applications), then the flow of multicast frames will probably cause the client radios to stay awake indefinitely. This draws battery power as if the power-save mode was not enabled. Even with DTIM intervals of two or three, battery life may still suffer. For example, with DTIMs occurring every other frame (a DTIM interval of two), the radio may be awake 50 percent of the time.

Even if you have changed the DTIM interval in the past, it may still be too high. For example, I've seen some DTIM intervals set to 30, which means that wireless clients with power-save mode enabled will not receive multicast traffic until after 30 beacon intervals. This might be great for battery life, but it only allows the delivery of multicast traffic every three seconds (assuming the default 100-millisecond beacon interval). The impact of this is highly application-specific, though. For example, the transmission of voice would likely have long and annoying skips or quiet intervals, but the delivery of text messages may not experience any impairment noticeable to humans.

What DTIM interval is best? Unfortunately, there's no straightforward answer to this. In order to optimize the DTIM interval, you should gain a good understanding of how your multicast applications work. You'll probably not find this in user manuals, and even the vendor may not want to tell you much about it, to avoid disclosing company secrets. In these cases, you might need to do some testing.

Most likely, the best DTIM setting will be the one that provides maximum battery life while allowing delivery of multicast often enough to provide good performance. You should determine the highest DTIM interval that can be set and still allow the multicast applications to work properly. First, try setting the DTIM interval to one, and then use the application while monitoring the quality of the transmission (such as voice quality). In terms of DTIM settings, this should offer the best quality. You can use this as a baseline for comparison purposes when setting the DTIM interval to higher values. Now, try increasing the DTIM interval to higher values while monitoring the transmission quality. Keep increasing the DTIM interval until the quality is just above the minimum tolerable level. At this point, you'll have the highest DTIM interval that you can use to maintain required performance while also offering the best power savings.

CHAPTER 2

Port-Based
Authentication Concepts

This chapter focuses on concepts dealing specifically with 802.1X and port-based authentication. It introduces you to the applicable terminology and protocols, such as EAPOL, EAP, EAP-Methods, and RADIUS, that make up a port-based authentication system. The following chapters cover these protocols in detail, but for now you'll learn how they work together and how they enable an 802.1X port-based authentication system to operate.

802.1X Port-Based Authentication Terminology

Authentication is the process of identifying a person or thing (see Figure 2-1). For example, Sally arrives at an airport and attempts to check in for her flight to Dallas. The airline agent asks to see Sally's driver's license to ensure that the person claiming to be Sally is indeed Sally. The agent looks at the driver's license and verifies that Sally is the person in the photo on the license, and the name on the license is Sally. This information is Sally's *credentials,* which is accepted for many transactions, such as checking in for airline flights. The process as just described, which we're all very familiar with, is *authentication.* The airline agent has verified Sally's identity through credentials, thus authentication has taken place. Based on the credentials, the airline clerk can either authorize or not authorize Sally to continue checking into the flight.

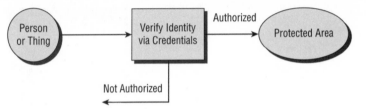

Figure 2-1: Simple example of authentication

Based on the airport analogy, authentication seems pretty simple. You merely verify that someone or something is who or what they claim to be, assuming the person or thing has the right credentials. That's really all there is to the basic definition of authentication.

An authentication system for a computer network can get more complex, though. Machines (such as Ethernet switches and network interface cards) must be told exactly what to do, and the precision and complexity of the necessary instruction set leaves no room for error. Incompatible protocols and even very slight misunderstandings in communications with machines generally results in non-interoperability—the system doesn't function correctly and ceases to be of any value. Humans, though, can apply reason to make adjustments when communication gets rough. For example, assume that Sally is checking into an international flight and she speaks only French, whereas the airline agent speaks only Spanish. The airline agent may ask in Spanish for Sally to produce her passport. Sally wouldn't understand this, and may instead show the airline agent her driver's license. The airline agent doesn't accept the driver's license, but despite the language difficulties, the airline agent may use some other means, such as body language, to impress on Susan that she must produce a passport. This may seem like a trivial example, but the point is that humans can adapt very easily based on the situation. Machines have some capability to adapt, but machines must be programmed and configured to adapt to specific situations. The designers of the network components, for instance, may not have thought of every conceivable situation, so the system has a tendency to break when unforeseen circumstances occur.

In addition to the standard, run-of-the mill issues just described, the standards and specifications that form a complete 802.1X port-based authentication system are written by different organizations: the Institute of Electrical and Electronic Engineers (IEEE) and the Internet Engineering Task Force (IETF). The IEEE standard that applies to port-based authentication is 802.1X, which addresses EAPOL, and the IETF provides RFCs for EAP, EAP-Methods, and RADIUS. All of these standards and specifications are needed. Thus, no single integrated standard specifies all of the components needed to implement a complete port-based authentication system. This results in a complexity that in turn often results in interoperability issues. In fact, the multiple standards that make up a port-based authentication system are what makes learning 802.1X and related specifications relatively difficult. You could download a copy of 802.1X and study it for weeks, but without references to several other documents, you probably wouldn't have a clue how port-based authentication really works. Standards and specifications also often change, and you must be careful to ensure that what you implement is backwardly compatible with versions that you choose for parts of the system. So, again, the point here is that 802.1X is much more difficult than what the definition of simple authentication implies.

Another term that must be understood in the realm of port-based authentication is "port," which is a Layer 2 (Data Link) connection in a computer network. For wired networks, the word "port" in port-based authentication refers to a port on an Ethernet switch, as shown in Figure 2-2. Of course, many different hardware devices, such as desktop PCs, laptops, servers, cameras, access points, and hubs, can connect to an Ethernet port. The complete link connection, in relation to networks, is made at Layer 1 (Physical Layer) and Layer 2 (Data Link Layer). The Ethernet cable that provides the interconnection establishes the physical part of the link. Port-based authentication attempts to verify the identity of these devices connected to the Ethernet port via a physical cable, and the authentication takes place at Layer 2 (Data Link Layer).

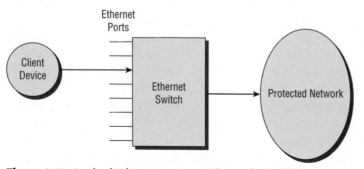

Figure 2-2: A wired Ethernet port provides a physical link.

Ports also apply to wireless LANs, but in the wireless world, the port is an association with an access point. Instead of producing a physical connection, a wireless client device, such as Wi-Fi-enabled laptop, goes through a process of associating with an *access point*. All access points in a wireless LAN periodically broadcast an 802.11 beacon frame. When a wireless client equipped with an 802.11 client radio first boots up, the client radio scans all channels and identifies the presence of access points in the surrounding area. The client radio then attempts to associate with the access point having the strongest signal. The association process involves a series of 802.11 frame transmissions between the client device and the access point, which results in the associated state shown in Figure 2-3. A successful association with an access point allows the wireless client, based on its MAC address, to communicate through the access point to other devices on the network infrastructure. As with an Ethernet port connection, the association provides a link whereby a device can be authenticated before being allowed access to the network.

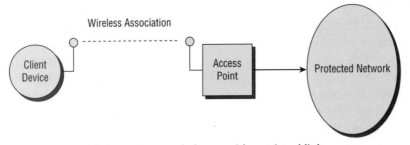

Figure 2-3: A wireless LAN association provides a virtual link.

Keep in mind that authentication is different from authorization. They're often treated closely together. Using the preceding analogy, when Susan showed valid credentials to the airline agent when checking into her flight, she was authenticated and then authorized to continue checking in. *Authorization* is a process of granting privileges to a person or device based on the outcome of the authentication. Imagine that John from the accounting department is attempting to log in to a network, and he is prompted to enter his username and password. After entering this information, the system verifies that John's username and password match what's contained in a database. So far, this has only involved authentication. Based on John's username, however, the system allows John access only to the servers belonging to the accounting department, and not any of the warehouse and human resources applications. This latter step of admitting John onto the network deals with authorization. Authorization is certainly important, but avoiding it for now will make learning authentication processes much easier.

Authentication Benefits

Port-based authentication keeps unauthorized users and client devices from accessing protected resources on the network, such as servers, corporate applications, and databases. Without authentication, a hacker could easily access the LAN by connecting a laptop to an Ethernet port within the facility, or associate with a wireless LAN access point from the parking lot of the company. If a hacker is allowed to connect to the network, they'll look for any and all ways to exploit security weaknesses.

Once connected to the network, a hacker has a surprisingly wide variety of tools and methods available to crack into corporate resources. A hacker, for example, could run a TCP (Layer 4) port scanner that causes all port 80 (http) devices connected to the network to echo back their IP address and other information, such as SNMP port status. Many of these port 80 IP addresses are http administration interfaces for access points, servers, and printers. Scores of companies fail to configure login security for administration interfaces on printers, which allows the hacker to aim their browser at a printer's administration port and reconfigure the printer. This may not sound like a big problem, but some printers allow you to configure the printer to print to a file, such as one located on the hacker's laptop, instead of (and in some cases in addition to) printing the associated document. Thus, a hacker connecting to the network may be able to passively redirect printed documents to their laptop. This is a significant compromise in security, especially when the printed documents contain employee social security numbers, competitive proposals, and sensitive intellectual property. There are dozens and possibly hundreds of ways that a seasoned hacker can breach security if they're able to connect to the network. Port-based authentication, however, will significantly reduce these risks and even prevent them from happening.

Implementing port-based access control constitutes a big step toward securing a wired or wireless network. It's not a silver bullet for providing network security, however. In addition, you must employ other methods, such as data packet encryption, intrusion detection, denial of service prevention, security awareness programs, and facility access controls in order to cover all possible security vulnerabilities.

In addition to keeping unauthorized people off the corporate network, a port-based authentication system also supports the following:

- **User location information:** An application can easily track the location of users, for instance, based on the switch or access point where the applicable client device was authenticated. The location information can map to a wide variety of applications. For example, a hospital can use this information to track the location of doctors and nurses using wireless client computing devices.

- **Billing and accounting mechanisms:** Port-based authentication, when combined with billing and accounting mechanisms, enables Internet service providers (ISPs) to implement fee-based Internet access. If the user is not authorized, they can be directed to pay for service via a credit card and then be given credentials (username and password) that the subscriber can use when logging into the system. Port-based authentication prompts users to enter their username and password, which the system uses to authenticate them. If the credentials match what the system has stored in a database, then a user will be authorized to access the protected side of the network, which is the Internet. Figure 2-4 illustrates this concept.

▪ **Personalized network access:** Based on credentials offered during authentication, the system can authorize the user to access certain applications.

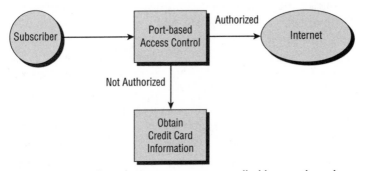

Figure 2-4: Fee-based Internet access controlled by port-based authentication

Primary Components

Until now, we've been looking at port-based authentication from a generic point of view, but now we should start using the proper names and actual protocols that you'll find in the 802.1X standards and specifications. As shown in Figure 2-5, the primary components of a port-based authentication system include supplicants, authenticators, and authentication servers.

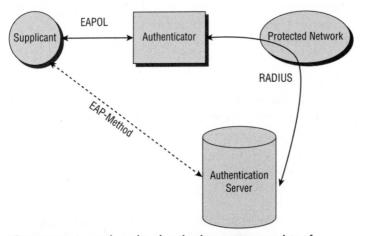

Figure 2-5: A port-based authentication system consists of a supplicant, authenticator, and authentication server.

Supplicant

A *supplicant* is a client device that needs to be authenticated before being allowed access to the network. Think of the supplicants as unknown users. Their identity is in question until they can produce valid credentials to the authentication server.

In order to be considered a valid supplicant, a typical client device, such as a laptop or IP phone, would need to implement 802.1X and a specific EAP-Method. For example, Windows XP comes with 802.1X built in with a variety of EAP-Methods, such as EAP-TLS. (Sometimes EAP-Methods are referred to as *EAP types*.) The supplicant communicates with the authentication server using EAP as the transport and a specific EAP-Method that provides the actual authentication mechanism. As explained later in this chapter, the actual communications between the supplicant and the authenticator is accomplished via EAPOL, which is defined by 802.1X. EAPOL delivers (encapsulates) the EAP and EAP-Method frames as data.

Authenticator

An *authenticator* is a Layer 2 network device, such as an Ethernet switch or a wireless LAN access point. In an enterprise network, all switch ports may implement 802.1X in order to support company-wide 802.1X port-based authentication. The authenticator acts as a security gate between the supplicants and the protected network. The gate (actually, port) stays closed until the authentication system verifies the credentials of the supplicant and deems that the supplicant is authorized to access the protected network. Once the system authenticates the supplicant, the authenticator will open a port so that the supplicant can access the protected network.

In addition, the authenticator is a translator between the supplicant and the authentication server. As the supplicant and authentication server converse, all communications flow through the authenticator. For example, the supplicant will send its credentials to the authentication server by encapsulating the credentials (based on the specific EAP-Method) in an EAP frame, which is all encapsulated in an EAPOL frame. The EAPOL frame is sent to the authenticator, which then removes the EAP-Method data from the EAPOL frame. The authenticator sends the EAP-Method data encapsulated in a RADIUS frame directly to the authentication server. Thus, the conversation between the supplicant and the authentication server is based on a common language.

Authentication Server

As mentioned above, the authenticator and the supplicant have a conversation regarding the authentication. The authentication server, for instance, will at some point request the credentials from the supplicant. The supplicant will then offer the credentials to the authentication server. The port-based authentication standards and specifications don't make any particular type of authentication server mandatory, but nearly all implementations utilize RADIUS. As a result, RADIUS is the de facto standard recognized by the networking industry.

In an enterprise system, the authentication server is likely a separate component attached to the network. There will probably be multiple authentication servers to improve availability and performance. Each authenticator points to a primary authentication server, with possibly several others listed as secondary servers that can be called upon if the primary authentication server is unresponsive.

In some cases, the authentication server may be embedded in the authenticators. This distributed authentication server model significantly reduces authentication traffic over the network, which is desirable for wireless networks where roaming frequently occurs. This can improve performance for all clients. In addition, smaller networks may strongly benefit from using a switch or access point that also provides authentication server functions. This is cost effective for smaller networks because it reduces hardware costs.

A Simple Analogy: Getting the Protocols Straight

As you can see, 802.1X port-based authentication involves several different protocols—namely, EAPOL, EAP, EAP-Methods, and RADIUS. In addition, a lot of layering takes place with these protocols. With no single standard to refer to, it's easy to get lost and not make any sense of the details that the rest of this book will cover. Therefore, let's explore an analogy that should help you fully understand where the protocols apply and how the transfer of data takes place.

Imagine that Rob (supplicant), located in Bangor, Maine, writes and mails a letter (EAP-Method data) to his friend Tony (authentication server), who lives in Houston, Texas. Rob mails the letter via a special courier who will deliver the letter by truck (EAPOL/EAP) to Dayton, Ohio (authenticator), which is approximately halfway between Bangor and Houston. In Dayton, the courier continues delivery of the letter to Houston by airplane (RADIUS). Tony receives and reads the letter successfully. Figure 2-6 illustrates this process.

The delivery process for the letter is similar to the layering process that takes place in an 802.1X port-based authentication system. The overall goal of the system is to allow the supplicant (Rob) to communicate with the authentication server (Tony) via a particular EAP-Method, which includes the sending of EAP-Method data back and forth between the supplicant (Rob) and the authentication server (Tony). In order to funnel the EAP-Method data through the system, EAPOL (delivery truck) carries the letter to the authenticator (Dayton), and

RADIUS (airplane) delivers the EAP-Method data (letter) to the authentication server (Tony). Figure 2-7 depicts the actual 802.1X layering process. In addition, another layer, not depicted in the figure, would include the specific LAN protocols, such as 802.3 or 802.11.

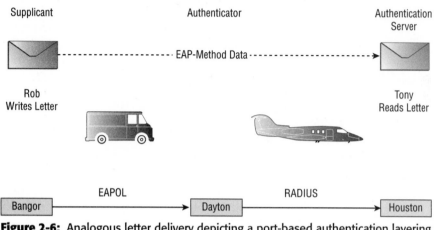

Figure 2-6: Analogous letter delivery depicting a port-based authentication layering process

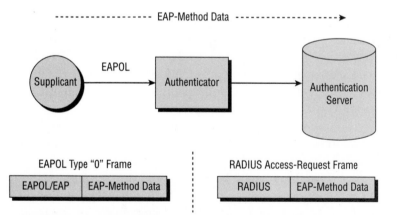

Figure 2-7: 802.1X port-based authentication system layering

The layering is done to allow different protocols between the supplicant and authenticator (EAPOL), and the authenticator and the authentication server (RADIUS). This enables the protocols to address the varying needs of each link in the system and at the same time allow a conversation to occur between the supplicant and authentication server (EAP-Method).

Port-Based Authentication Operation

The operation of an 802.1X-based port-based authentication system makes use of a variety of standards and specifications, which the previous sections identify. You now know what 802.1X port-based authentication does and what components and protocols are involved. Let's take a closer look at how the overall system operates.

A Simple Analogy—Understanding the Overall System

At the beginning of this chapter, an analogy describing Sally checking in for a flight at an airport defined authentication. This particular analogy was very simple and doesn't include all of the components of a port-based authentication system. As the following analogy unfolds, parenthetical terms and phrases map the analogy to an actual 802.1X port-based authentication system.

Assume that Terry (supplicant) arrives at the White House (protected network) in order to meet with the president (see Figure 2-8). As Terry enters the driveway (switch port), a gate guard (authenticator) orders Terry to stop the car. The gate guard blurts out, "Why are you here?" Terry says, "I'm here to see the president." The guard then calls Eva (authentication server), the primary point of contact for the President's security unit and lets Terry talk directly with Eva, who's inside the White House. Terry can be seen by Eva through a security video camera, and Eva asks Terry to put his passport in front of the camera so that Eva can clearly see his name, picture, and passport number (EAP-Method data). After verifying that Terry is who he claims to be (authenticated), Eva finds Terry's name on the list of authorized meeting attendees and tells the gate guard to issue him a pass to the meeting room (authorized services). The guard then lets Terry drive through and access the meeting room.

Several variations on this analogy often pop up in actual port-based authentication systems. If Eva doesn't find Terry's name on the authorized list, then she would tell the guard to not let Terry through (unauthorized access). The gate guard would use force if needed to keep Terry from entering the White House grounds. If Terry were a tourist (visitor), the guard would tell Terry that he could park down the street and arrange for a tour of the White House (guest access).

When Eva asks Terry to show his passport, Terry might not have one. Terry could negotiate with Eva and possibly use his driver's license instead. This comes up with port-based authentication methods when the supplicant doesn't support the primary EAP-Method. When this happens, the supplicant and the authentication server can negotiate use of a different EAP-Method. There's a possibility, however, that Eva may not accept a driver's license as a valid form of identification. If this were the case, then she would, obviously, inform the gate guard to not let Terry through, and the guard would probably offer Terry guest access by signing up for a White House tour.

If Eva doesn't answer the phone when the guard calls, then the guard could try calling other people in the security unit. Eventually, the guard may reach a different security person, who can talk directly with Terry and handle the identification (authentication) process. The guard may not, however, reach anyone in the security unit. The phones may be down or the security unit may be so busy that they can't service any new requests. Terry would then need to wait until the guard puts him in touch with someone from the security unit.

Alternatively, Terry may arrive at the security gate, but the guard doesn't notice Terry is there. The guard may be yakking with another guard about last night's game. In this case, Terry may say, "Excuse me!" This would probably get the attention of the guard, who will then ask, "Why are you here?" The process then continues from that point on as described above.

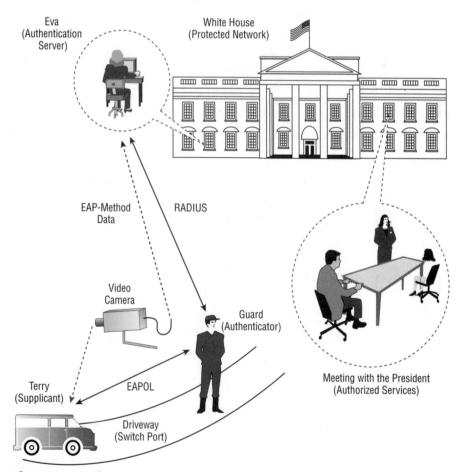

Figure 2-8: Analogous security gate authentication system

Supplicant to Authentication Server: EAP-Methods

The actual conversation regarding authentication occurs between the supplicant and the authentication server. This is similar to the conversation occurring between Terry and Eva in the preceding analogy, where Terry is the supplicant and Eva is the authentication server. In a port-based authentication system, a specific EAP-Method defines how the authentication takes place between the supplicant and the authentication server. The conversation between the supplicant and authentication server includes EAP-Method data, which represents various elements, such as the supplicant's credentials. Figure 2-9 illustrates communications between the supplicant and the authentication server. The conversation between the supplicant and the authentication server includes multiple exchanges of EAP data, depending on the type of EAP-Method.

The implementation and result of an EAP-Method is the goal of the port-based authentication system. The process that Terry and Eva completed when verifying that Terry, based on the information supplied in his passport, was indeed the person he said he was, is what an EAP-Method provides. In actual 802.1X port-based authentication systems, EAP-Methods make use of different types of credentials, such as username/passwords, encryption keys, and digital certificates.

The standards require implementation of the following EAP-Methods:

- MD5 challenge
- One-Time Passwords (OTP)
- Generic token card

In addition, there are many proprietary and RFC-based EAP-Methods, such as EAP-TLS, EAP-TTLS, EAP-FAST, and EAP-LEAP. Chapter 5, "EAP-Methods," discusses details of the various EAP-Methods.

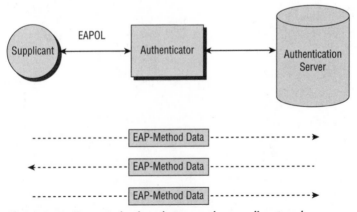

Figure 2-9: Communications between the supplicant and authentication server

Supplicant to Authenticator: 802.1X / EAPOL

802.1X only applies between the supplicant and the authenticator. This is analogous to communications between Terry and the gate guard in the White House example. A complete 802.1X port-based authentication system makes use of other protocols, such as RADIUS. 802.1X is only part of the overall system.

Figure 2-10 illustrates the communications between a supplicant and an authenticator.

EAP was designed as a point-to-point protocol (PPP) for communications over a serial link. EAPOL is defined in the 802.1X standard to adapt EAP for operation over LANs.

To do this, EAPOL adds three additional fields to EAP:

▪ Version

▪ Type

▪ Length

As a result, EAPOL encapsulates EAP frames as data. Chapter 3 explains the details of these fields. For now, in this chapter, it's important to learn the different types of EAPOL frames to understand the basics of 802.1X operation.

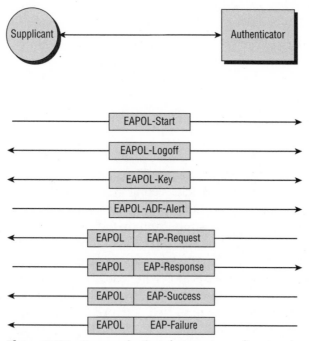

Figure 2-10: Communications between supplicant and authenticator

A Type "0" EAPOL frame means that the frame is carrying an EAP frame. This requires the destination, whether it's the supplicant or the authenticator, to merely strip off the EAPOL header and process the EAP frame. Thus, Type "0" EAPOL frames merely pass through EAP frames, which are generally carrying EAP-Method data.

In addition to carrying EAP-Method data, other EAP frames manage the authentication information. For example, EAP provides a mechanism for the supplicant and the authentication server to negotiate which EAP-Method to use. This is similar to the previous analogy when determining whether a driver's license could be used instead of a passport for verifying Terry's identity to Eva. In addition, other EAP frames provide the means for exchanging credentials and declaring the success or failure of the authentication. The exchange of these frames can be found in the analogy in which the gate guard tells Terry that either he can or he can't enter the White House grounds.

EAP doesn't have any security features, such as encryption of data carried in the EAP frame bodies. This requires designers to implement security in other layers. For example, if the link between the supplicant and the authenticator is wireless, then it would be best to implement some sort of link encryption, such as 802.11i. In this case, 802.11i would encrypt the data portion of the 802.11 frame, which contains the 802.1X protocols.

There are four EAP frame types:

■ Request

■ Response

■ Success

■ Failure

As mentioned earlier, EAPOL always carries these EAP frames in EAPOL Type "0" frames.

The supplicant can only issue EAP Response frames, and the authenticator can perform EAP Request, Success, and Failure frames. The authenticator issues EAP Request frames to deliver EAP-Method data traveling from the authentication server to the supplicant, and the supplicant issues EAP Response frames to deliver EAP-Method data going from the supplicant to the authentication server. An authenticator will send an EAP Success frame to the supplicant if the authentication server informs the authenticator that the supplicant is authorized to access the protected network. The authenticator will send an EAP Failure frame to the supplicant if the result of the authentication process indicates that the supplicant is not authorized to access the protected network. The EAP Success frames and Failure frames are sent in response to the EAP-Method outcome. In some cases, an authenticator may issue EAP Failure frames to the supplicant to initiate the authentication process because the EAP Failure frame causes the supplicant to reset its link.

EAP provides correct ordering of the EAP frames through a "lock-step" mechanism. This is a simple process whereby the authenticator, for example, sets a value in the Identifier field of the EAP frame when sending an EAP Request frame to the supplicant. The supplicant sets the same value in the Identifier field of the EAP Response frame. This informs the authenticator that the supplicant has received the EAP Request frame and to move on to the next frame.

After the link between the supplicant and the authenticator becomes active, the authenticator sends an EAP Request frame (again, encapsulated in an EAPOL Type "0" frame) to demand the identity of the supplicant. The authenticator will not let any non-EAP-Method traffic through to the protected side of the network at this point. Based on the process defined in the EAP-Method, the supplicant and authentication server will converse using the EAP-Method. The communications between the supplicant and the authenticator include transfers of EAPOL Type "0" frames carrying EAP and EAP-Method data. The authenticator simply acts as a translator and keeps the EAP-Method data flowing between the supplicant and the authentication server until the authentication server decides whether to authorize or not authorize the supplicant.

Ultimately, the authenticator may assign the supplicant to an authorized VLAN. If the supplicant ends up not being authorized, then the authenticator can assign the supplicant to an unauthorized port (e.g., guest VLAN), such as one providing access to the Internet only, if this feature is available (see Figure 2-11). In some cases, the switch may support dynamic VLAN assignment so that the supplicant can be connected to one of several authorized VLANs based on authorization that applies to the credentials configured in the authentication server.

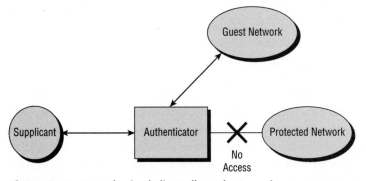

Figure 2-11: Unauthorized client allowed connection to a guest network

After the authenticator sends the initial EAP Request frame to the supplicant, there may be no response from the supplicant. Returning to the analogy presented earlier, Terry may have his car stereo turned up too loud and can't hear the guard. In a real network, the network interface card, such as the Ethernet card or 802.11 adapter, may be faulty or may not support 802.1X. After waiting for a specific period of time (which is configurable), the authenticator will attempt to resend the EAP Request frame. If the authenticator doesn't get any response from the supplicant after sending multiple EAP Request frames (the number is configurable), then the authenticator may shut down the link or connect the client to a guest VLAN, depending on configuration. In a wireless LAN, the authenticator disassociates the wireless client (supplicant) when shutting down the link.

So far, we've only discussed the EAPOL Type '0' frames for carrying EAP and EAP-Method data. Other types of EAPOL frames include the following:

- EAPOL-Start
- EAPOL-Logoff
- EAPOL-Key
- EAPOL-Encapsulated-ADF-Alert

These frames are outside the scope of EAP and don't carry EAP or EAP-Method data. Why, then, do we need them? They provide additional functionality needed to make EAP work on a LAN. EAP wasn't specifically designed for LANs; therefore, 802.1X devised EAPOL to wrap around EAP (EAPOL type "0" frames) and provide additional LAN functionality.

For example, a supplicant can send an EAPOL Start frame. This gets the attention of the authenticator, which responds immediately with an EAP Request frame that requests the identity of the supplicant. In the preceding analogy, this is the case where Terry drives up to the gate guard and the guard is busy talking to someone. Terry must get the guard's attention in order to start the process of checking into the White House grounds. A similar event can happen in real networks because the supplicant may be downstream from other devices, such as hubs, that have been authenticated, and the link is already active. The authenticator wouldn't know if the supplicant comes online; therefore, the supplicant must alert the authenticator with an EAPOL Start frame. Chapter 3 describes the other EAPOL frame types.

802.1X (i.e., EAPOL) applies to Layer 2 in order to keep a supplicant from connecting to the network before authenticating. If authentication is done at Layer 4, for instance, then a network connection would have to be made before starting the authentication process, making the network vulnerable to a hacker. As explained earlier in this chapter, a connection to the network at Layer 2 offers many opportunities for a hacker to exploit the security of the network.

In order to accomplish integration at Layer 2, 802.1X takes advantage of access controls offered by 802.1D, which defines MAC bridges. 802.1D is required by all 802 LANs, including 802.3 (Ethernet) and 802.11 (Wi-Fi). As a result, 802.1X will work with any of the LAN types. The integration is done is a way that keeps 802.1X traffic from disrupting other LAN protocols and allows 802.1X frames to be the first ones sent on the link.

802.1X makes use of the addressing reserved for the 802.1D Spanning-Tree Protocol. 802.1D owns several reserved group addresses. With group addresses, every member of the group processes the frame. 802.1X has been assigned one of the unused 802.1D Spanning-Tree group addresses, which is 01:80:C2:00:00:03. This address is often referred to as the *802.1X Port Access Entry (PAE)* address. All 802-based devices (client cards, switches, access points, etc.) are designed to receive and process frames having this group address.

NOTE When using a packet sniffer, you can easily trace 802.1X communications by filtering the trace on the group MAC address: 01:80:C2:00:00:03, which is uniquely assigned to all 802.1X frames.

Authenticator to Authentication Server: RADIUS

Figure 2-12 illustrates communications between the authenticator and the authentication server using RADIUS. Similar to EAP, RADIUS frames are sent using a lock-step process. RADIUS frame types include the following:

- Access-Request
- Access-Accept
- Access-Reject
- Access-Challenge
- Accounting-Request
- Accounting-Response

Most communications between the authenticator and the authentication server consist of RADIUS Access-Request and Access-Challenge frames. The authenticator sends EAP-Method data to the authentication server via RADIUS Access-Request frames. The authenticator will have removed the EAP-Method data from an EAPOL/EAP frame that it received from the supplicant. If the authentication server receives a RADIUS Access-Request and the IP address of the authenticator, and a shared secret provided by the authenticator matches what the authentication server is expecting, then the authentication server will process the request. If these items don't match, then the authentication server remains silent and doesn't respond at all. The authenticator will likely keep repeating the RADIUS Access-Request frame multiple times, however. If configured properly, the authenticator will eventually give up and try communicating with a connection with a different RADIUS server. The authentication server sends EAP-Method data to the authenticator (and bound for the supplicant) via RADIUS Access-Challenge frames. Of course, the supplicant will extract the EAP-Method data from the RADIUS frame and send the EAP-Method data to the supplicant via EAPOL/EAP.

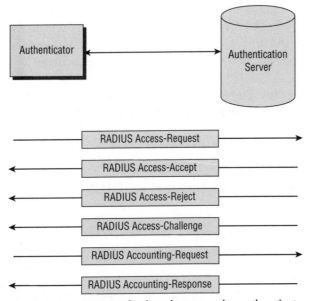

Figure 2-12: Communications between the authenticator and the authentication server

NOTE IETF RFCs 2865 and 3579 extend RADIUS into 802.1X, and RFC 3780 identifies RADIUS attributes.

After the EAP-Method results in deeming the supplicant either authorized or not authorized, the authentication server sends an applicable RADIUS Access-Accept or Access-Reject frame to the authenticator. The authenticator then issues the corresponding EAPOL Success or EAPOL Failure frame to the supplicant. At that point, if the request was successful, then the authenticator opens the port for the supplicant to have access to the protected network.

NOTE Refer to Chapter 4 for details on communications between the authenticator and the authentication server.

A Historical Perspective

The first IEEE 802 standard LANs came about in the early 1980s. As these networks began to proliferate and replace terminal-host mainframe systems, network component vendors and standards bodies were motivated to create a security gate to the networks. At first, this wasn't too important for wired corporate networks because the walls of the facility offered physical access control. If a hacker couldn't get inside the building, then it was nearly impossible to connect to the network. The thrust toward port-based authentication started when employees started accessing the corporate network from remote locations, such as hotel rooms and homes. The opening of the corporate network to the Internet, to enable higher-speed connections than the dial-up telephone provides, required tighter access control. Thus, port-based authentication became a critical component, which drove the writing of related IEEE standards and IETF specifications.

Nowadays, nearly all corporate networks interface with the Internet; and despite the use of firewalls, fears remain that hackers can still get into the network. In addition, many companies and organizations have wireless LANs, either as their entire network or as an extension to existing wired networks. These wireless networks make it even easier for hackers to gain access to the corporate network. In most cases, a hacker can be sitting inside a car located in the parking lot of the company or even down the street in a hidden location.

The first big move toward port-based authentication specifications was the creation of the Extensible Authentication Protocol (EAP), approved in 1998 as IETF RFC 2284, titled "PPP Extensible Authentication Protocol." EAP provides communications between the client device being authenticated and an authentication server. As you learn more details later in this chapter, EAP is really just a point-to-point protocol that carries actual authentication elements. Specific EAP-Methods actually provide the authentication mechanism, such as definition of credentials. There are a few mandatory EAP-Methods that EAP must support, but there are many proprietary EAP-Methods.

Another big step came in 2001 when the IEEE ratified the 802.1X standard (often referred to as 802.1X-2001). This initial 802.1X standard is based largely on EAP. In fact, 802.1X merely extends EAP to operate over LANs. 802.1X defines the EAP over LANs (EAPOL) protocol to accomplish this. 802.1X (and EAPOL) only applies to the interface between the client device being authenticated and the Ethernet switch or wireless LAN access points to which the client device is connecting. In 2004, EAP and 802.1X documents underwent significant revision, which resulted in RFC 3748 for EAP and 802.1X-2004. These are the most current versions and the basis for this book. RADIUS is another major component of a port-based authentication system. RADIUS was more formally introduced into port-based authentications documents around 2003.

Today 802.1X, RADIUS, EAP, and EAP-Methods are fairly well coupled through formal standards and specifications. This leads to the deployment of secure port-based authentication systems that provide much better interoperability than was possible in the earlier days.

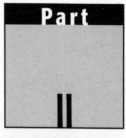

Part

II

Standards and Protocols

In This Part

EAPOL Protocol

In this chapter, we to dive into the details of the EAPOL (Extensible Authentication Protocol over Wireless LAN) packet structure. With this, along with the overview provided in Chapter 2, you'll have a good understanding of how EAPOL works. This will provide a basis for implementing and troubleshooting port-based authentication systems.

EAPOL Recap

EAPOL is defined in the 802.1X standard to adapt EAP communications for operation over LANs. In order to do this, EAPOL provides additional header fields to EAP packets and creates some specialized EAP packet types. In addition, EAPOL transports EAP packets as data in the packet body of EAPOL packets. As shown in Figure 3-1, EAPOL is the primary communications link between a supplicant and an authenticator in a port-based authentication system.

The EAPOL protocol operates at Layer 2 to prevent a supplicant from connecting to the network before authenticating. This is achieved by exploiting access controls offered by IEEE 802.1D, which defines MAC bridges and is required by all 802 LANs. The protocol ensures that EAPOL packets are the first ones sent on the link.

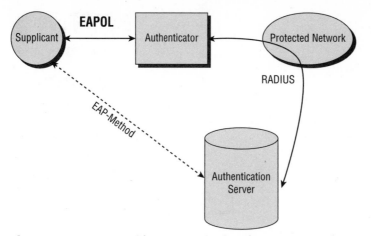

Figure 3-1: EAPOL provides communications between a supplicant and an authenticator.

EAPOL Encapsulation

It's important to keep in mind the encapsulation that takes place in order to support communications between the supplicant and the authenticator. This is particularly important when you're first learning how port-based authentication works and when troubleshooting problems. The layering process is similar to other computer network architectures. Figure 3-2 illustrates this encapsulation that takes place between the supplicant and the authenticator. The collection of these protocols comprises an 802.1X port-based authentication system. EAPOL is the overall port-based authentication entity that requires transportation by a link protocol.

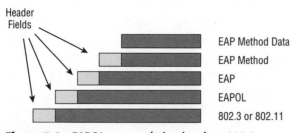

Figure 3-2: EAPOL encapsulation involves 802.3 (or 802.11), EAP, and EAP-Method data.

The primary goal of port-based authentication communications is to transport EAP-Method data, which implements the actual authentication process. The specific EAP-Method in use defines this EAP data. EAP packets (EAP-Request and EAP-Response packets) carry the EAP-Method protocol headers and data. EAPOL packets transport the EAP packets, and 802.3 (or 802.11) data frames carry the EAPOL packets. In addition to carrying the higher-layer protocol as data, as you'll see in the subsequent sections, each one of the protocols (EAPOL, EAP, etc.) has its own function and defines packets that might not carry any of the higher-layer protocols. A simple analogy that describes encapsulation is a transportation company delivering goods from Miami (suppliant) to Tampa (authenticator). The item being delivered is a gold watch (EAP Method data) contained within a cardboard box (EAP) that is wrapped with brown paper (EAPOL).

EAPOL Packet Structure

EAPOL adds three additional fields to EAP packets, as shown in Figure 3-3. These fields add several functions needed for integrating with LANs and effectively transporting EAP packets (and EAP-Method data). The following sections explain each of these fields.

Octets:	1	1	2	Variable
	Version	Type	Length	Packet Body

Figure 3-3: EAPOL packets include Version, Type, Length, and Packet Body fields.

Version Field

The Version field of an EAPOL packet identifies the version of the EAPOL protocol that the sender of the EAPOL packet supports. The value contained in this field is one octet in length. The Version field in all 802.1X implementations contains the value "0000 0002." As with other communication protocols, the implementation of the Version field enables development of components and systems that are backwardly compatible.

NOTE All values contained within EAPOL packets are unsigned binary numbers.

Type Field

The Type field of an EAPOL packet, represented by a value one octet in length, identifies the type of packet being sent. Table 3-1 identifies the various types of EAPOL packets based on the Type field value. EAPOL doesn't specify use of any of the other possible values at this time. Future extensions to the protocol may utilize additional values, however. Refer to the section "EAPOL Packet Types," later in this chapter, for a description of each packet type.

Table 3-1: EAPOL Type Field Values

PACKET TYPE	TYPE FIELD VALUE
EAP-Packet	0000 0000 (Hex "00")
EAPOL-Start	0000 0001 (Hex "01")
EAPOL-Logoff	0000 0010 (Hex "02")
EAPOL-Key	0000 0011 (Hex "03")
EAPOL-Encapsulated-ASF-Alert	0000 0100 (Hex "04")

Length Field

The Length field of an EAPOL packet is two octets in length and defines the length of the Packet Body field. The value contained within the Length field represents length as a number of octets. For example, an EAPOL Length field value of "0000 0000 0001 1011" indicates that the Packet Body field of the EAPOL packet contains 27 octets of data. A value of "0000 0000 0000 0000" in the Length field means that the EAPOL packet has no Packet Body field, which is the case with EAPOL-Start and EAPOL-Logoff packets.

NOTE The maximum length of the EAPOL packet depends on limitations of the link transport protocol, such as IEEE 802.3 or 802.11.

NOTE An octet, sometimes referred to as a "byte," includes eight bits of data. Each bit can be either a "0" or a "1."

Packet Body Field

The Packet Body field is the payload portion of the EAPOL packet and is present for EAP-Packet, EAPOL-Key, and EAPOL-Encapsulated-ASF-Alert type packets. The Packet Body field, for example, contains exactly one EAP packet if the packet type is EAP-Packet. If the packet type is EAPOL-Key, then the Packet Body field carries a single Key Descriptor. Refer to the following section for an explanation of Key Descriptors. For EAPOL-Encapsulated-ASF-Alert packet types, the Packet Body includes exactly one ASF-Alert packet.

EAPOL Packet Types

The following sections describe each of the EAPOL packets types.

EAP-Packet

Figure 3-4 illustrates an EAP-Packet. An EAP-Packet, sometimes referred to as a Type "0" EAPOL packet or EAPOL data packet, is carrying, as you might guess, an EAP packet. This requires the destination, whether it's the supplicant or the authenticator, to merely strip off the EAPOL header and process the EAP packet. Thus, Type "0" EAPOL packets merely pass through EAP packets, which are generally carrying EAP-Method data. After link initiation, the most common EAPOL packets are EAP-Packet entities.

Octets:	1	1	2	Variable
	Version	Type	Length	Packet Body
Values:		"00"		(EAPOL/EAP Packet)

Figure 3-4: An EAP-Packet is identified by a "0000 0000" (Hex value "00") in the Type field.

EAPOL-Start

The normal authentication process kicks off when the link state goes from down to up. The authenticator generally initiates the authentication process when this transition from down to up occurs, such as when a user on an Ethernet network first boots up their computer. If the link is already up, and the supplicant needs to authenticate, then the supplicant must initiate the authentication process by sending an EAPOL-Start packet to grab the attention of the authenticator. The authenticator will then know to initiate the authentication process. Figure 3-5 illustrates the EAPOL-Start packet.

Octets: 1   1   2   Variable

Version	Type	Length	Packet Body

Values: "01"   "00"   (no packet body)

Figure 3-5: An EAPOL-Start packet is identified by a "0000 0001" (Hex value "01") in the Type field.

EAPOL-Logoff

Figure 3-6 illustrates an EAPOL-Logoff packet. The supplicant sends an EAPOL-Logoff packet to the authenticator to gracefully return the authenticated port to an unauthorized state. This could occur when the user decides to log off from a particular system residing on the protected side of the network. The use of EAPOL-Logoff packets is ideal because it makes efficient use of authenticator resources.

Octets: 1   1   2   Variable

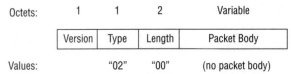

Version	Type	Length	Packet Body

Values: "02"   "00"   (no packet body)

Figure 3-6: An EAPOL-Logoff packet is identified by a "0000 0010" (Hex value "02") in the Type field.

EAPOL-Key

Figure 3-7 illustrates an EAPOL-Key packet, which can be sent by either the supplicant or the authenticator. The EAPOL-Key packet is optional. If the 802.1X implementation requires the transport of keys between the supplicant and the authenticator, the Packet Body of an EAPOL-Key packet contains a Key Descriptor with the format illustrated in Figure 3-8.

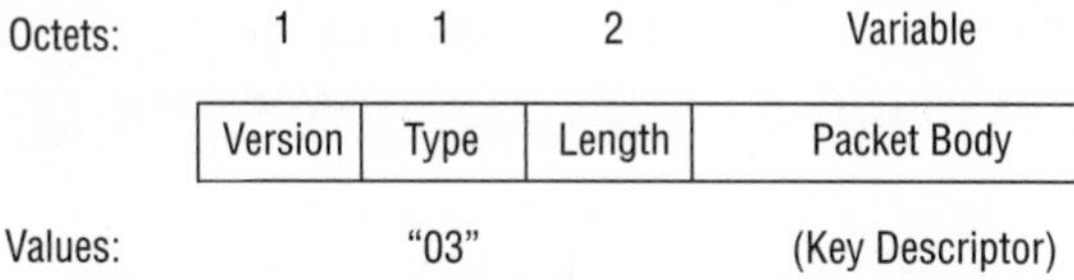

Octets: 1   1   2   Variable

Version	Type	Length	Packet Body

Values: "03"   (Key Descriptor)

Figure 3-7: An EAPOL-Key packet is identified by a "0000 0011" (Hex value "03") in the Type field.

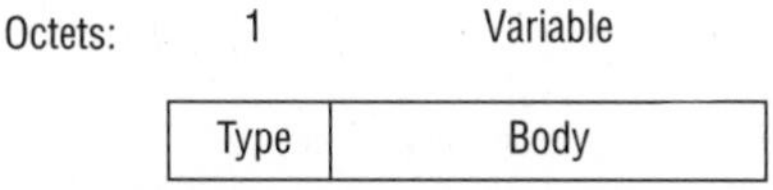

Octets: 1   Variable

Type	Body

Figure 3-8: Format for the Key Descriptor contained within EAPOL-Key packets.

Descriptor Type Field

The Descriptor Type field of an EAPOL-Key packet is one octet in length and represents the type of Key Descriptor being carried by the EAPOL-Key packet. The Descriptor Type value allows the receiving end of the packet to correctly interpret the Key Descriptor. Table 3-2 identifies the current Key Descriptor values.

Table 3-2: EAPOL Descriptor Types

DESCRIPTOR TYPE	VALUE
RC4 Key Descriptor	1
IEEE 802.11 Key Descriptor	2

Descriptor Body Field for RC4

Figure 3-9 illustrates the format of the RC4 Descriptor Body of an EAPOL-Key packet. This type descriptor may be found in earlier implementations of 802.1X. The definition of each field is shown in Table 3-3.

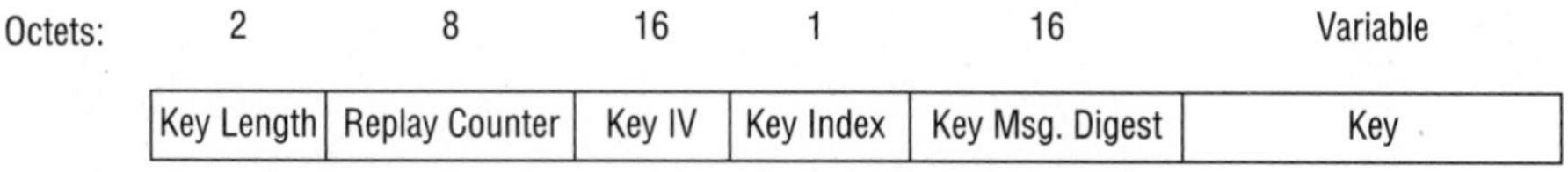

Octets: 2   8   16   1   16   Variable

Key Length	Replay Counter	Key IV	Key Index	Key Msg. Digest	Key

Figure 3-9: EAPOL-Key Packet Body contents for RC4 descriptors

Table 3-3: EAPOL-Key Packet Body contents

EAPOL-KEY FIELDS	SIZE	VALUE
Key Length	2 octets	Equals the number of octets in the key. For example, a key length of 40 bits has a Key Length field value of 5.
Replay Counter	8 octets	A counter value to detect and avoid replaying of key messages
Key IV (Initialization Vector)	16 octets	128-bit random number that represents the IV value used to generate the RC4 encryption key
Key Index	1 octet	The authenticator generates this value, which is used to differentiate multiple keys in use. 7 bits of the field represent an integer 0–127, which is the key index. A single bit flag in the field is interpreted as follows: flag = 1 means that the key is a unicast key, flag = 0 means that the key is a broadcast key.
Key Message Digest	16 octets	Digest of all the fields of the EAPOL packet
Key		The actual key

EAPOL-Encapsulated-ASF-Alert

Figure 3-10 illustrates an EAPOL-Encapsulated-ASF-Alert packet. This packet is useful when the supplicant must send information to the protected side of the network before authentication is complete. For example, the supplicant may need to send a status message to a server. The contents of the EAPOL-Encapsulated-ASF-Alert are generally proprietary.

Octets:	1	1	2	Variable
	Version	Type	Length	Packet Body
Values:		"04"		(Alert Data)

Figure 3-10: An EAPOL-Encapsulated-ASF-Alert packet is identified by a "0000 0100" (Hex value "04") in the Type field.

EAP Packet Structure

An EAP packet includes the fields shown in Figure 3-11. The following sections describe each of the EAP packet fields.

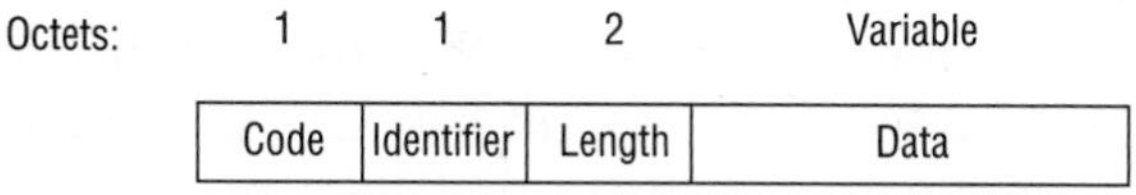

Octets: 1   1   2   Variable

| Code | Identifier | Length | Data |

Figure 3-11: EAP packets include Code, Identifier, Length, and Data fields.

EAP Code Field

Similar to the Type field in EAPOL packets, the EAP Code field identifies the type of EAP packet. This field is one octet long. Table 3-4 identifies the various types of EAP packets based on the Code field value. EAP in the 802.1X standard doesn't specify use of any of the other possible values at this time. Future extensions to the protocol may utilize additional values, however. Refer to the section "EAP Packet Types," later in this chapter, for a description of each packet type.

Table 3-4: EAP Code Field Values

PACKET TYPE	CODE FIELD VALUE
EAP-Request	0000 0001 (Hex "01")
EAP-Response	0000 0010 (Hex "02")
EAP-Success	0000 0011 (Hex "03")
EAP-Failure	0000 0100 (Hex "04")

EAP Identifier Field

The EAP Identifier field is one octet in length. The Identifier field makes it possible to match EAP-Response packets to the applicable EAP-Request packets.

If the Identifier field in an EAP-Request packet sent from the authentication server to the supplicant contains the value "0000 0101," for example, the supplicant will respond with an EAP-Response packet with the EAP Identifier set to "0000 0101." In addition, the authenticator uses the same Identifier values when retransmitting EAP packets. For example, an authenticator may initially send an EAP-Request packet to the supplicant with the Identifier field set to "0000 1100." If no response is heard from the supplicant, then the authenticator will retransmit the EAP-Request packet with the Identifier field set to "0000 1100." This ensures that the supplicant knows that a particular packet is a retransmission, which avoids processing duplicate packets. A typical 802.1X implementation has a maximum of three to five retransmissions.

EAP Length Field

The EAP Length field is two octets long and identifies the number of octets comprising the EAP packet. The EAP Length field value includes the EAP Code, Identifier, Length, and Data fields, which is the length of the entire EAP packet. Thus, the EAP Length field value is the same as the EAPOL length field value. For example, an EAP Length field value of "0000 0100 1001 1110" indicates that the EAP packet contains 1,182 total octets. In this case, the EAP Data field contains 1,178 octets of data, which are the 1,182 total octets minus 4 header octets. If an entity such as a supplicant or authenticator receives an EAP packet with an actual received length that is less than the Length field value, then the entity must silently discard the packet. For example, a received EAP packet having a total of 1,179 octets would be discarded if the EAP Length field were 1,182 octets.

NOTE As with EAPOL, the maximum length of the EAP packet depends on limitations of the link transport protocol, such as IEEE 802.3 or 802.11.

EAP Data Field

The contents of the Data field of an EAP packet depends on the packet type. For instance, EAP-Request and EAP-Response packets have Data fields. In some cases, the EAP Data field may not include any data.

EAP Packet Types

The following sections describe each of the EAP packet types.

EAP-Request

Figure 3-12 illustrates an EAP-Request packet. The authenticator communicates with the supplicant using EAP-Request packets. For example, the authenticator issues EAP-Request packets to deliver EAP-Method data traveling from the authentication server to the supplicant. Or, the supplicant may send an EAP-Request packet to demand the identity of the authenticator for mutual authentication, depending on the EAP-Method in use.

Octets: 1   1   2   Variable

Code	Identifier	Length	Data

Values: "01"   (EAP Method Data)

Figure 3-12: An EAP-Request packet is identified by a "0000 0001" (Hex value "01") in the Type field.

EAP-Response

Figure 3-13 illustrates an EAP-Response packet. The supplicant issues an EAP Response packet to communicate with the supplicant, such as when sending EAP-Method data or credentials requested by the supplicant.

Octets: 1   1   2   Variable

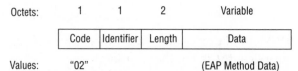

Code	Identifier	Length	Data

Values: "02"   (EAP Method Data)

Figure 3-13: An EAP-Response packet is identified by a "0000 0010" (Hex value "02") in the Type field.

EAP Request/Response Types

The EAP specification defines an initial set of EAP types that define the structure of the EAP-Request and EAP-Response packets. The EAP type controls what the EAP packet carries. Table 3-5 identifies the standards-based EAP types. Types 1, 2, and 3 are special case types, and the remaining types are for authentication exchanges. All EAP implementations must support types 1, 2, 3, and 4. The EAP type is represented in the Code field of an EAP-Method packet as a single octet value (see Figure 3-14). Chapter 5 explains details of these EAP types as well as several others that have been developed since ratification of the 802.1X and EAP standards.

Table 3-5: Standards-Based EAP Types

VALUE (DECIMAL AND BINARY)	EAP TYPE
1 (0000 0001)	Identity
2 (0000 0010)	Notification
3 (0000 0011)	NAK
4 (0000 0100)	MD5-Challenge
5 (0000 0101)	One-Time Password (OTP)
6 (0000 0110)	Generic Token Card (GTC)
254 (1111 1110)	Expanded Types
255 (1111 1111)	Experimental use

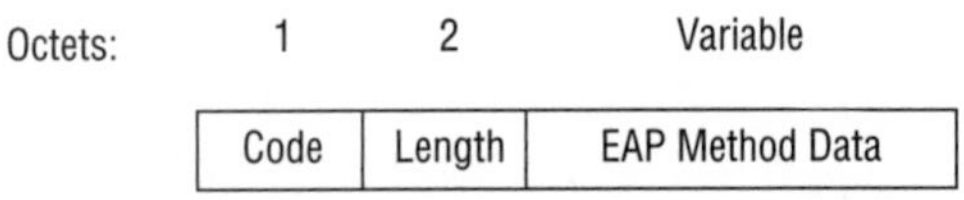

Octets: 1   2   Variable

Code	Length	EAP Method Data

Figure 3-14: An EAP-Method packet consists of Code, Length, and EAP Method Data fields.

EAP-Success

Based on the outcome of the EAP-Method procedures, the authenticator sends an EAP-Success packet to the supplicant if the authentication server informs the authenticator that the supplicant is authorized to access the protected network. Figure 3-15 illustrates an EAP-Success packet. This packet doesn't contain an EAP Data field.

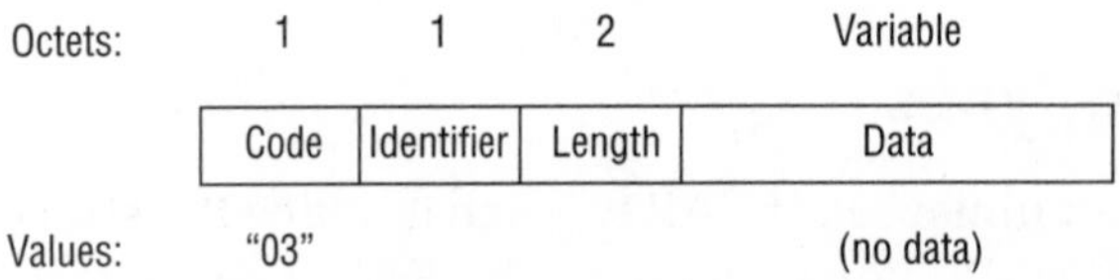

Octets: 1   1   2   Variable

Code	Identifier	Length	Data

Values: "03"   (no data)

Figure 3-15: An EAP-Success packet is identified by a "0000 0011" (Hex value "03") in the Type field.

EAP-Failure

The authenticator sends an EAP-Failure packet to the supplicant if the result of the authentication process indicates that the supplicant is not authorized to access the protected network. Figure 3-16 illustrates an EAP-Failure packet. This packet doesn't contain an EAP Data field.

Octets: 1   1   2   Variable

Code	Identifier	Length	Data

Values: "04"   (no data)

Figure 3-16: An EAP-Failure packet is identified by a "0000 0100" (Hex value "04") in the Type field.

802.3 Frame Structure

The IEEE 802.3 (Ethernet) standard defines a wired local area network (LAN). If users are stationary, 802.3 will likely provide the Physical Layer and Data Link Layer connectivity between the supplicants and authenticator. In this case, user computing devices (supplicant) will be equipped with Ethernet cards, which communicate using the 802.3 protocol with an Ethernet switch (authenticator). An advantage of Ethernet is that it offers a very reliable connection between the supplicant and the authenticator. The Data field within the 802.3 Data frame, which Figure 3-17 illustrates, carries the EAPOL/EAP packets. Table 3-6 describes each field of the 802.3 Data frame.

Octets: 7   1   6   6   2   Variable   4

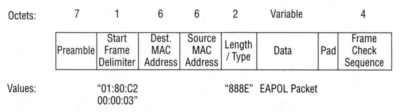

Preamble	Start Frame Delimiter	Dest. MAC Address	Source MAC Address	Length / Type	Data	Pad	Frame Check Sequence

Values: "01:80:C2 00:00:03"   "888E"   EAPOL Packet

Figure 3-17: The IEEE 802.3 Data frame carries EAPOL/EAP packets in wired networks.

Table 3-6: 802.3 Data Frame Fields

FIELD	SIZE	VALUE
Preamble	7 octets	Used by the receiving station to synchronize on the incoming data
Start Frame Delimiter	1 octet	A value of "1010 1011," which indicates the start of the frame
Destination MAC Address	6 octets	For 802.1X, the value is always 01:80:C2:00:00:03 (hex format).
Source MAC Address	6 octets	MAC address of the sending station
Length/Type	2 octets	For 802.1X frames, this value is 888e (hex format) and indicates the nature of the protocol (i.e., Data field contains an EAPOL/EAP packet).
Data	Variable packets	Encapsulated EAPOL, EAP, and EAP-Method
Pad	Variable	Variable number of octets based on 802.3 specifications
Frame Check Sequence	4 octets	Value generated prior to transmitting the frame for the destination station to determine whether errors occurred during transmission over the medium

As mentioned in Chapter 2, 802.1X makes use of the MAC addressing reserved for the 802.1D Spanning-Tree Protocol. 802.1X has been assigned one of the unused 802.1D Spanning-Tree group addresses, which is 01:80:C2:00:00:03. All 802-based devices receive and process frames having this group address.

Before sending an 802.3 frame, a station, which could be the Ethernet card (station) in the supplicant or authenticator, must first listen on the wired medium (i.e., the Ethernet cable connecting the supplicant and authenticator) to determine whether any other station is currently transmitting a frame. Frames are transmitted over Ethernet networks using digital signals, which are electrical impulses that represent the 1s and 0s (data) of the EAPOL, EAP, and EAP-Method packets. If no other station is transmitting, then the station can send the data. The station will hold off transmission if another station is transmitting. This is often referred to as *carrier sense multiple access (CSMA)* or *listen-before-talk protocol*. The resulting sharing of the wired medium can lead to delays if there is heavy traffic on the network, but Ethernet is very efficient and these delays only infrequently impact the operation of 802.1X in a significant manner.

802.11 Frame Structure

The IEEE 802.11 (Wi-Fi) standard defines a wireless LAN, which offers an effective wire-free interface between supplicants and authenticators. An advantage of Wi-Fi is that it offers mobility, but resulting wireless connections between the supplicant and the authenticator may be unreliable at times. Radio frequency (RF) interference from microwave ovens, cordless phones, and other wireless systems may interfere with the operation of Wi-Fi networks. Figure 3-18 illustrates the Data field within the 802.11 Data frame. As with 802.3, the 802.11 Data frames carry the EAPOL/EAP packets in the Frame Body field.

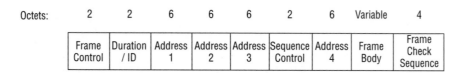

Octets:	2	2	6	6	6	2	6	Variable	4
	Frame Control	Duration / ID	Address 1	Address 2	Address 3	Sequence Control	Address 4	Frame Body	Frame Check Sequence

Figure 3-18: The IEEE 802.11 Data frame carries EAPOL/EAP packets in wireless networks.

Similar to 802.3, 802.11 networks also use CSMA for controlling access to the wireless medium. With wireless networks, however, radio waves provide a mechanism for sending the data. The radio waves generally represent the 1s and 0s of the EAPOL, EAP, and EAP-Method packets through the use of different frequencies or phase shifts. The resulting sharing of the wireless medium can lead to longer delays than with 802.3 because 802.11 is not as efficient.

The combination of RF interference and limited capacity can sometimes impact the operation of 802.1X port-based authentication systems unless special consideration is given to the design of the wireless network. For example, installers must ensure that adequate signal coverage is available in all areas where users will need to access the network. In addition, preventative measures, such as RF channel settings, should be established to limit exposure of the system to RF interference.

CHAPTER 4

RADIUS Protocols

This chapter continues the discussion of 802.1X port-based authentication protocols begun in Chapters 2 and 3 and provides a closer look at RADIUS, which is by far the most common authentication server protocol. As you'll see, the RADIUS protocol is fairly straightforward, but there are many RADIUS attributes common to 802.1X systems that are beneficial to know. This chapter will help you understand RADIUS protocols to provide a basis for configuring and troubleshooting port-based authentication systems.

RADIUS Recap

As you might recall from Chapter 2, "Port-Based Authentication Concepts," RADIUS is the primary communications mechanism between an authenticator and an authentication server in a port-based authentication system (see Figure 4-1). Sometimes the authentication server that implements RADIUS is called a "RADIUS server." The RADIUS protocols between the authenticator and the authentication server transport the EAP-Method data in encrypted format. The 802.1X standard and EAP specification do not require RADIUS as the authentication server, but RADIUS is by far the most commonly used. Therefore, this book focuses on implementing RADIUS for port-based authentication systems.

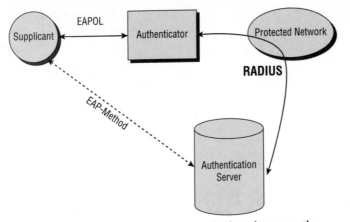

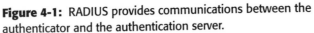

Figure 4-1: RADIUS provides communications between the authenticator and the authentication server.

The authentication server carries on a two-way conversation, one with the authenticator via RADIUS protocols and one with the supplicant via EAP-Methods. The use of RADIUS protocols is somewhat of a physical process, whereas communications with EAP-Methods is logical. RADIUS protocols provide the physical "transportation" of the EAP-Methods between the authenticator and the authentication server. EAP-Methods, on the other hand, offer the "intelligence" to the communications. As discussed in Chapter 2, most communications between the authenticator and the authentication server consist of RADIUS Access-Request and Access-Challenge packets. The authenticator sends EAP-Method data to the authentication server via RADIUS Access-Request frames, and the authentication server sends EAP-Method data to the authenticator in Access-Challenge packets.

NOTE Be certain that the RADIUS server you choose supports the EAP-Methods that you plan to implement.

RADIUS Packet Structure

All RADIUS packets have the same basic structure, which consists of Code, Identifier, Length, Authenticator, and Attributes fields (see Figure 4-2). The EAP-Method packet is carried in the Data field of an EAP packet. Each of the subsequent subsections explains the fields of the EAP-Method packet.

Octets:	1	1	2	16	Variable
	Code	Identifier	Length	Authenticator	Attributes

Figure 4-2: A RADIUS packet consists of Code, Identifier, Length, Authenticator, and Attributes fields.

Code Field

The RADIUS Code field is one octet in length and identifies the type of RADIUS packet. Table 4-1 identifies the various Code values and corresponding packet types. For example, if the Code field value is "1," the packet is a RADIUS Access-Request.

Table 4-1: RADIUS Code Field Values

CODE	PACKET TYPE
1	RADIUS Access-Request
2	RADIUS Access-Accept
3	RADIUS Access-Reject
4	RADIUS Accounting-Request
5	RADIUS Accounting-Response
11	RADIUS Access-Challenge
12	Status-Server (experimental)
13	Status-Client (experimental)
255	Reserved

Identifier Field

The RADIUS Identifier field is one octet in length. Similar to the like-named field in the EAP protocol, the Identifier field of a RADIUS packet makes it possible to match RADIUS Access-Challenge packets with Access-Request packets. The Identifier field in a RADIUS Access-Request packet sent from the authenticator, for example, may contain the value "0000 1101." The authentication server will respond with a RADIUS Access-Challenge packet Identifier field set to "0000 1101." In addition, the authenticator would use the same Identifier value if retransmitting the same corresponding RADIUS Access-Request packet.

For example, an authenticator may initially send a RADIUS Access-Request packet to the authentication server with the Identifier field set to "0001 1100." If no response is heard from the authentication server, the authenticator will retransmit the RADIUS Access-Request packet with the Identifier field set to "0001 1100." This ensures that the authentication server knows that a particular packet is a retransmission, which avoids processing duplicate packets.

Length Field

The RADIUS Length field is two octets long and identifies the number of octets comprising the RADIUS packet. The maximum length of the RADIUS packet is 4,096 octets. The RADIUS Length field value includes the EAP Code, Identifier, Length, Authenticator, and Attributes fields. For example, a RADIUS Length field value of "0000 0100 1001 1110" indicates that the EAP packet contains 1,182 total octets. In this case, the RADIUS Attributes field, which is variable in length, contains 1,162 octets of data, which are the 1,182 total octets minus 20 header octets. As with EAP packets, if an entity such as an authenticator or authenticator server receives a RADIUS packet with an actual received length that is less than the Length field value, then the entity must silently discard the packet.

For example, a received RADIUS packet with a total of 1,179 octets would be discarded if the EAP Length field were 1,182 octets. If the received RADIUS packet has a length that is greater than identified in the Length field, then the entity receiving the packet must discard the additional octets. For example, an authentication server receiving a RADIUS packet with a total of 1,029 octets and a Length field indicating a packet of 1,022 octets would process the packet but discard the last seven octets of the packet.

NOTE As with EAPOL, the maximum length of the EAP packet depends on limitations of the link transport protocol, such as IEEE 802.3 or 802.11.

Authenticator Field

The Authenticator field is 16 octets long and contains a value corresponding to the RADIUS packet type being sent. Figure 4-3 illustrates the contents of the Authenticator field for various packet types.

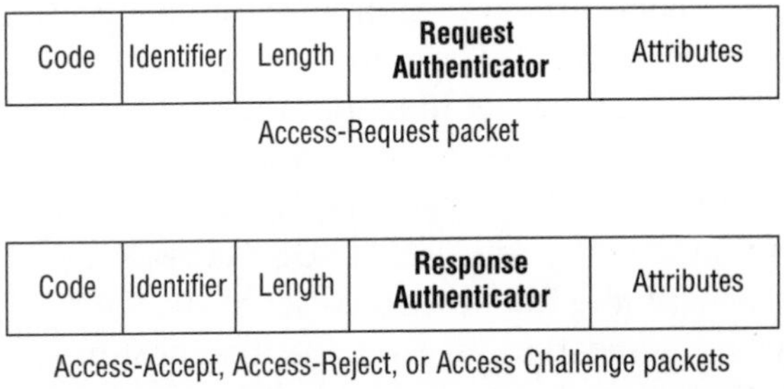

Code	Identifier	Length	Request Authenticator	Attributes

Access-Request packet

Code	Identifier	Length	Response Authenticator	Attributes

Access-Accept, Access-Reject, or Access Challenge packets

Figure 4-3: The Authenticator field of a RADIUS packet contains a Request Authenticator or Response Authenticator, depending on the RADIUS packet type.

Request Authenticator

In RADIUS Access-Request packets, the content of the Authenticator field is the Request Authenticator. This value is a random number and should be unpredictable and unique. The shared secret configured in the authenticator and the authentication server is combined with the Request Authenticator and put through a one-way MD5 hash to create the digest value (16 octets in length) that is XORed with the user's password. The RADIUS Access-Request packet carries this result in the User-Password attribute. The Request Authenticator value is changed whenever the Identifier field changes.

Response Authenticator

The Response Authenticator resides in the Authenticator field of RADIUS Access-Accept, Access-Reject, and Access-Challenge packets. The Response Authenticator is a one-way MD5 hash calculated over the entire length of the corresponding RADIUS Access-Request packet and the shared secret. Figure 4-4 shows how this works.

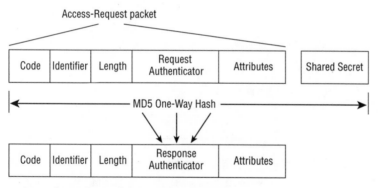

Figure 4-4: The Response Authenticator consists of a one-way MD5 hash of the RADIUS Access-Request packet and shared secret.

NOTE The shared secret for use between the authenticator and the RADIUS server should be at least 16 octets in length and unguessable.

Attributes Field

The Attributes field of a RADIUS packet is variable in length and contains specific data elements being communicated between the authenticator and the authentication server. The section "RADIUS Attributes" explains many of the common attributes that RADIUS uses.

RADIUS Packet Types

Figure 4-5 illustrates communications between the authenticator and the authentication server using RADIUS. Similar to EAP, RADIUS frames are sent using a lock-step process.

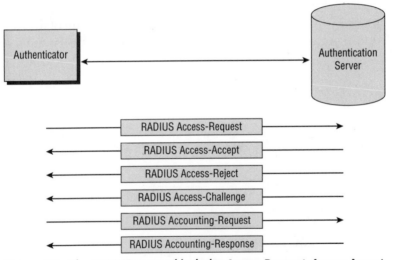

Figure 4-5: The RADIUS protocol includes Access-Request, Access-Accept, Access-Reject, Accounting-Request, Accounting-Response, and Access-Challenge packets.

RADIUS Access-Request

Figure 4-6 illustrates a RADIUS Access-Request packet, which is sent from the authenticator to the RADIUS server to carry data pertinent to the EAP-Method in use. For example, the Access-Request packet could include the supplicant's credentials. All authentication implementations must issue an Access-Request packet when authenticating the supplicant. The Access-Request generally contains the User-Name attribute and the NAS-IP-Address attribute (or a NAS-Identifier attribute). When containing the User-Password attribute, the password is hidden using a method based on RSA MD5.

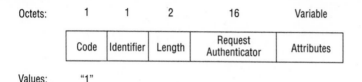

Values: "1"

Figure 4-6: A RADIUS Access-Request packet is identified by a decimal "1" in the Code field.

RADIUS Access-Challenge

Figure 4-7 illustrates a RADIUS Access-Challenge packet, which is sent from the RADIUS server to the authenticator in response to an Access-Request packet. The Identifier field value of the Access-Challenge must match the Identifier value in the corresponding Access-Request packet. The Attributes field of an Access-Challenge packet may have one or more of the following attributes: State, Reply-Message, Vendor-Specific, Idle-Timeout, Session-Timeout and Proxy-State.

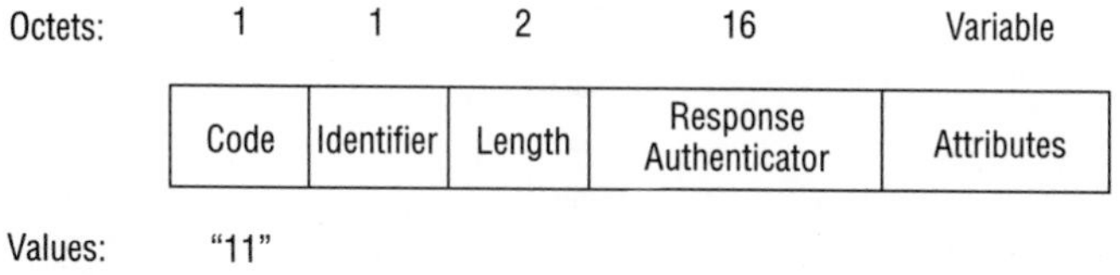

Octets:	1	1	2	16	Variable
	Code	Identifier	Length	Response Authenticator	Attributes

Values: "11"

Figure 4-7: A RADIUS Access-Challenge packet is identified by a decimal "11" in the Code field.

NOTE If an authenticator for some reason does not support challenge/response protocols, the authenticator must treat an Access-Challenge packet as an Access-Reject packet regardless of the contents of the Access-Challenge packet.

RADIUS Access-Accept

Figure 4-8 illustrates a RADIUS Access-Accept packet, which is sent from the RADIUS server to the authenticator in response to a RADIUS Access-Request. For example, the Access-Accept packet may carry an acceptance or configuration information for a particular supplicant. The Identifier field value of the Access-Accept packet must match the Identifier value in the corresponding Access-Request packet. The Attributes field of an Access-Accept packet may have one or more attributes similar to the those identified for the RADIUS Access-Challenge packet.

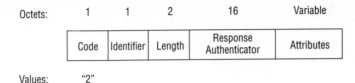

Octets: 1   1   2   16   Variable

Code	Identifier	Length	Response Authenticator	Attributes

Values: "2"

Figure 4-8: A RADIUS Access-Accept packet is identified by a decimal "2" in the Code field.

RADIUS Access-Reject

Figure 4-9 illustrates a RADIUS Access-Reject packet, which is sent from the RADIUS server to the authenticator in response to a RADIUS Access-Request. The Access-Reject packet is sent when any of the attributes in the Access-Request are not acceptable. The Identifier field value of the Access-Accept must match the Identifier value in the corresponding Access-Request packet. The Attributes field of an Access-Reject packet may include one or more Reply-Message attributes with a text message, which the authenticator can display to the user.

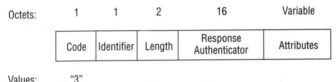

Octets: 1   1   2   16   Variable

Code	Identifier	Length	Response Authenticator	Attributes

Values: "3"

Figure 4-9: A RADIUS Access-Accept packet is identified by a decimal "3" in the Code field.

RADIUS Accounting-Request

Figure 4-10 illustrates a RADIUS Accounting-Request packet, which is sent from the authenticator to the RADIUS server to request accounting information.

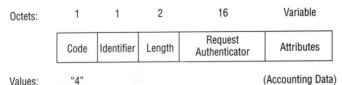

Octets: 1   1   2   16   Variable

Code	Identifier	Length	Request Authenticator	Attributes

Values: "4"   (Accounting Data)

Figure 4-10: A RADIUS Accounting-Request packet is identified by a decimal "4" in the Code field.

RADIUS Accounting-Response

Figure 4-11 illustrates a RADIUS Accounting-Response packet, which is sent from the RADIUS server to the authenticator in response to the RADIUS Accounting-Request packet. The Accounting-Response packet must match the Identifier value in the corresponding Accounting-Request.

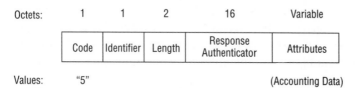

Figure 4-11: A RADIUS Accounting-Response packet is identified by a decimal "5" in the Code field.

> **NOTE** For details on RADIUS Code field values 4 (Accounting-Request) and 5 (Accounting-Response), refer to RFC 2866.

> **NOTE** Refer to RFC 2865 for more details on RADIUS packet structure and packet types.

RADIUS Attributes

The RADIUS attributes contained within a RADIUS packet are elements of data communicated between the authenticator and the RADIUS server. More than 100 attributes are defined in a combination of RFC 2865 and vendor documentation.

RADIUS Attributes Format

Each attribute contained in the Attributes field of a RADIUS packet has the format shown in Figure 4-12. Some RADIUS packets carry several attributes. As a result, the format shown in Figure 4-12 is repeated within the Attributes field of the RADIUS packet.

Octets:	1	1	Variable
	Type	Length	Value

Figure 4-12: The Attributes field of a RADIUS packet contains Type, Length, and Value fields.

Type Field

The Type field of a RADIUS attribute is one octet in length and identifies a specific attribute. Type values 192–223 are for experimental use, values 224–240 are for implementation-specific use, and values 241–255 are reserved and should not be used. RADIUS servers are designed to ignore attributes with an unknown value in the Type field of the RADIUS packet. RFC 2865 defines an initial set of attributes as shown in Table 4-2. There are many other RADIUS attributes defined in other publications. For instance, RADIUS attribute "EAP Message" (Type field = "79") is one defined in RFC 2284 that encapsulates EAP packets (and EAP-Method data) sent between the authenticator and the authentication server.

Table 4-2: List of RADIUS Attributes Defined in RFC 2865

ATTRIBUTE NUMBER	ATTRIBUTE NAME
1	User-Name
2	User-Password
3	CHAP-Password
4	NAS-IP-Address
5	NAS-Port
6	Service-Type
7	Framed-Protocol
8	Framed-IP-Address
9	Framed-IP-Netmask
10	Framed-Routing
11	Filter-Id
12	Framed-MTU
13	Framed-Compression
14	Login-IP-Host
15	Login-Service
16	Login-TCP-Port
17	(unassigned)

Table 4-2 *(continued)*

ATTRIBUTE NUMBER	ATTRIBUTE NAME
18	Reply-Message
19	Callback-Number
20	Callback-Id
21	(unassigned)
22	Framed-Route
23	Framed-IPX-Network
24	State
25	Class
26	Vendor-Specific
27	Session-Timeout
28	Idle-Timeout
29	Termination-Action
30	Called-Station-Id
31	Calling-Station-Id
32	NAS-Identifier
33	Proxy-State
34	Login-LAT-Service
35	Login-LAT-Node
36	Login-LAT-Group
37	Framed-AppleTalk-Link
38	Framed-AppleTalk-Network
39	Framed-AppleTalk-Zone
40–59	(reserved for accounting)
60	CHAP-Challenge
61	NAS-Port-Type
62	Port-Limit
63	Login-LAT-Port

Length Field

The Length field of a RADIUS attribute is one octet and indicates the length of the defined attribute. The length includes the Type, Length, and Value fields. If the RADIUS server receives an attribute in a RADIUS Access-Request packet with an invalid length, then the RADIUS server should respond with a RADIUS Access-Reject packet. If the authenticator receives an attribute in a RADIUS Access-Accept, Access-Reject, or Access-Challenge packet with an invalid length, then the authenticator will either regard the received packet as an Access-Reject or silently discard the packet.

Value Field

The Value field of a RADIUS attribute is zero or more octets in length and includes attribute-specific data. The Value field can include the following different data types:

- **Text:** 1–253 octets containing UTF-8 encoded characters. If no text is sent, then the entire attribute will be discarded by most RADIUS servers and authenticators.
- **String:** 1–253 octets containing binary data. If no data is sent, then the entire attribute will be discarded by most RADIUS servers and authenticators.
- **Address:** 32-bit value
- **Integer:** 32-bit unsigned value
- **Time:** 32-bit unsigned value representing the number of seconds since 00:00:00 UTC, January 1, 1970. The standard attributes in RFC 2865 do not use this data type, but other attribute types might.

The following sections summarize some of the common RADIUS attributes used with 802.1X port-based authentication systems.

EAP-Message Attribute

The RADIUS EAP-Message attribute (Type field = "79") in RADIUS packets is the primary attribute for 802.1X because it encapsulates the EAP-Method data between the authenticator and the authentication server (see Figure 4-13). As described in other chapters, EAP-Methods are communications between the supplicant and the authentication server. The EAP-Message attribute actually contains the EAP-Method packet. All other RADIUS attributes in 802.1X port-based authentication implementations are peripheral to the EAP-Message attribute.

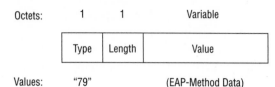

Octets: 1   1   Variable

| Type | Length | Value |

Values: "79"   (EAP-Method Data)

Figure 4-13: An EAP-Message attribute encapsulates EAP-Method data.

EAP-Message attributes are sent from the authenticator to the RADIUS server within RADIUS Access-Request packets. EAP-Message attributes are sent from the RADIUS server to the authenticator in RADIUS Access-Challenge packets. A RADIUS Access-Request or Access-Challenge packet may contain multiple EAP packets. If this is the case, then they must be in order and in consecutive EAP-Message attributes. RADIUS Access-Accept and Access-Reject packets generally only carry a single EAP-Message attribute. As examples, the Access-Accept packet would contain an EAP-Success packet and the Access-Reject packet would contain an EAP-Failure packet. If a RADIUS server receives an EAP packet that it doesn't understand, then it will normally respond with a RADIUS Access-Reject packet.

When implementing the EAP-Message attribute, the Message-Authenticator attribute protects all Access-Request, Access-Challenge, Access-Accept, and Access-Reject packets containing EAP-Method data. In fact, a RADIUS server receiving a RADIUS Access-Request packet including an EAP-Message attribute without a valid Message-Authenticator will silently discard the packet. In addition, RADIUS servers not supporting the EAP-Message attribute will also discard the corresponding RADIUS Access-Request packets containing EAP-Message attributes.

NOTE Refer to RFC 2284 for details on RADIUS support for delivery of EAP packets.

Message-Authenticator Attribute

In general, the RADIUS Message-Authenticator attribute (Type field = "80") may be used by the RADIUS server in any RADIUS Access-Request packet to authenticate RADIUS Access-Requests. In addition, the Message-Authenticator attribute may check the integrity of Access-Requests to prevent spoofing. When supporting EAP-Message attributes, all Access-Request, Access-Accept, Access-Reject, or Access-Challenge packets must include the Message-Authenticator attribute.

Figure 4-14 illustrates the format of the Message-Authenticator attribute. The length of the Message-Authenticator attribute is always 18 octets. For Access-Request packets, the Value field of the Message-Authenticator attribute is an HMAC-MD5 hash of the Access-Request packet, using the shared secret as the key.

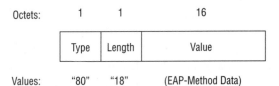

Octets: 1   1   16

Type	Length	Value

Values: "80"   "18"   (EAP-Method Data)

Figure 4-14: A RADIUS Message-Authenticator attribute in a RADIUS packet provides authentication for RADIUS packets implementing EAP-Message attributes.

NOTE Refer to RFC 2104 for details on calculating the HMAC-MD5 hash used with the RADIUS Message-Authenticator attribute.

Password-Retry Attribute

The RADIUS Password-Retry attribute (Type field = 75) can be included in a RADIUS Access-Reject packet to indicate the number of authentication attempts a user can perform before being disconnected. Figure 4-15 shows the format of the Password-Retry attribute. This attribute is always six octets in length. The Value field is four octets and includes an integer specifying the number of password retry attempts the user can utilize. For the example shown in Figure 4-15, the supplicant has three attempts to authenticate. If the third attempt fails, then the supplicant will be disconnected from the network.

Octets: 1   1   4

Type	Length	Value

Values: "75"   "6"   "3"

Figure 4-15: A RADIUS Password-Retry attribute includes the number of password attempts that a user can perform before being disconnected from the network.

User-Name Attribute

The User-Name attribute (Type Field = "1") identifies the name of the user being authenticated and is sent from the authenticator to the RADIUS server in a RADIUS Access-Request packet. This is a very common attribute. The username is one or more octets in length. Figure 4-16 illustrates the format of a User-Name attribute.

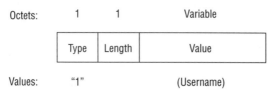

Figure 4-16: A RADIUS User-Name attribute carries the username.

The username generally has one of the following forms:

- **Text:** UTF-8 encoded with 10646 different characters
- **Network access identifier:** Identifier as defined in RFC 2486
- **Distinguished name:** Name in ASN.1 form used in Public Key authentication systems

User-Password Attribute

The User-Password attribute (Type Field = "2") identifies the password of the user being authenticated and is sent from the authenticator to the RADIUS server in a RADIUS Access-Request packet. The user password is one or more octets in length. Figure 4-17 illustrates the format of the User-Password attribute. The password is hidden prior to transmission in the Access-Request packet. The password is first padded with nulls to a multiple of 16 octets. A one-way MD5 hash is then calculated over the shared secret and Request Authenticator. The result of this calculation is XORed with the first 16 octets of the password and placed at the beginning of the User-Password attribute Value field.

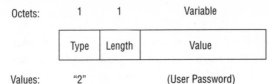

Octets: 1   1   Variable

Type	Length	Value

Values: "2"   (User Password)

Figure 4-17: A RADIUS User-Name attribute is identified by a decimal "2" in the Type field of the attribute and carries a hidden version of the user password.

NAS-IP-Address Attribute

The NAS-IP-Address attribute (Type field = "4") indicates the IP address of the authenticator that is requesting authentication of the supplicant. The NAS-IP-Address attribute is only used in RADIUS Access-Request packets. Either the NAS-IP-Address attribute or the NAS-Identifier attribute must be present in an Access-Request packet. Figure 4-18 illustrates the format of the NAS-IP-Address attribute. This attribute is always six octets in length, and four octets are allocated to the IP Address field.

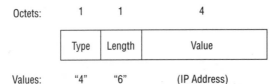

Octets: 1   1   4

Type	Length	Value

Values: "4"   "6"   (IP Address)

Figure 4-18: A RADIUS NAS-IP-Address attribute includes the IP address of the authenticator.

NAS-Port Attribute

The NAS-Port attribute (Type field = "5") includes the physical port number (not TCP or UDP port) of the authenticator that is requesting authentication of the supplicant. The NAS-Port attribute is only used in RADIUS Access-Request packets. Figure 4-19 illustrates the format of the NAS-Port attribute. This attribute is always six octets in length, and four octets are allocated to the Port Number field.

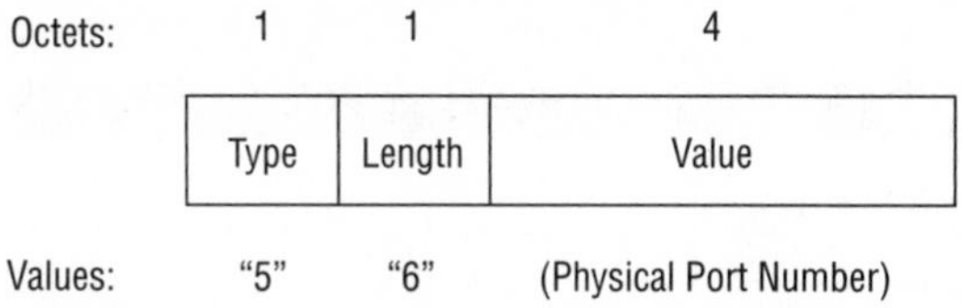

Octets: 1   1   4

Type	Length	Value

Values: "5"   "6"   (Physical Port Number)

Figure 4-19: A RADIUS NAS-Port attribute includes the physical port number of the authenticator.

Service-Type Attribute

The Service-Type attribute (Type field = "6") identifies the type of service that either the supplicant is requesting or the RADIUS server is granting. The Service-Type attribute is used in both Access-Request and Access-Accept packets. Figure 4-20 illustrates the format of the Service-Type attribute. This attribute is always six octets in length, and the Value field is four octets. The authenticator treats any unsupported service types granted by the RADIUS server as Access-Reject packets.

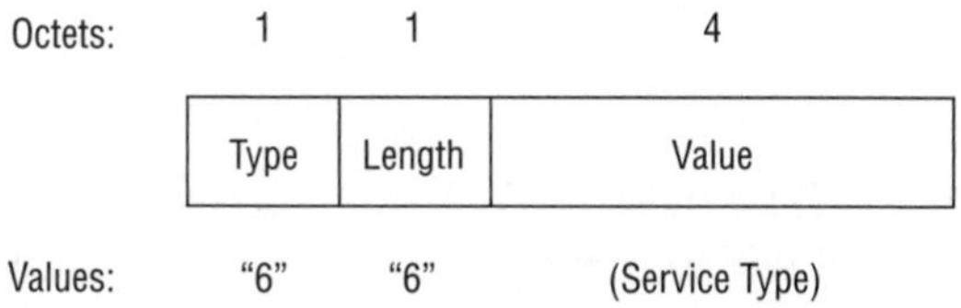

Octets: 1   1   4

Type	Length	Value

Values: "6"   "6"   (Service Type)

Figure 4-20: A RADIUS Service-Type attribute identifies a request or granting of a particular service.

The Value field of the Service-Type attribute can be one of the ones shown in Table 4-3.

Table 4-3: Value Field Services for the Service-Type Attribute

VALUE	SERVICE
1	Login
2	Framed
3	Callback Login

Continued

Table 4-3 *(continued)*

VALUE	SERVICE
4	Callback Framed
5	Outbound
6	Administrative
7	NAS Prompt
8	Authenticate Only
9	Callback NAS Prompt
10	Call Check
11	Callback Administrative

NOTE Refer to RFC 2865 for definitions of each of the service types for the RADIUS Service-Type attribute.

Vendor-Specific Attribute

The RADIUS Vendor-Specific attribute (Type field = "26") enables vendors to implement proprietary attributes not suitable for general usage. The inclusion of additional attributes, however, doesn't interfere with the operation of the RADIUS protocol. If a RADIUS server receives a RADIUS packet containing a Vendor-Specific attribute that it doesn't understand, the RADIUS server will discard the attribute and likely send an applicable message to the authenticator. Figure 4-21 illustrates the format of the Vendor-Specific attribute.

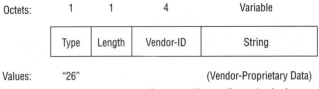

Figure 4-21: A RADIUS Vendor-Specific attribute includes vendor-proprietary data.

Vendor-ID Field

The Vendor-ID field of the Vendor-Specific attribute is four octets in length. The high-order octet contains all zeros, and the low-order three octets include the SMI Network Management Private Enterprise Code of the vendor.

String Field

The String field of the Vendor-Specific attribute is one or more octets in length.

Session-Timeout Attribute

The RADIUS Session-Timeout attribute (Type field = "27") establishes the maximum number of seconds the supplicant will have service. This attribute is only sent from the RADIUS server to the authenticator in RADIUS Access-Accept or Access-Challenge packets. Figure 4-22 shows the format of the Session-Timeout attribute. The length of the Session-Timeout attribute is always six octets. The Value field is four octets and contains a 32-bit unsigned integer, which represents the maximum number of seconds the applicable supplicant can have service.

Octets: 1   1   4

| Type | Length | Value |

Values: "27"   "6"   (Maximum Session Seconds)

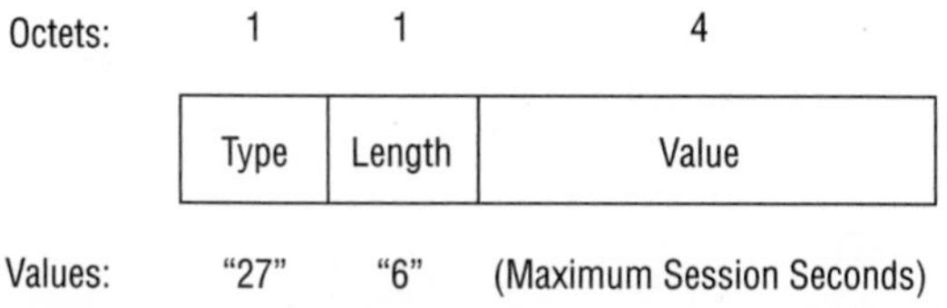

Figure 4-22: A RADIUS Session-Timeout attribute identifies the maximum number of seconds that the supplicant can have service.

Idle-Timeout Attribute

The RADIUS Idle-Timeout attribute (Type field = "28") establishes the maximum number of seconds the supplicant can be in an idle state before being disconnected from the network. This attribute is only sent from the RADIUS server to the authenticator in RADIUS Access-Accept or Access-Challenge packets. Figure 4-23 shows the format of the Idle-Timeout attribute. The length of the Idle-Timeout attribute is always six octets. The value field is four octets and contains a 32-bit unsigned integer, which represents the maximum number of seconds the applicable supplicant can be idle.

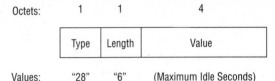

Octets: 1   1   4

Type	Length	Value

Values: "28"   "6"   (Maximum Idle Seconds)

Figure 4-23: A RADIUS Idle-Timeout attribute identifies the maximum number of seconds that the supplicant can be idle before being disconnected from the network.

Termination-Action Attribute

The RADIUS Termination-Action attribute (Type field = "29") indicates what action the authenticator should take when the specified service is completed. The Termination-Action attribute is only used in Access-Accept packets. Figure 4-24 shows the format of the Termination-Action attribute. The Value field is four octets in length and can either be "0" for Default or "1" for Radius Request. If the Value Field is "Radius Request," then the authenticator may send a new Access-Request to the RADIUS server after the service is terminated.

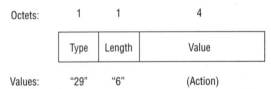

Octets: 1   1   4

Type	Length	Value

Values: "29"   "6"   (Action)

Figure 4-24: A RADIUS Termination-Action attribute identifies the action an authenticator should take when service is completed.

Authentication Server Selection Considerations

When implementing 802.1X port-based authentication systems, you need to choose a particular authentication server. In nearly all situations, RADIUS will likely satisfy all authentication requirements. In fact, the enterprise you're working with will probably already have a RADIUS server installed on the network.

Attributes

When determining which RADIUS server to select, be certain to consider the RADIUS attributes that must be supported. For example, if the authenticator can make use of proprietary features, then it's likely that you'll need the RADIUS server to support the applicable Vendor-Specific attributes. Of course, the RADIUS server will need to support the EAP-Message attribute in order to work with EAP-Methods in general, but nearly all RADIUS servers include the EAP-Message attribute.

EAP-Methods

The RADIUS server you select also needs to support the EAP-Methods you're planning to use. Many of the standard ones are integrated within all RADIUS servers, but take a closer look if you're planning to deploy a less popular EAP-Method.

CHAPTER 5

EAP-Methods Protocol

This chapter completes our exploration of port-based authentication protocols by looking at the details of the EAP (Extensible Authentication Protocol) Method types and packet structures. The protocols of EAP-Methods are what actually accomplish the authentication processes, and there are many options. This chapter will help clarify which EAP-Method is best for your implementation.

EAP-Methods Recap

EAP-Methods are the primary end-to-end, logical communications mechanism between a supplicant and an authenticator server in a port-based authentication system (see Figure 5-1). Sometimes an EAP-Method is called an "EAP Authentication type" or just simply "EAP type." An EAP-Method actually implements the authentication process, whereas other protocols, such as EAPOL and RADIUS, merely transport the EAP-Method data.

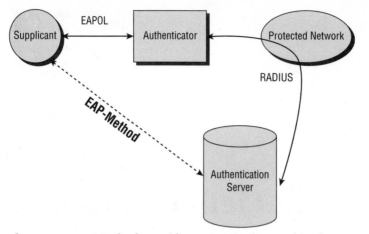

Figure 5-1: EAP-Methods provide communications and implement an authentication process between a supplicant and an authenticator server.

EAP-Method Encapsulation

Figure 5-2 highlights EAP-Method encapsulation based on the analogy of the truck and airplane introduced in Chapter 2. EAP-Method data is sent between the supplicant and authenticator in EAP packets. An authenticator, for example, will communicate EAP-Method data via an EAP Request packet. An EAP packet, which is the letter shown in Figure 5-2, flows between the supplicant and the authenticator physically within EAPOL packets (called EAP Data packets), which is the truck illustrated in Figure 5-2. EAPOL, the only one of these protocols defined by the IEEE 802.1X standard, adapts EAP to operate over a LAN, rather than a point-to-point system as EAP was originally intended. EAP Response packets carry EAP-Method data from the supplicant to the authenticator, as illustrated by the example shown in Figure 5-2, and EAP Request packets carry EAP-Method data from the authenticator to the supplicant. When traveling between the authenticator and authentication server, EAP-Method data is sent in RADIUS packets, represented by the airplane in the figure. RADIUS Access-Request packets carry EAP-Method data from the authenticator to the authentication server (refer to Figure 5-2), and RADIUS Access-Accept packets carry EAP-Method data from the authentication server to the authenticator. Together, EAPOL and RADIUS packets effectively transport EAP-Method Data among the supplicant, authenticator, and authentication server.

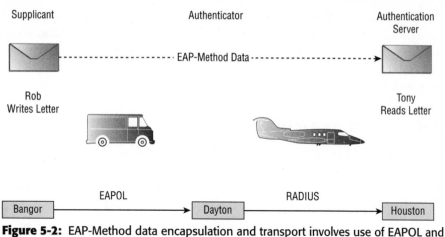

Figure 5-2: EAP-Method data encapsulation and transport involves use of EAPOL and RADIUS protocols.

EAP-Method Packet Structure

All EAP-Method packets have the same basic structure, which consists of Type and EAP-Method Data fields (see Figure 5-3). The EAP-Method packet is carried in the Data field of an EAP packet. Each of the subsequent subsections explains the fields of the EAP-Method packet.

Octets: 1   Variable

Type	EAP Method Data

Figure 5-3: An EAP-Method packet consists of Type and EAP-Method Data fields.

EAP-Method Type Field

The EAP-Method Type field, an eight-octet value, identifies a specific EAP-Method. There are many EAP-Methods, some of which were originally defined by the EAP specification (RFC 3748) and many others that are optional and proprietary. Table 5-1 lists many of the EAP-Method types. The value of the EAP-Method Type field indicates what the EAP packet carries. For example, a Type field value of "13" means that the EAP-Method data consists of data relevant to the EAP-TLS authentication process, which is one of the more popular ones. The decimal Type number for each EAP-Method represents the value that fits in the Type field. For example, a Type field decimal value of "5" is included in the Type field in binary format as "0000 0101."

EAP-Method Data Field

The EAP-Method Data field contains information corresponding to the particular EAP-Method type and applicable protocol exchanges. For example, the EAP-Method Data field may be carrying credentials, such as a digital certificate, from the supplicant to the authentication server (see Figure 5-4).

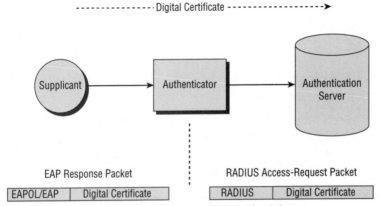

Figure 5-4: EAP-Method packets carry EAP-Method data.

Table 5-1: EAP-Method Types

TYPE	EAP-METHOD
1	Identity [RFC 3748]
2	Notification [RFC 3748]
3	NAK [RFC 3748]
4	MD5-Challenge [RFC 3748]
5	One-Time Password (OTP) [RFC 3748]
6	Generic Token Card (GTC) [RFC 3748]
9	RSA Public Key Authentication
10	DSS Unilateral

Table 5-1 *(continued)*

TYPE	EAP-METHOD
11	KEA
12	KEA-VALIDATE
13	EAP-TLS
14	Defender Token (AXENT)
15	RSA Security SecureID EAP
16	Arcot Systems EAP
17	EAP-Cisco Wireless
18	GSM Subscriber Identity Modules (EAP-SIM) [RFC4186]
19	SRP-SHA1
21	EAP-TTLS
22	Remote Access Service
23	EAP-AKA Authentication [RFC4187]
24	EAP-3Com Wireless
25	PEAP
26	MS-EAP-Authentication
27	Mutual Authentication w/Key Exchange (MAKE)
28	CRYPTOCard
29	EAP-MSCHAP-V2
30	DynamID
31	Rob EAP
32	Protected One-Time Password [RFC4793]
33	MS-Authentication-TLV
34	SentriNET
35	EAP-Actiontec Wireless
36	Cogent Systems Biometrics Authentication EAP
37	AirFortress EAP
38	EAP-HTTP Digest

Continued

Table 5-1 *(continued)*

TYPE	EAP-METHOD
39	SecureSuite EAP
40	DeviceConnect EAP
41	EAP-SPEKE
42	EAP-MOBAC
43	EAP-FAST [RFC4851]
44	ZoneLabs EAP (ZLXEAP)
45	EAP-Link
46	EAP-PAX
47	EAP-PSK [RFC4764]
48	EAP-SAKE [RFC4763]
254	Expanded Types [RFC 3748]
255	Experimental use [RFC 3748]

NOTE Because of the variations of EAP based on the many different EAP-Method types, there is a high risk of interoperability issues when deploying 802.1X port-based authentication systems. As a result, ensure that you choose compatible EAP-Method types for all components.

Original EAP-Method Types

RFC 3748, which is the basis for the initial set of EAP-Method types, describes support for the following EAP-Methods:

- Identity (Type 1)
- Notification (Type 2)
- Legacy NAK (Type 3)
- MD5-Challenge (Type 4)
- One-Time Password (Type 5)
- Generic Token Card (Type 6)
- Expanded Types (Type 254)
- Experimental Use (Type 255)

MD5-Challenge, One-Time Password, and Generic Token Card types implement authentication processes. The others are considered to be special case types. The following sections give an overview of each of these EAP-Method types.

Identity

The EAP-Method Identity packet is represented by a decimal "1" in the Type field of an EAP-Method packet, as shown in Figure 5-5. The EAP-Method Identity packets may be used before or during an authentication process. For example, with specific EAP-Methods that implement mutual authentication, the EAP-Method Identity packets generally convey information regarding the credentials of the supplicant or the authentication server. In other cases, the EAP-Method Identity packets only convey credentials of the supplicant.

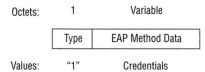

Octets: 1   Variable

| Type | EAP Method Data |

Values: "1"   Credentials

Figure 5-5: An EAP-Method Identity packet consists of a Type field with a value of "1" and a Data field that may contain credentials.

Figure 5-6 illustrates a typical use of EAP-Method Identity packets. At the beginning of a particular EAP-Method authentication process, the authenticator will request credentials from the supplicant by sending an EAP-Method Identity packet to the supplicant. In some cases, the request may include a message that the supplicant displays to the user, such as when the user must enter a username and password in order to complete the authentication process. In response to the Identity request, the supplicant will send an EAP-Method Identity packet to the authenticator. This packet contains the credentials of the supplicant.

Figure 5-6 shows how the EAP-Method Identity data is sent between the supplicant and the authenticator. An EAP Request packet carries the EAP Method Identity packet from the authenticator to the supplicant. An EAP Response packet then carries the EAP-Method Identity packet (containing the credentials) from the supplicant to the authenticator. If the credentials received by the supplicant are invalid, then the authenticator will usually resend the EAP-Method Identity packet several times. The resent Identity packet generally includes the reason why the credentials are invalid. It's important not to retry the identity request too many times, to avoid a hacker from breaking into the network. Some implementations require the authenticator to forward the credentials to the authentication server for verification, and in some cases the authenticator will verify the supplicant without reference to an authentication server.

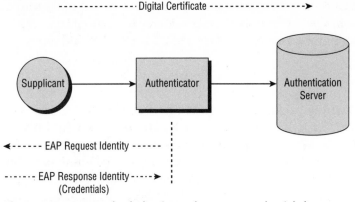

Figure 5-6: EAP-Method Identity packets carry credentials between the supplicant and the authenticator.

NOTE Some authentication processes reduce overhead by piggybacking various functions (as special data bits) in EAP-Method packets, such as Identity Requests, after a null character at the end of the EAP-Method data.

Notification

The EAP-Method Notification type is represented by a decimal "2" in the Type field of an EAP-Method packet, as shown in Figure 5-7. The Notification packets may be used before or during an authentication process. The reception of a Notification packet causes the receiving entity to send a Notification packet in response. For example, an authentication server may send a notification to the supplicant to provide authentication status. A Notification packet, for instance, could alert the supplicant that the user must reenter his or her password because it didn't match what's stored in the authentication server. The supplicant would then respond with the credentials.

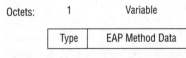

Figure 5-7: An EAP-Method Notification packet consists of a Type field with a value of "2" and a Data field that may contain human-readable text.

The Notification packet can carry up to 1,015 octets of human-readable text for displaying messages to the user. The supplicant generally displays this message to the user. If that's not possible, the supplicant stores the message in a log file.

Figure 5-8 shows the transmission of a notification from the authentication server to the supplicant. This Notification packet indicates that a password will soon expire, prompting the supplicant to initiate the process of acquiring a new password. A RADIUS Access-Accept packet carries the Notification packet from the authentication server to the authenticator, and an EAP Request packet carries the Notification packet from the authenticator to the supplicant. The supplicant displays a message to the user to enter a new password.

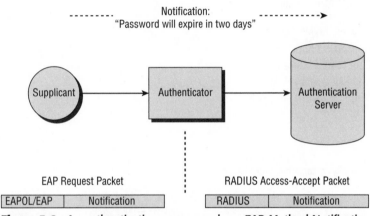

Figure 5-8: An authentication server sends an EAP-Method Notification packet to the supplicant to provide a status message to the user.

NOTE Some authentication methods don't utilize EAP-Method Notification type packets. If a supplicant, for example, receives a Notification packet in this case, the supplicant will discard the Notification packet.

Legacy NAK

The EAP-Method Legacy NAK type is represented by a decimal "3" in the Type field of an EAP-Method packet, as shown in Figure 5-9. A supplicant, for example, sends a Legacy NAK packet when the supplicant is unable to support an authentication type (EAP-Method) that the authentication server proposes. The Legacy NAK packet identifies one or more EAP-Method types that the supplicant can support. Figure 5-10 illustrates the sending of a NAK from a supplicant to an authentication server.

If the Legacy NAK identifies EAP-Method Type "0," then the authenticator has no viable alternatives and the authenticator should not send any more requests (see Figure 5-11). The Legacy NAK type is very limited in allowing the supplicant to request a different authentication method because the Legacy NAK can only be sent in EAP Response packets. The Expanded NAK, explained below, is much better equipped for the supplicant to propose authentication methods.

Octets: 1   Variable

Type	EAP Method Data

Values: "3"   Supported EAP-Method Types

Figure 5-9: An EAP-Method NAK packet consists of a Type field with a value of "3" and a Data field that may contain EAP-Method types that the supplicant supports.

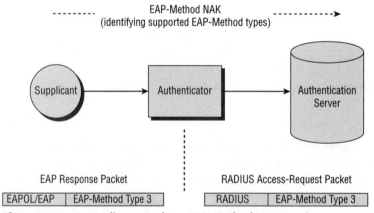

Figure 5-10: A supplicant sends an EAP-Method NAK to reject a proposed EAP-Method and identify supported alternative EAP-Method types to the authentication server.

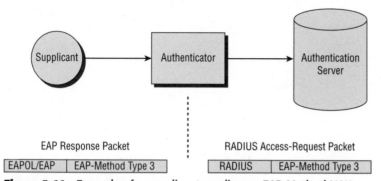

Figure 5-11: Example of a supplicant sending an EAP-Method NAK (identifying Type = "0") to the authentication server to reject a proposed EAP-Method and indicate no EAP-Method alternatives.

Expanded NAK

The EAP-Method Expanded NAK is represented by a decimal "254" in the Type field of an EAP-Method packet. As the name implies, the Expanded NAK expands the capability of the Legacy NAK and conforms to the general Expanded Type packet structure discussed later in this chapter. Similar to the Legacy NAK, the Expanded NAK allows the supplicant, for example, to propose an authentication method to the authentication server, but the Expanded NAK is much more flexible. The Expanded NAK allows a port-based authentication system to have a much larger possible number of EAP-Method types, well beyond the limits of the eight-octet limit (maximum 255) of the EAP-Method Type field. An Expanded NAK is sent in an EAP Response packet only after receiving an Expanded NAK in an EAP Request packet.

Figure 5-12 illustrates the format of an Expanded NAK packet. The Expanded NAK includes a structured table in its Data field, with each row of the table being eight octets in length and representing an EAP-Method that the supplicant supports. Each Expanded NAK begins with an initial eight-octet field group with Type field = "254" (Expanded Type), Vendor-ID= "0" (IETF), and Vendor-Type = "3" (NAK). The initial field is then followed by one or more eight-octet field groups that identify proposed EAP-Methods in expanded format. For example, Figure 5-12 identifies the IETF's GTC and the MIT's OTP as proposed EAP-Methods. Figure 5-13 shows the packet structure of an Expanded NAK for which there is no desired alternative EAP-Method.

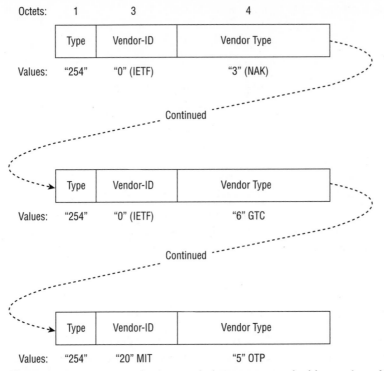

Figure 5-12: An EAP-Method Expanded NAK structured table consists of a succession of EAP-Method Type, Vendor-ID, and Vendor-Type fields.

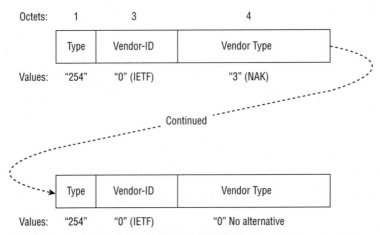

Figure 5-13: An EAP-Method Expanded NAK can specify no desired alternative EAP-Method by setting the Vendor-Type = "0."

MD5-Challenge

The EAP-Method MD5-Challenge type is represented by a decimal "4" in the Type field of an EAP-Method packet. MD5-Challenge is one of the original authentication processes defined by EAP. MD5 provides only one-way authentication, which allows supplicants to authenticate themselves with an authentication server through the use of a user password. When a user initially types in his or her password to establish an account on the authentication server, the authentication server actually stores the hash of the password instead of the password itself to avoid storing the password in unencrypted form. The hash is a 128-bit fingerprint often called a *message digest*. Later, whenever the user logs into the system, the supplicant computes the hash of the password that the user inputs when logging into the system and sends the hash value to the authentication server for verification. The authentication server verifies the password by performing an MD5 hash of the user password.

The MD5-Challenge type is similar to PPP CHAP (RFC 1994), with the algorithm specified as MD5. The authentication process is a three-way handshake between the supplicant and the authentication server (see Figure 5-14). The authentication server will challenge the supplicant by issuing a challenge via a RADIUS-Access Challenge packet. The supplicant then responds by sending an EAP Response packet containing an MD5-challenge message, Legacy NAK, or Expanded NAK. If the response is an MD5-Challenge, then the contents will contain the value resulting from a one-way hash of the password entered by the user. The authentication server receives the hash value and determines whether the hash function was completed correctly by the supplicant, and, if so, acknowledges the authentication. The supplicant can reply to the MD5-Challenge with a Legacy or Expanded NAK to recommend different EAP-Method types.

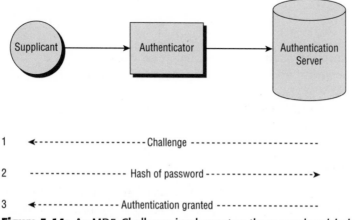

1   ◄- Challenge -

2   - - - - - - - - - - - - - - - - - - Hash of password -►

3   ◄- - - - - - - - - - - - - - - - Authentication granted - - - - - - - - - - - - - - - - - -

Figure 5-14: An MD5-Challenge implements a three-way handshake that provides one-way authentication.

MD5 is not suitable for wireless LANs and public Ethernet networks because a hacker can easily sniff the password hashes, which allows the hacker to derive the password and compromise the security of the network. The structure of the MD5-Challenge packet is shown in Figure 5-15, and the following sections describe the Value-Size, Value, and Name fields.

Octets:	1	1	1 or more	1 or more
	Type	Value-Size	Value	Name

Values: "4"

Figure 5-15: An MD5-Challenge packet includes Type, Value-Size, Value, and Name fields.

Value-Size Field

The Value-Size field of an EAP-Method MD5-Challenge packet is one octet in length and identifies the length of the Value field.

Value Field

The Value field of an EAP-Method MD5-Challenge packet is one or more octets in length. In EAP Requests that are sent from the authenticator to the supplicant, the Value field contains the challenge value. This value is generally changed each time it is sent. In the EAP Response sent from the supplicant to the authenticator, the Value field contains the one-way hash value, which is 16 octets in length.

Name Field

The Name field of an EAP-Method MD5-Challenge packet is one or more octets identifying the entity sending the MD5-Challenge packet.

NOTE For details on the MD5 algorithm, refer to RFC 1321.

One-Time Password

The EAP-Method One-Time Password (OTP) type is represented by a decimal "5" in the Type field of an EAP-Method packet. OTP is one of the original authentication processes defined by EAP. OTP provides only one-way authentication, which allows supplicants to authenticate themselves with an authentication server. When receiving a OTP authentication request, the supplicant responds with a OTP response, Legacy NAK, or Expanded NAK.

NOTE Refer to RFC 2289 for more details on the OTP EAP-Method.

Generic Token Card

The EAP-Method Generic Token Card (GTC) type is represented a decimal "6" in the Type field of an EAP-Method packet. As with MD5-Challenge and OTP, GTC is one of the original authentication processes defined by EAP. GTC also provides only one-way authentication, which allows supplicants to authenticate themselves with an authentication server. With GTC, an authentication request from the authenticator contains a displayable message, and the authentication response from the supplicant includes token card data read from a token card device that's needed for authentication. When receiving a GTC authentication request, the supplicant can respond with a Legacy NAK or Expanded NAK instead of the GTC response.

Expanded Types

An Expanded EAP-Method type is represented by a decimal "254" in the Type field of an EAP-Method packet. As discussed earlier in this chapter, the EAP-Method Expanded NAK is an Expanded EAP-Method type. The Expanded NAK, as previously mentioned, allows a port-based authentication system to have a much larger possible number of EAP-Method types, well beyond the limits of the eight-octet limit (maximum 255) of the EAP-Method Type field. In general, the Expanded Types are intended for the vendors in order to support their own EAP-Methods that are not suitable for general usage. Figure 5-16 illustrates the general format of an Expanded EAP-Method type packet.

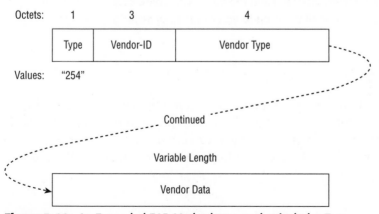

Figure 5-16: An Expanded EAP-Method type packet includes Type, Vendor-ID, Vendor-Type, and Vendor Data fields.

Vendor-ID Field

The Expanded Type Vendor-ID field is three octets and identifies the organization that supports the proposed EAP-Method identified in the Expanded Type Vendor-Type field. The Vendor-ID is an SMI Network Management Private Enterprise Code of the vendor as allocated by the IANA (Internet Assigned Number Authority). The Vendor-ID indicates a specific vendor's version of the proposed EAP-Method type identified in the Expanded Type Vendor-Type field.

> **NOTE** For a current list of SMI Network Management Private Enterprise Codes (Vendor-ID codes), go to www.iana.org/assignments/enterprise-numbers.

Vendor-Type Field

If the Vendor-Type field contains a value equal to "0," then the Expanded Type Vendor-Type field contains an EAP-Method Type value that is currently one of the 256 EAP-Method types allocated within the EAP-Method Type field (i.e., Table 5-1) or some value larger than 255. The capability to have values larger than 255 allows for a larger set of EAP-Method number assignments beyond the 256 limitation of the single-octet EAP-Method Type field. For Vendor-ID field values that are greater than "0," the Vendor-Type field may identify any of the EAP-Method types shown in Table 5-1 or any other value. This enables vendors to offer vendor-specific EAP-Method types not available from the IETF. Thus, vendors can alter the EAP-Method types in ways that best satisfy solution needs.

> **NOTE** Most protocol analyzers ("sniffers") will only indicate the EAP-Method type and may or may not correctly decode the vendor code or vendor-specific type. In order to fully decode the meaning of these fields, you may need to request detailed documentation from the vendor. In some cases, the vendor may not provide this documentation to you because of security concerns.

Experimental

An EAP-Method Experimental type is represented by a decimal "255" in the Type field of an EAP-Method packet. The Experimental type has no standardized format or content. Anyone is free to structure the packets as they wish to allow for experimentation. Figure 5-17 illustrates the format of an Experimental type packet.

Octets: 1   Variable

Type	Experimental fields

Values: "255"

Figure 5-17: An EAP-Method Experimental type packet includes Type and Experimental fields.

Additional EAP-Method Types

The 8-bit Type field in EAP-Method packets allows additional EAP-Method types beyond the original types explained in the previous section. These additional EAP-Methods that warrant their own Type code are meant for widespread implementation. Table 5-1 identifies many of these EAP-Methods. In addition, as explained before, the Expanded Type EAP-Method has provisions for even more EAP-Methods that may not be intended for widespread implementation. In general, most of the additional EAP-Method types exchange credentials based on user passwords or digital certificates. Some establish a secured tunnel for another EAP-Method to utilize. The following sections provide an overview of the more common EAP-Method types defined outside the scope of RFC 3748.

EAP-TLS

EAP with Transport Layer Security (EAP-TLS), EAP-Method Type "13," provides mutual authentication, whereby both the supplicant and the authentication server prove their identities to each other. EAP-TLS makes use of public key cryptography for authentication purposes, which could involve smart cards or digital certificates. EAP-TLS by far has the broadest support in supplicants and authentication servers. As examples, Cisco, FreeRADIUS, Funk, Interlink, Meetinghouse, Microsoft, and Radiator have RADIUS server support for EAP-TLS.

Communications between the supplicant and the authentication server is achieved via an encrypted TLS tunnel. This makes EAP-TLS very secure. EAP-TLS is best for enterprises that have digital certificates already deployed and that utilize Microsoft Windows-based supplicants, especially those equipped with Windows XP, Windows 2000, and Windows Vista. If your clients are already equipped with Windows, then you're in a good position to implement EAP-TLS.

The following describes the general EAP-TLS authentication process (see Figure 5-18):

1. The authenticator sends an EAP-Request/Identity packet to the supplicant.

2. The supplicant responds by sending an EAP-Response/Identity packet, containing the peer's user ID, to the authenticator.

3. The authenticator sends the peer's identity to the authentication server.

4. The authentication server sends an EAP-TLS/Start packet.

5. The supplicant sends an EAP-Response packet with Type=EAP-TLS, and the data field of that packet contains one or more TLS records in TLS record layer format.

6. The authentication server then responds with an EAP-Request packet with Type=EAP-TLS, and the Data field contains one or more records in TLS record layer format.

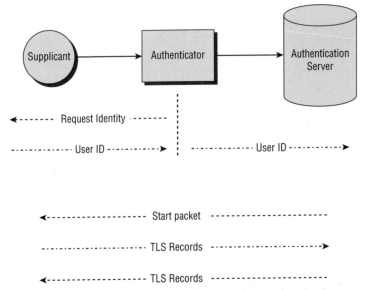

Figure 5-18: EAP-TLS allows a supplicant and an authentication server to authenticate each other.

When digital certificates are deployed, certificates are installed on both the supplicants and the authentication server (see Figure 5-19). As a result, a significant disadvantage of EAP-TLS is that it is difficult to manage the certificates in a large enterprise network. For example, the IT staff must install a new certificate after purchasing a new laptop or any other device that will make use of EAP-TLS authentication.

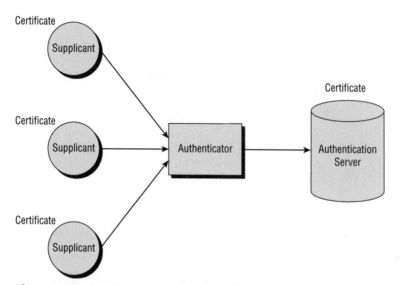

Figure 5-19: EAP-TLS requires digital certificates on the authentication server and all supplicants.

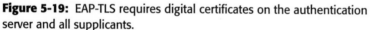 **NOTE** Refer to RFC 2716 for details on the EAP-TLS authentication process.

EAP-TTLS

EAP-TTLS (Tunneled Transport Layer Security), EAP-Method Type "21," was developed by Funk Software and Certicom as an extension of EAP-TLS. Similar to EAP-TLS, EAP-TTLS is a certificate-based, mutual authentication system. EAP-TTLS, however, requires only server-side certificates (see Figure 5-20). This is done by connecting the supplicant to the authentication server via TLS through a secure tunnel. The users can then authenticate themselves through the use of a password, rather than a certificate. This greatly reduces the complexity of the port-based authentication system because there's no need to install and manage certificates on the client devices. Funk Software is the primary supporter of EAP-TTLS. In order to utilize EAP-TTLS, you must usually install third-party 802.1X supplicant software.

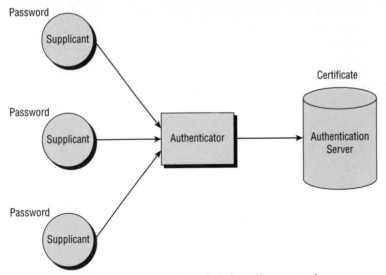

Figure 5-20: EAP-TTLS only requires digital certificates on the authentication server.

PEAP

PEAP (Protected Extensible Authentication Protocol), EAP-Method Type "25," which is similar to EAP-TTLS, was developed by Microsoft, Cisco, and RSA Security. As with EAP-TTLS, PEAP doesn't require certificates on the client devices. PEAP offers a secure transport of authentication data, which could include legacy passwords. PEAP accomplishes this by using tunneling between PEAP clients and an authentication server. The advantage of PEAP is that Microsoft offers it free of charge.

NOTE Cisco and Microsoft have distributed different versions of PEAP, so if you are implementing PEAP be sure that the actual authentication method is compatible.

LEAP

LEAP (Lightweight Extensible Authentication Protocol), EAP-Method Type "17," was developed by Cisco for wireless LANs. LEAP provides encryption through dynamically generated WEP (Wired Equivalent Privacy) keys and makes use of strong user passwords for authenticating supplicants. You can count on LEAP being available for most Cisco devices, as well as some vendor devices that license the use of LEAP. Note that it's possible to fairly easily crack LEAP with a tool called ASLEAP; however, you might find some authentication systems using LEAP. For new implementations, strongly consider a different protocol. If you want to stay with the Cisco line, then consider EAP-FAST.

EAP-FAST

EAP-FAST (Flexible Authentication via Secure Tunneling), EAP-Method Type "43," was developed by Cisco as a replacement for LEAP. In fact, some of the Cisco access points and client radio cards readily support EAP-FAST. EAP-FAST provides mutual authentication through the use of a Protected Access Credential (PAC) instead of digital certificates. An administrator can distribute the PACs manually or automatically via the authentication server. The advantage of EAP-FAST is that an enterprise doesn't need to deploy any digital certificates.

NOTE Refer to RFC 4851 for details on the operation of EAP-FAST.

EAP-SIM

EAP-SIM (Subscriber Identity Module) offers mutual authentication for SIM cards installed in GSM cellular telephones. EAP-SIM allows the card to authenticate with a GSM authentication server and vice-versa. Smart phones with EAP-SIM can also authenticate with Wi-Fi hotspots when roaming from a GSM network to the hotspot.

NOTE Refer to RFC 4886 for details on the operation of EAP-SIM.

Wi-Fi Alliance Certification

The Wi-Fi Alliance currently performs interoperability testing with the following EAP-Method types:

- EAP-TLS
- EAP-TTLS
- PEAP
- EAP-SIM

For a listing of Wi-Fi client radio cards and access points that support each of these EAP-Method types, refer to the Appendix of this book.

EAP-Method Selection Considerations

Choosing the appropriate EAP-Method type will probably be your biggest decision when designing a port-based authentication system. The following sections describe some points you should consider when further researching and choosing an EAP-Method type.

Security Policies

Before getting too far with evaluating EAP-Method types, determine whether there are any company security policies that mandate the use of any particular type. In some cases, the company may have already spent the time and money evaluating the various EAP-Method types and found significant advantages of using one over the others. It may not be worthwhile going through the entire selection process again. If policies dictate which one to use, however, always consider whether changes in requirements may point the implementation toward a different choice.

Existing Security Infrastructure

Take a close look at the existing system infrastructure and determine whether any elements might favor a particular EAP-Method. For example, if digital certificates are already in use on client devices, then it may be fairly easy to move forward to take advantage of an authentication process, such as EAP-TLS, that uses certificates on both supplicants and authentication servers. Conversely, a company might not implement certificates at all. For this case, an authentication process that only uses certificates on the authentication server, such as EAP-TTLS, or one that doesn't use certificates at all, such as EAP-FAST, may be a better choice because they avoid the overhead of managing certificates.

Client Devices

The type of client devices that will play the role of supplicant may affect your choice of EAP-Method type. This task may be easy where there is only one client device to support. For example, if the client devices run Microsoft Windows, then EAP-TLS may be fairly easy to implement because of integrated support. If the system has other client device types, such as Cisco wireless IP phones, then you may find it desirable to implement EAP-FAST on the phones. Ideally, you should strive to choose a common EAP-Method type that all supplicants can support. In some cases, however, you may need to support several different types of EAP-Method types, which complicates the authentication server implementation. This forces you to find an authentication server that supports the specific EAP-Method types that you need to implement. Refer to Chapter 8, "Configuring Authentication Servers," for more details on implementing authentication servers.

NOTE The rollout of a port-based authentication system can be very complex. It's definitely worthwhile to perform pilot testing with the chosen EAP-Method type before installing the entire system.

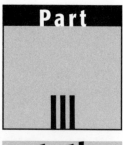

Part

III

Implementation

In This Part

Configuring Supplicants

This chapter looks at configuring 802.1X supplicants, which interface with an authenticator. The chapter covers general configuration parameters commonly found on supplicants and then goes through the process of setting up real-world components. An example is given for configuring a Microsoft Windows XP supplicant, which provides a good overview of the general configuration process that you can apply when configuring most other supplicants.

Supplicant Recap

As explained in Chapter 2, "Port-Based Authentication Concepts," a supplicant is a client device that needs to be authenticated before being allowed access to the network. In order to be considered a valid supplicant, a typical client device, such as a laptop or IP phone, must implement 802.1X and a specific EAP-Method. Windows XP, for example, comes with 802.1X built in with a variety of EAP-Methods, such as EAP-TLS. In addition, recall that the actual communications between the supplicant and the authenticator is accomplished via EAPOL, which is defined by 802.1X. EAPOL delivers (encapsulates) the EAP and EAP-Method frames as data. Figure 6-1 illustrates how a supplicant interfaces with the other components of an 802.1X port-based authentication system.

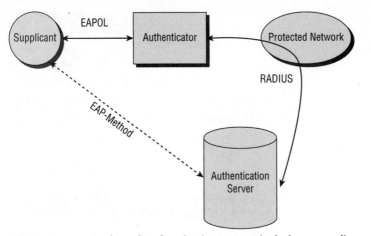

Figure 6-1: A port-based authentication system includes a supplicant, which interfaces the user to a protected network.

Choosing Supplicants

In order to integrate a particular client device into an 802.1x port-based authentication system, the client device must have 802.1X client software and some sort of network connectivity, such as Wi-Fi or Ethernet. The client's 802.1X software must support the EAP-Method type that you've chosen to use. For example, Windows XP and Vista by default support 802.1X for all network devices, but the choice of native EAP-Methods is somewhat limited to EAP-TLS, EAP-PEAP, and smart cards. If you want to support additional EAP-Methods, then you'll probably need to install additional software or use different supplicant software.

NOTE Sometimes loading client card software will automatically install various EAP-Methods other than those provided by default in Microsoft Windows. For example, with Cisco equipment, the installation process makes LEAP available. When upgrading the client card drivers, the 802.1X supplicant software is upgraded as well.

The following sections provide a brief overview of the various types of supplicant software.

Windows Authentication Client

Microsoft Windows Vista, Windows XP, and Windows Server 2003 have built-in support for 802.1X authentication using the Extensible Authentication Protocol (EAP). The Microsoft 802.1X Authentication Client uses 802.1X to authenticate Wi-Fi and Ethernet connections by using either EAP-TLS or PEAP. Windows XP Service Pack 1 also supports PEAP-TLS and PEAP-MS-CHAPv2. Because of native support, the Windows Authentication Client is preferred if you plan to use Windows operating systems on client devices.

> **NOTE** If you find that EAP-PEAP is not available on a Windows XP computer, then be sure that Service Pack 2 is installed.

> **NOTE** If the client device operating system is relatively old (pre-XP or Vista), then you'll likely need to use third-party supplicant software to enable the client device to operate on an 802.1X port-based authentication system. In this case, consider recommendations from the authentication server manufacturer that you plan to use. That will provide the highest degree of compatibility and allow supplicant software updates to occur more easily.

SecureW2

SecureW2 is the open-source EAP-TTLS client for Microsoft Windows platforms. If the Windows Authentication Client doesn't fulfill your requirements, then consider using SecureW2 to create a custom 802.1X/EAP solution. Refer to the following website to download SecureW2 software and documentation: www.securew2.com/.

Juniper Odyssey Access Client

Juniper Networks' Odyssey Access Client (OAC) provides enterprise-class 802.1X access client software, which is compatible with Juniper Networks' Odyssey Access Server (retired in May 2007) or Steel-Belted Radius. A specialized version of OAC has been FIPS 140-2 Level 1 validated, which meets the security requirements of government agencies.

Juniper Networks now recommends interfacing OAC with only Steel-Belted Radius or Juniper's Infranet Controller. The Juniper OAC is a good choice for high-end security.

> **NOTE** Consider implementing the same supplicant software on each client device to facilitate effective support.

wpa_supplicant

wpa_supplicant is a free software implementation of the IEEE 802.11i (WPA2) supplicant for Linux, BSD, and Microsoft Windows. Wpa_supplicant supports a wide range of EAP-Methods:

- EAP-TLS
- EAP-PEAP/MSCHAPv2 (both PEAPv0 and PEAPv1)
- EAP-PEAP/TLS (both PEAPv0 and PEAPv1)
- EAP-PEAP/GTC (both PEAPv0 and PEAPv1)
- EAP-PEAP/OTP (both PEAPv0 and PEAPv1)
- EAP-PEAP/MD5-Challenge (both PEAPv0 and PEAPv1)
- EAP-TTLS/EAP-MD5-Challenge
- EAP-TTLS/EAP-GTC
- EAP-TTLS/EAP-OTP
- EAP-TTLS/EAP-MSCHAPv2
- EAP-TTLS/EAP-TLS
- EAP-TTLS/MSCHAPv2
- EAP-TTLS/MSCHAP
- EAP-TTLS/PAP
- EAP-TTLS/CHAP
- EAP-SIM
- EAP-AKA
- EAP-PSK
- EAP-FAST
- EAP-PAX
- EAP-SAKE
- EAP-GPSK
- LEAP

If you're having trouble finding supplicant software that supports a particular EAP-Method for Wi-Fi implementations, then consider using wpa_supplicant. For up-to-date information on wpa_supplicant, refer to the following website: `http://hostap.epitest.fi/wpa_supplicant/`.

NOTE Mac OS X has had native support for 802.1X since Mac OS 10.3.

Open1X

Open1X is an open-source project for Linux platforms for implementing 802.1X solutions. Open1X supports both authenticators and supplicants. It is an alternative solution for implementing 802.1X on Linux platforms. Refer to `http://open1x.sourceforge.net/` for an update on Open1X.

Common Supplicant Configuration Parameters

This section discusses the common configuration parameters for 802.1X supplicants.

802.1X Activation

In order to enable a supplicant for 802.1X communications, you must enable the supplicant for 802.1X service. In Windows XP, refer to the Wireless Zero Configuration to enable 802.1X support. After starting the 802.1X service, it's possible to configure 802.1X parameters.

Configuring Windows XP 802.1X Wi-Fi Clients

The following explains the steps necessary for configuring 802.1X for Windows XP Wi-Fi clients:

1. Open the Network Connections window, shown in Figure 6-2.
2. Select the applicable Wireless Network Connection. This corresponds to a specific client radio installed in the client device. A separate wireless network connection icon will appear for each client radio installed in the client device.
3. Under Network Tasks, select "Change settings of this connection."

Figure 6-2: Selecting a specific wireless network connection (client radio)
for configuring 802.1X

NOTE To configure 802.1X settings in Windows, you must be an administrator
or a member of the administrators group.

4. Select the Wireless Networks tab. The window shown in Figure 6-3 will
   appear.

5. Select the wireless network that you'd like to configure for 802.1X, such
   as Wireless-Nets as shown in Figure 6-3, and click the Properties button.
   The wireless networks listed in this window correspond to SSIDs of specific wireless networks. The 802.1X configuration will only apply to the
   wireless network you choose.

6. Select the Authentication tab, and the window shown in Figure 6-4 will
   appear.

7. Select the check box for "Enable IEEE 802.1X authentication for this network" (see Figure 6-4). This activates 802.1X authentication.

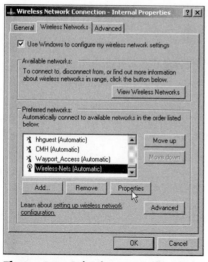

Figure 6-3: Selecting a specific wireless network (SSID) to configure for 802.1X

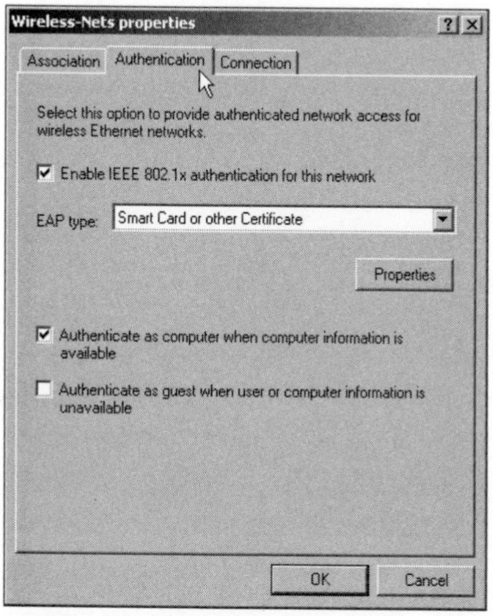

Figure 6-4: Selecting the Authentication window and enabling 802.1X authentication services

8. Select the EAP type (EAP-Method) that you'd like to implement, such as PEAP, as shown in Figure 6-5.

NOTE If the Authentication tab on the client device is not visible, the 802.1X service is likely not activated.

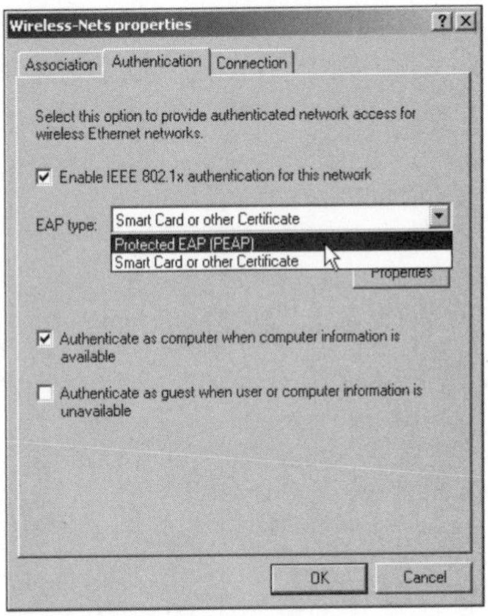

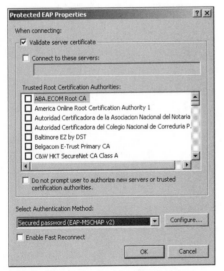

Figure 6-5: Choosing Protected EAP (PEAP) as the EAP-Method for 802.1X authentication

Figure 6-6: Window for configuring Protected EAP (PEAP)

9. Click the Properties button to configure the chosen EAP type. Refer to instructions in Windows documentation, and configure the chosen EAP-Method, such as PEAP (see Figure 6-6) or smart cards (see Figure 6-7).

10. Click OK to activate the settings.

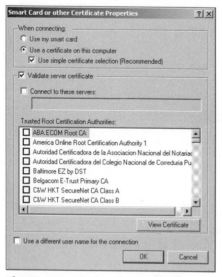

Figure 6-7: Window for configuring a smart card

Configuring Windows XP 802.1X Ethernet Clients

The following steps explain how to configure 802.1X for Windows XP Ethernet clients:

1. Open the Network Connections window, shown in Figure 6-8.

2. Select the applicable local area connection (LAN). This corresponds to a specific Ethernet card installed in the client device. A separate local area connection icon will appear for each client Ethernet card installed in the client device.

3. Under Network Tasks, select "Change settings of this connection" (refer to Figure 6-8).

4. Select the Authentication tab. The window shown in Figure 6-9 will appear.

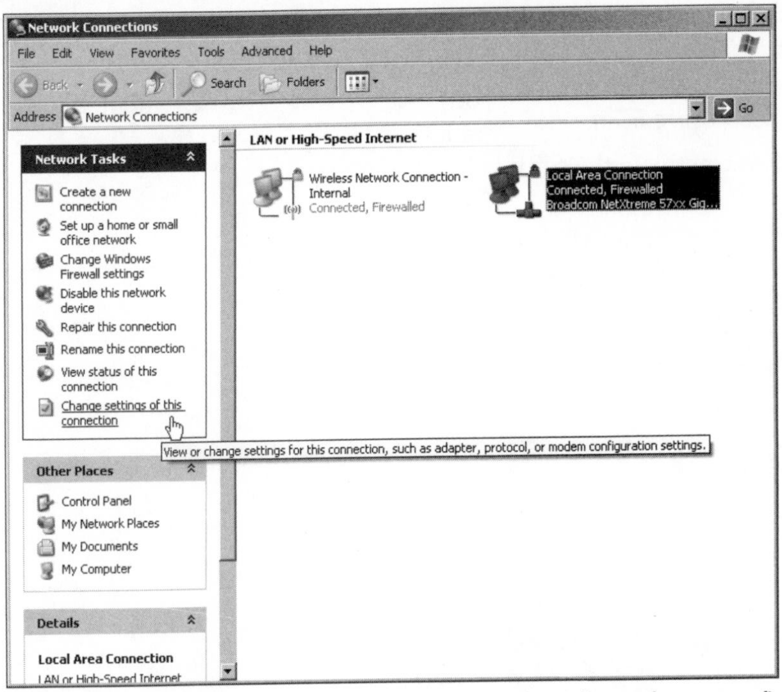

Figure 6-8: Selecting a specific local area connection (client Ethernet card) for configuring 802.1X

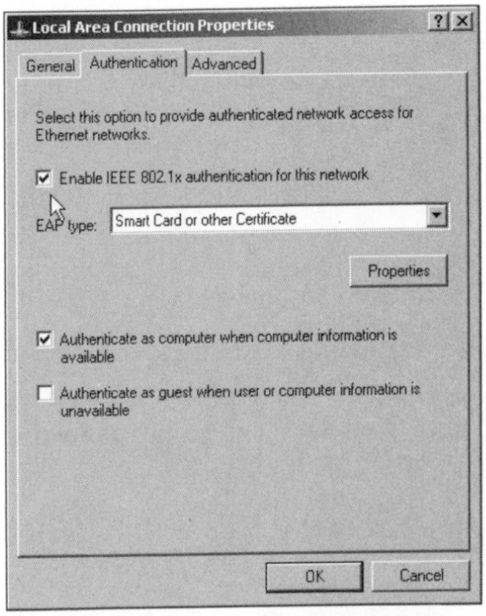

Figure 6-9: Enabling 802.1X authentication

5. Select the check box for "Enable IEEE 802.1X authentication for this network." This activates 802.1X authentication.

6. Select the EAP type (EAP-Method) that you want to implement, and refer to the Windows documentation for specific configuration properties and information.

7. Click the OK button to activate the settings.

Windows XP is fairly common and represents many of the configuration parameters that you can configure for 802.1X supplicants.

NOTE Before configuring Windows for a particular EAP-Method, you'll likely need to install the EAP-Method before it appears in the EAP-Method list.

Configuring Client Radios

In this section, we'll examine common configuration approaches and settings for client radios that implement 802.1X. Because of their security vulnerabilities, the majority of 802.1X port-based authentication systems make use of wireless client cards installed in the client device. As with wireless LAN access points, covered in Chapter 7, "Configuring Authenticators," it's useful to understand how to best configure the corresponding wireless client cards.

Configuration Update Approaches

There are several approaches you can take for configuring wireless client devices. The following subsections provide an overview of the distributed and centralized approaches.

Distributed Update Approach

It's possible to implement the configuration of client cards through the client device itself (see Figure 6-10). This is a common approach when you have relatively few client devices to configure or when you're first experimenting with 802.1X port-based authentication systems, and it's the approach used as an example later in this chapter. If there are a relatively large number of client devices to support, however, then this approach is not very efficient. Imagine needing to configure several hundred laptops with 802.1X! This may be the only approach to use, though, if you have a mix of client device operating systems.

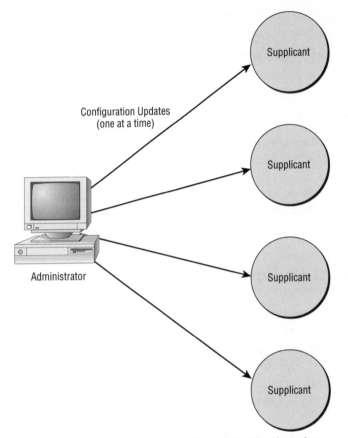

Configuration Updates
(one at a time)

Administrator

Figure 6-10: Configuring client radios via the distributed approach

Centralized Update Approach

The centralized management software approach (see Figure 6-11) is crucial when rolling out hundreds of client devices configured for 802.1X. In this case, you might find that when you are configuring each of the following settings, you'll need to interface with the access point in some manner in order to issue configuration commands or view configuration screens.

Client Radio Settings

This section discusses client radio settings that you should consider when implementing 802.1X solutions. There are several radio settings on a wireless client card. As with the access point, most of the default settings enable the client card to operate effectively, but you might consider changing them depending on requirements.

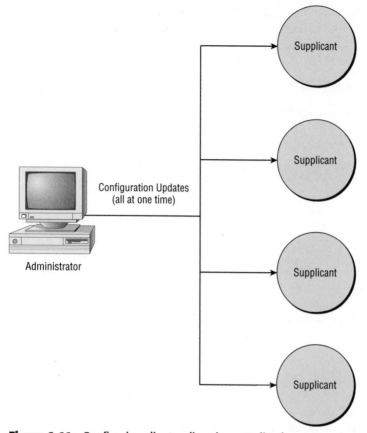

Figure 6-11: Configuring client radios via centralized management software

To configure a client radio with Windows XP, open the Wireless Network Connection window, select the Wireless Network Connection corresponding to the client radio you want to configure, and select "Change settings of this connection" in the pane on the left (see Figure 6-12). A window similar to the one shown in Figure 6-13 will appear. With this utility, you can configure all the settings on the client radio.

IP Address

One of the first things you should configure on a client radio is its IP address. In most cases, the network to which the client will be connecting will be implementing dynamic host configuration protocol (DHCP). For enterprise systems, there is likely to be a centralized DHCP server located somewhere on the network. With DHCP set on the client radio, the client radio automatically receives a valid IP address after connecting to the access point. For smaller networks, the

DHCP server may be located on the access point (in this case, probably a Wi-Fi router), but the automatic assignment of IP address to the client radio works the same as if the DHCP server is centralized.

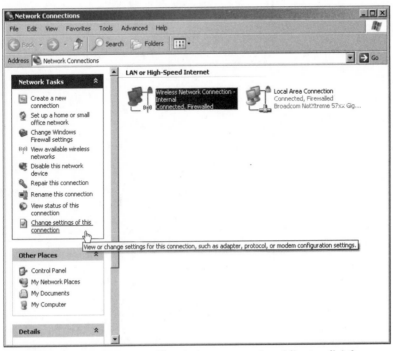

Figure 6-12: Selecting a specific wireless connection (client radio) for configuring radio settings

In order to configure the client radio for DHCP, perform the following steps:

1. As shown in Figure 6-12, open the Wireless Network Connection window for the client radio that you want to configure. A window similar to the one shown in Figure 6-13 will appear.

2. Select the General tab.

3. Scroll down the list of connection items and choose Internet Protocol (TCP/IP).

4. Click the Properties button. The window shown in Figure 6-14 will appear.

5. Select the General tab.

6. Enable the check boxes "Obtain an IP address automatically" and "Obtain DNS server address automatically."

7. Click the OK button, and the client radio will be configured to receive valid IP addresses automatically.

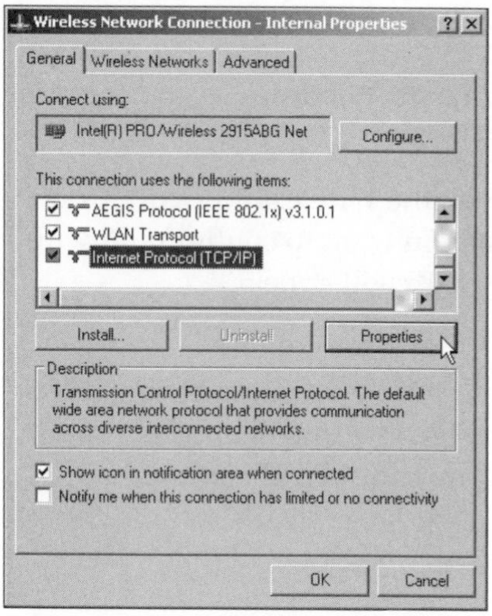

Figure 6-13: Selecting the TCP/IP for configuring the IP address of the client

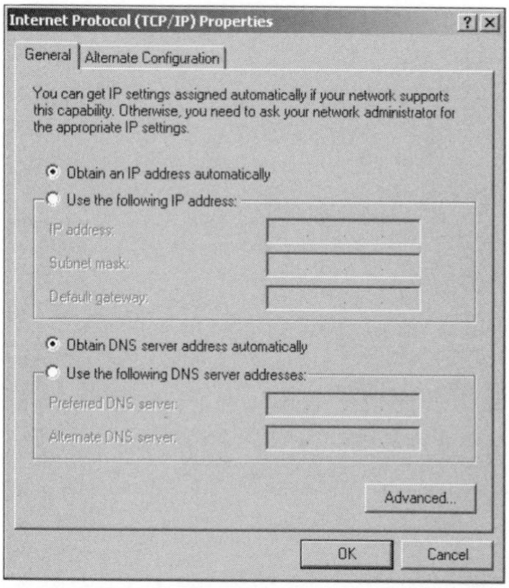

Figure 6-14: Enabling automatic IP address assignments using DHCP

If the network uses static IP addresses for clients, then you'll need to configure a valid IP address for the client radio. To do this, select "Use the following IP address" in the window shown in Figure 6-14, and configure the IP address, subnet mask, and default gateway (if applicable).

Wireless Network Connection Properties

In order to configure 802.11 radio parameters with Windows XP, perform the following steps:

1. As shown previously in Figure 6-12, open the Wireless Network Connection window for the client radio that you want to configure. A window similar to the one shown in Figure 6-15 will appear.

2. Select the General tab.

3. Click the Configure button, and a Wireless Network Connections Properties window similar to that shown in Figure 6-15 will appear. From this window, you'll be able to configure specific 802.11 settings.

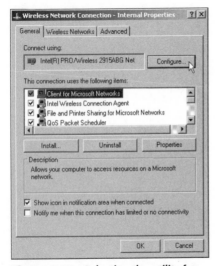

Figure 6-15: Selecting the utility for configuring the client radio

Transmit Power

In most cases, it's advantageous to set the transmit power of the client radio to the highest value. This maximizes the uplink range between the client and the access point. If there's a need to support high capacity with the wireless LAN, then lower transmit power settings may be beneficial to decrease the cell size of the network, which improves capacity.

In order to adjust the transmit power of the client radio with Windows XP, perform the following steps (refer to Figure 6-16 unless otherwise noted):

1. Open the Wireless Network Connection Properties for the client radio you want to configure (refer to Figure 6-15).

2. Choose the Advanced tab. The window that appears will be similar to the one shown in Figure 6-16.

3. Scroll through the Property list and select Transmit Power.

4. Unselect the Use Default Value option (if applicable).

5. Move the slider bar to Highest.

6. Click the OK button to activate the settings.

The client radio will now transmit at the highest power available. In most cases, this is 30 milliwatts, which is somewhat lower than access point transmit power levels.

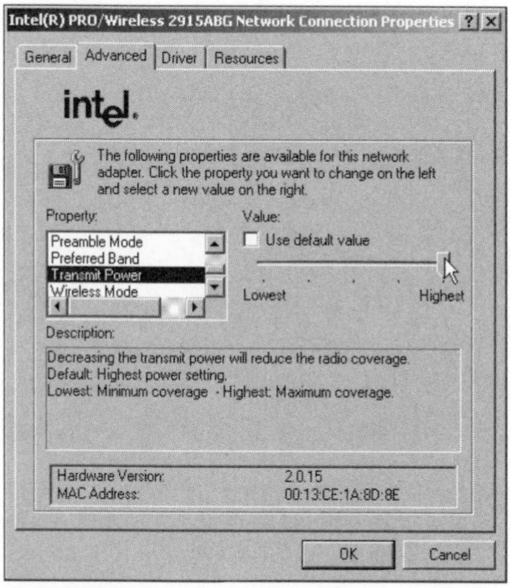

Figure 6-16: Configuring the transmit power of the client radio

Data Rate

The 802.11 standard includes a feature for client radios and access points to automatically adjust their data rate. This enables the radio to decrease its transmission data rate when excessive retransmissions are occurring or the received signal levels are too low. By lowering the data rate, wireless communications can operate over a longer range or in the midst of RF interference.

In most cases, the data rate on the client radio should be set to Auto or Best Rate, depending on the name the manufacturer gives to the automatic data rate feature. This is the most effective setting if the client will roam throughout the network and experience varying signal levels. For stationary applications, a fixed data rate may be best. For example, you may want to choose the highest fixed data rate if it's desirable to limit the effective range of the network for security purposes.

In order to adjust the data rate of the client radio with Windows XP, perform the following steps (refer to Figure 6-17 unless otherwise noted):

1. Open the Wireless Network Connection Properties for the client radio you want to configure (refer to Figure 6-15).

2. Choose the Advanced tab. The window that appears will be similar to the one shown in Figure 6-17.

3. Scroll through Property list and select Data Rate.

4. Unselect the Use Default Value option (if applicable).

5. Select Best Rate or whatever name the manufacturer has used for this feature. Sometimes it's referred to as Auto.

6. If a fixed data rate is desired, then choose the applicable data rate.

7. Click the OK button to activate the settings.

The client radio will now operate at the data rate selected.

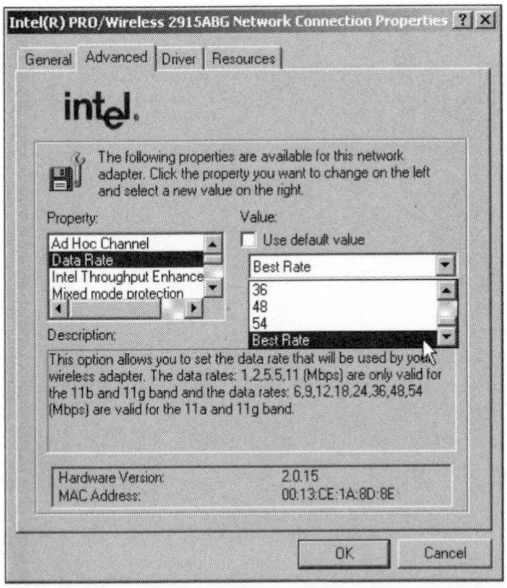

Figure 6-17: Configuring the data rate of the client radio

Wireless Modes

Many client radio manufacturers have implemented multiple-mode radios, whereby the radio can interface with a combination of 802.11a, 802.11b, and 802.11g networks. If the client radio supports multiple modes, then there will likely be a configuration setting for identifying the combination of network types with which the client radio will interface.

The default setting generally reflects the ability of the client radio to interface with all network types (802.11a, 802.11b and 802.11g), and this is the setting that you should probably use. However, it may be effective to operate in 802.11g-only mode if all client radios support 802.11g, and it's worthwhile to avoid having 802.11b devices associating with the network and lowering overall performance (due to the need for protection mechanisms in a mixed 802.11b/g network). In some cases, though, forcing all client radios to operate in 802.11b-only mode may improve overall range if the access points are also set to 802.11b-only mode.

In order to configure the wireless modes of the client radio with Windows XP, perform the following steps (refer to Figure 6-18 unless otherwise noted):

1. Open the Wireless Network Connection Properties for the client radio you want to configure (refer to Figure 6-15).

2. Choose the Advanced tab. The window that appears will be similar to the one shown in Figure 6-18.

3. Scroll through Property list and select Wireless Mode.

4. Unselect the Use Default Value option (if applicable).

5. Select the wireless mode that you want to use.

6. Click the OK button to activate the settings.

The client radio will now operate in the mode that you selected.

Figure 6-18: Configuring the wireless mode of the client radio

Ad Hoc Channel

The 802.11 standard defines both infrastructure and ad hoc (peer-to-peer) wireless LANs. The infrastructure wireless LAN involves the use of access points and is by far the most common. With infrastructure wireless LANs, you set the channel of the network in the access point, and the client radio automatically tunes to that channel before associating with the access point. The client radio is configured for operation over an infrastructure by default. As a result, you don't have to configure the channel for the client radio.

With ad hoc networks, however, you must configure the channel in the client radio. In order to tune the ad hoc channel of the client radio with Windows XP, perform the following steps (refer to Figure 6-19 unless otherwise noted):

1. Open the Wireless Network Connection Properties for the client radio you want to configure (refer to Figure 6-15).

2. Choose the Advanced tab. The window that appears will be similar to the one shown in Figure 6-19.

3. Scroll through Property list and select Ad Hoc Channel.

4. Select the channel that applies for 802.11b/g and 802.11a.

5. Click the OK button to activate the settings.

The client radio will now operate on the selected channel when configured for ad hoc mode.

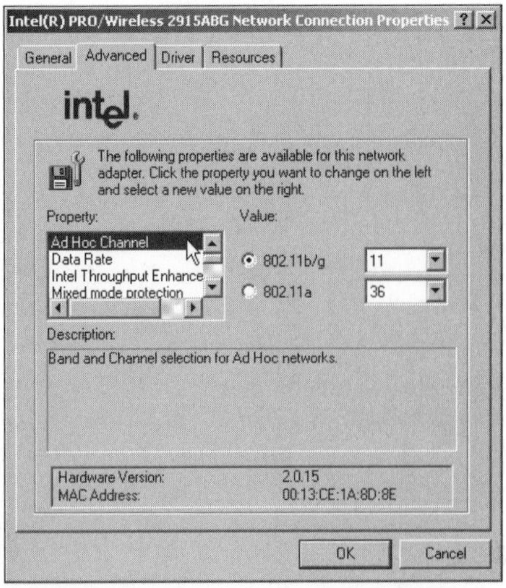

Figure 6-19: Configuring the RF channel of the client radio for ad hoc mode operation

Power Management

The 802.11 standard includes a power management feature called *power save mode*, which enables the client radio to conserve battery power when data does not need to be sent. For battery-powered clients, such as laptops, set the power management function to the greatest power-saving capability unless application requirements require the client radio to remain active at all times.

In order to adjust the power management function of the client radio to the greatest power-saving capability with Windows XP, perform the following steps (refer to Figure 6-20 unless otherwise noted):

1. Open the Network Connection Properties for the client radio you want to configure (refer to Figure 6-15).

2. Choose the Advanced tab. The configuration window that appears will be similar to the one shown in Figure 6-20.

3. Scroll through the Property list and select Power Management.

4. Unselect the Use Default Value option (if applicable).

5. Move the slider bar to Lowest.

6. Click the OK button to activate the settings.

The client radio will now operate with maximum power savings.

Figure 6-20: Configuring power management of the client radio

Protection Mechanisms

The 802.11 standard includes the optional use of protection mechanisms for when an 802.11g network accepts associations from 802.11b client radios. This is necessary to reduce collisions between 802.11g and 802.11b radios when transmitting data. Generally, the CTS-to-self setting is best because it minimizes overhead on the network, which improves the performance of a mixed 802.11b/g network. With CTS-to-self, a client radio transmits a CTS (clear to send) frame to itself with a value in the duration field of the 802.11 frame header that informs other stations to hold off transmitting for a period of time long enough for the sending station to transmit its data. This function only requires the transmission of one overhead frame (the CTS frame), whereas the RTS/CTS function requires the transmission of two overhead frames (the RTS frame and the CTS frame).

In order to configure the client radio protection mechanisms to the CTS-to-self setting with Windows XP, perform the following steps (refer to Figure 6-21 unless otherwise noted):

1. Open the Network Connection Properties for the client radio you want to configure (refer to Figure 6-15).

2. Choose the Advanced tab. The configuration window that appears will be similar to the one shown in Figure 6-21.

Figure 6-21: Configuring protection mechanisms for the client radio

3. Scroll through the Property list and select Mixed Mode Protection.

4. Unselect the Use Default Value option (if applicable).

5. Move the slider bar to CTS-to-self enabled.

6. Click the OK button to activate the settings.

The client radio will now operate using the CTS-to-self protection mechanism.

NOTE Refer to Chapter 7, "Configuring Authenticators," for details on configuring 802.11 access points.

Configuring Authenticators

In this chapter, we'll continue exploring the primary port-based authentication components by looking at how to choose and configure an authenticator, such as a wired switch and wireless access point. The chapter covers general configuration parameters commonly found on authenticators and then explains the process of setting up real-world products. This provides a good overview of the configuration process that you can apply when setting up just about any authenticator.

Authenticator Recap

As explained in Chapter 2, "Port-Based Authentication Concepts," an authenticator is a device that works at Layer 2 and provides the function of a security gate between the supplicants and the protected network (see Figure 7-1). Each port of the authenticator remains closed until the authentication system verifies the credentials of the supplicant and deems that the supplicant is authorized to access the protected network. Once the system authenticates the supplicant, the authenticator opens a port so that the supplicant can access the protected network. When the supplicant and authentication server converses, all communications flows through the authenticator.

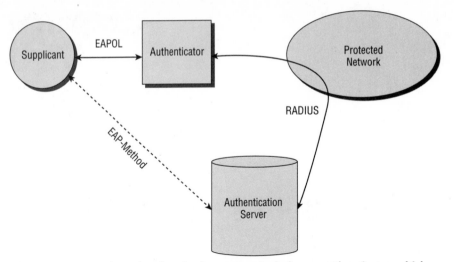

Figure 7-1: A port-based authentication system includes an authenticator, which provides a security gate function between the supplicant and the protected network.

The authenticator may be a wired switch or a wireless access point, depending on the implementation, that implements 802.1X port-based authentication protocols. A wired switch, which Figure 7-2 illustrates, requires the supplicant client devices to connect via a wired Ethernet cable. An example of a wired switch is Cisco's Catalyst 3750. Each port on the switch implements 802.1X, which allows each client access to the protected network on a case-by-case basis based on the outcome of each supplicant's authentication with an authentication server.

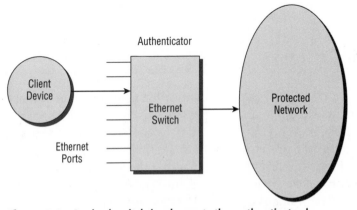

Figure 7-2: A wired switch implements the authenticator by authenticating physical client device connections to the switch.

The wireless access point manages wireless associations of client devices, which constitutes "connections" to the access point (see Figure 7-3). The Cisco 1240 is an example of a common enterprise-grade wireless access point. Instead of authenticating physical connections, the access point authenticates the wireless association between the client device and the access point. As with a switch, the access point will not let client device traffic through the access point, except for communications with the authentication server, until the wireless association is authenticated.

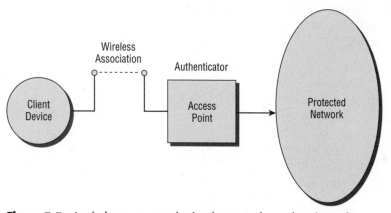

Figure 7-3: A wireless access point implements the authenticator by authenticating client device wireless associations to the switch.

Choosing Authenticators

Because the authenticator acts mostly as a pass-through component for port-based authentication, not many applicable options are available on wired switches and wireless access points. The following sections describe the primary features to be aware of when choosing an authenticator.

802.1X Support

Whether the authenticator is a wired switch or a wireless access point, the key feature that must be available is support for 802.1X protocols. This enables you to configure the authenticator for port-based authentication. Make sure that the authenticator supports the specific EAP-Methods that you plan to use. For example, the Cisco 1240 wireless access point supports EAP-FAST, PEAP, EAP-TLS, EAP-TTLS, EAP-SIM, and LEAP.

Authentication Server Support

Nearly all wired switches and wireless access points that support 802.1X protocols allow authentication to an external authentication server. Figure 7-4 illustrates this approach. With this architecture, communication between the supplicant/authenticator and the authentication server takes place over the protected network during the authentication process. This, of course, generates overhead traffic on the protected network, which can be significant if there are many supplicants and they are very mobile. In general, it's probably easiest to manage a single external authentication server (with backup feature) that services authentication requests from multiple authenticators located throughout a facility.

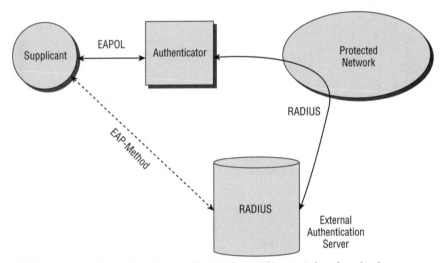

Figure 7-4: Port-based authentication system with external authentication server

Some wired switches and wireless access points that support 802.1X allow the authentication server or a replicated authentication database to reside within the same hardware as the switch or access point (see Figure 7-5). The local authentication can be configured as the primary means for authenticating supplicants or as a backup in case the external RADIUS server becomes unavailable. For example, an external authentication server may be located remotely on the other side of a WAN. If the WAN goes down, then the authentication server would not be reachable. In this case, the supplicant could authenticate with the authenticator instead. Generally only one of the wired switches or wireless access points on the network needs to be configured as the local authenticator.

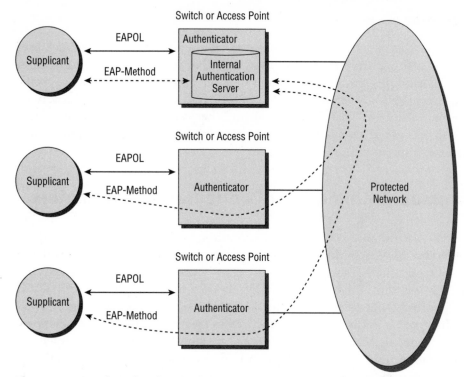

Figure 7-5: Port-based authentication system with internal authentication server

NOTE **In order to maximize the performance of a wireless network, configure a local authentication server in the access point that is projected to have the least amount of user traffic. In addition, be certain to secure this access point to ensure that no one can alter its configuration.**

This internal approach may be best for smaller organizations to avoid the need for supporting a dedicated and relatively expensive server for the authentication server functions. In addition, it may be best to improve performance by replicating the authentication server database at the same location as the authenticator in order to avoid delays in reaching an external authentication server. If the authenticator must communicate over a large network to reach an authentication server, then significant delays and lower performance may result. An internal authentication server solves this problem. Keep in mind that the internal approach may lead to roaming issues unless the distributed authentication servers share authorized user lists.

Miscellaneous Features

Of course, the switch or access point you choose also needs to have features that best satisfy requirements for functions other than port-based authentication. For example, requirements may call for an access point that has a specific type of encryption, such as AES, or multiple SSIDs may be needed to divide users into different classes of service. In other cases, the authenticator may need to be a wired switch or access point from a specific vendor so that it can implement special proprietary features.

Common Authenticator Configuration Parameters

Generally, there are no settings on the authenticator for the specific EAP-Method because EAP-Method data flows directly between the supplicant and the authentication server. Several system and port settings, however, are configurable on the authenticator. All of these settings apply to both wired switches and wireless access points. Many of the examples given in this section are specific to Cisco switches and access points, but these parameters are common among other vendor solutions. In fact, many vendors implement configuration naming conventions and commands that are very similar to what Cisco implements.

NOTE Many of the examples given for the configuration of the authenticator include Cisco IOS (Internetwork Operating System) commands. IOS is a command-line interface (CLI) for configuring Cisco switches and access points. The CLI includes a set of multiple-word commands. Other vendors use CLIs that are very similar to Cisco's.

The following is a list of IOS commands applicable to authenticators. They are explained in the following sections.

- dot1x system-auth-control
- dot1x guest-vlan supplicant
- dot1x guest-vlan <vlanid>
- dot1x port-control auto
- switchport access vlan <vlanid>

- dot1x host-mode multi-host
- dot1x max-req <number>
- dot1x timeout supp-timeout <seconds>
- dot1x timeout server-timeout <seconds>
- do1x timeout quite-period <seconds>
- dot1x re-authentication
- dot1x re-authenticate interface <interface-id>
- dot1x reauth-period <seconds>

802.1X Activation

Before an authenticator that supports 802.1X can actually handle port-based authentication, you must usually "turn on" 802.1X for the entire system by setting a specific configuration in the authenticator. Under default settings, most wired switches and wireless access points will not perform any port-based authentication functions. As an example, the Cisco IOS command for enabling 802.1X for a Cisco authenticator is as follows:

```
dot1x system-auth-control
```

NOTE Some authenticators, such as Cisco Airespace, have 802.1X set "on" for the system by default.

RADIUS Server Identification

In order for the authenticator to find the authentication server, the IP address of the RADIUS server must be configured in the authenticator. In addition, the authenticator must be configured with the shared secret password so that it can communicate with the authentication server. Figure 7-6 illustrates this setting.

As mentioned previously, some wired switches and wireless access points may perform authentication server functions locally to reduce delays. In this case, there may be other ways of identifying the authentication server without the need for supplying an IP address.

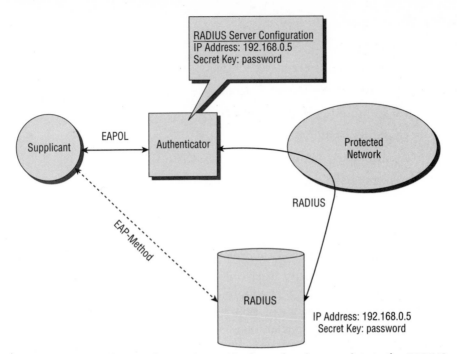

Figure 7-6: IP address and secret key set in the authenticator points to the RADIUS server

Local Authentication Server Configuration

If you plan to use one of the authenticators to host a local authentication server—sometimes referred to as a *local authenticator*—then you'll need to perform applicable configurations on all wired switches and wireless access points through which users (supplicants) may be interfacing with the network. In order to establish local authentication, you'll need to accomplish the following generic steps.

Enable the Local Authentication Server

On the authenticator you've chosen to provide authentication server functions, enable the wired switch or wireless access point to perform the local authentication function. For example, with Cisco components you would issue the following CLI command:

```
radius-server local
```

This establishes the local authentication server function and specifies a mode for configuring the authenticator.

Identify Authorized Access Points

Next, on the authenticator, you need to identify all access points that are authorized to use the authentication server to authenticate supplicants. This involves entering the IP address and shared key for each switch or access point that will interface with the local authentication server. The shared key allows the authentication server to authenticate the switches or access points. With Cisco components, for example, the following CLI command adds a switch or access point to the authorized list on the local authentication server:

```
nas <ip-address> key <shared-key>
```

To add multiple switches or access points, repeat the preceding step. If you don't configure all the devices, then a user attempting to connect with the network may fail the authentication process and not be allowed access to the protected network.

NOTE If you're configuring a Cisco wireless access point as a local authentication server, then you must also enter the access point as a network access server (NAS) so that client devices associating with the access point can authenticate with the authentication server.

Identify Authorized Users

When implementing local authentication, you need to configure the users (supplicants) in the authentication server. This generally requires the selection of a EAP-Method and identification of a username and password for each user. In addition, it may be necessary to enter the user's MAC address when implementing MAC-based authentication. In most cases, the authenticator will automatically perform all supported EAP-Methods by default.

Some local authentication servers allow you to optionally identify a period of time that users must wait after failing to authenticate after a specific number of attempts. The Cisco IOS command for this option is as follows:

```
Block count <count> time <seconds>
```

The <count> variable is the number of failed passwords that triggers the authenticator to block the applicable user. The <seconds> variable is the number of seconds that can elapse before the user is blocked from attempting to authenticate again. With Cisco (and this may be the same with other vendors), you can enter indefinite in the <seconds> field. This causes the authentication server to block the user from authenticating indefinitely. In this case, an administrator must manually unblock the user.

Guest VLAN Configuration

In many cases, the assignment of a guest VLAN is worthwhile. If the authentication process fails, then at least the client device can still interface with non-sensitive applications, such as web browsing, and possibly still make use of VPN interfaces. Figure 7-7 illustrates the guest VLAN approach.

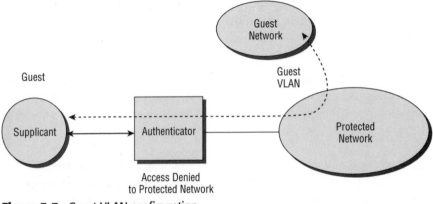

Figure 7-7: Guest VLAN configuration

Most authenticators have a global configuration setting for allowing non-authenticated supplicants to be placed on a special VLAN, such as a "guest" VLAN. For example, the Cisco IOS command for setting the global VLAN configuration is as follows:

```
dot1x guest-vlan supplicant
```

In addition to the global setting, you must set the guest VLAN number for the guest VLAN as well. With Cisco IOS, the command to set the guest VLAN number is as follows:

```
dot1x guest-vlan <vlanid>
```

These settings keep the protected network secure while letting clients have access to nonsensitive information and servers.

Some wireless access points don't support guest VLANs. If this is the case, then consider setting up a special SSID (service set identifier) in the access point for use with a guest VLAN. Figure 7-8 illustrates this configuration. If a user attempts to authenticate with the protected network, then the user can choose to associate with the access point via the guest SSID, which is tied to the guest VLAN.

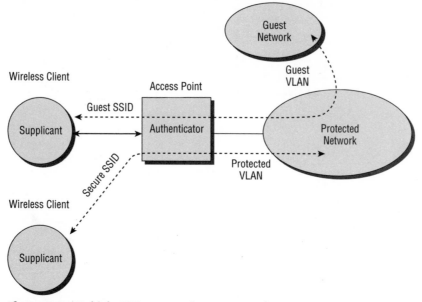

Figure 7-8: Multiple SSIDs supporting secure and guest VLANs

> **NOTE** For the latest Cisco IOS command reference guides, go to
> `www.cisco.com/univercd/cc/td/doc/product/software/`.

Port Activation

In addition to enabling 802.1X for the entire system, each port must be activated for 802.1X as well. Each port can generally be set to one of three different configurations: unauthorized, authorized, or auto. Figure 7-9 illustrates these different approaches.

Forced-Unauthorized

The forced-unauthorized configuration of an authenticator port disables the forwarding of traffic from all supplicants through that port. The switch or access point set to forced-unauthorized will ignore all authentication requests. This could be done to manually guard a particular port from all client devices. It locks down the port from potential attack.

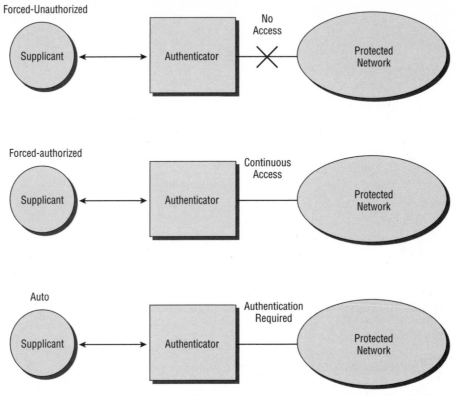

Figure 7-9: 802.1X ports can be configured as forced-unauthorized, forced-authorized, or auto.

Forced-Authorized

If a port on an authenticator is set to forced-authorized, then the authenticator will forward all traffic coming to that port. Thus, the port is forced to authorize all supplicants. This is usually the default configuration.

Auto

The auto configuration of a port requires that supplicants perform some sort of authentication. This means that the port has been activated for 802.1X protocols. The Cisco IOS command for setting a port to auto state, for example, is as follows:

```
dot1x port-control auto
```

Initially, a port set to auto will be in an unauthorized state, letting only EAP traffic enter the protected network to reach the authentication server. After the authentication process takes place and the supplicant is authorized to enter the protected network, the port will switch to an authorized state for that particular supplicant. Figure 7-10 illustrates this process. If the state of the link connected to the port goes down, then the port set to auto will generally switch to an unauthorized state.

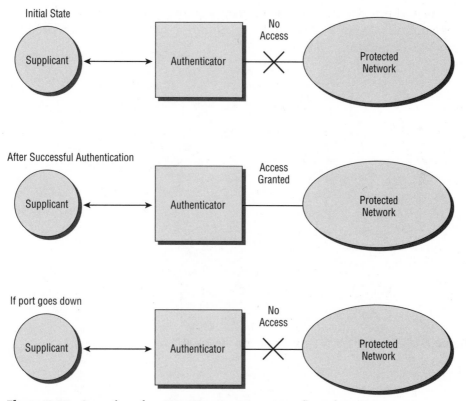

Figure 7-10: Operation of an 802.1X port set to autoconfiguration

NOTE With most vendor solutions, especially Cisco, you can't enable 802.1X on a trunk port. If you do, an error message appears and 802.1X will not be enabled.

VLAN Identification

In most enterprise deployments, it will be necessary to set the port's VLAN. The result is that traffic associated with the port becomes associated with the VLAN number set for the port. The following Cisco IOS command is an example of assigning a VLAN to a particular port:

```
switchport access vlan <vlanid>
```

Some port-based authentication implementations enable the RADIUS server to dynamically assign VLANs to the ports during the authentication process. Figure 7-11 shows this concept.

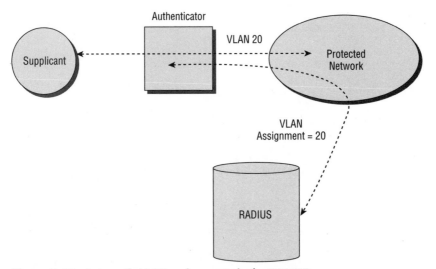

Figure 7-11: Automatic VLAN assignment via the RADIUS server

Multiple MAC Address Support

With most port-based authentication systems, the default configuration is for each 802.1X-enabled port to support only a single MAC address (i.e., single client device). When that particular supplicant authenticates through the port, only that supplicant is authorized. No other supplicants are allowed through the port unless they authenticate as well. If you wish to support more than one MAC address on each port, then you can generally do that by configuring the authenticator to accept multiple hosts. For example, the Cisco IOS command for allowing multiple MAC addresses is as follows:

```
dot1x host-mode multi-host
```

When the authenticator is configured for multiple hosts, the first supplicant that authenticates successfully with the port causes the port to be authorized for that particular supplicant and all other supplicants. This can drastically reduce the security of the network, so use it sparingly. It's also possible to set the maximum number of active MAC addresses per port and which specific MAC addresses are allowable. If re-authentication fails or the port receives an EAPOL-Logoff packet from one of the supplicants, then the port transitions to an unauthorized state for all of the supplicants on that port.

Retry Number

It's possible to set the number of times that the authenticator retries transmission of a packet to a supplicant or authentication server. This affects most or all of the instances when a packet needs to be retransmitted. For example, the authenticator may send an EAP Request packet to a supplicant, and if after a specified period of time (retry timeout value) the authenticator doesn't receive a corresponding EAP Response packet, the authenticator will resend the same EAP Request packet originally sent.

The typical default retry number is 2, but it can often be set to a range from 1 to 10. The Cisco IOS command for setting the retry number is as follows:

```
dot1x max-req <number>
```

This retry number applies to the 802.1X protocols, not necessarily other retry settings, such as those used with 802.11.

Retry Timeout Value

The retry timeout value is the amount of time that the authenticator will wait before resending a packet if no response is heard from the supplicant or authentication server. Most port-based authentication systems have a separate retry timeout value for the supplicants and authentication servers. If you're implementing a wireless system, then it may be beneficial to allocate a higher retry timeout value due to potential delays over the wireless network. The Cisco IOS command for setting the retry timeout value for the supplicant and authentication server, respectively, is as follows:

```
dot1x timeout supp-timeout <seconds>
dot1x timeout server-timeout <seconds>
```

The range for both retry timeout values is 1 to 65,535 seconds (just over 18 hours), with 30 seconds as the default value.

> **NOTE** Be careful when setting the retry number and retry timeout values. For example, a retry number of 4 and a retry timeout value of 30 seconds could lead to a two-minute delay before a user receives an indication of what's happening. That's a very long time that most users can't tolerate without having feedback from the system.

Quiet Period Value

The quiet period is the amount of time that can elapse before another attempt is made after an unsuccessful authentication. The following Cisco IOS command sets the quiet period value:

```
dot1x timeout quiet-period <seconds>
```

The range for the quiet period value is usually 1 to 65,535 seconds (just over 18 hours), with 60 seconds as the default value.

Re-authentication Activation

By default, most authenticators are set to not allow re-authentication. As a result, you must configure the authenticator to enable the re-authentication process. This could be beneficial for improving the security of the network. Periodically, with re-authentication enabled, the supplicants will be forced to re-authenticate in order to remain in the authorized state and reach into the protected network. The Cisco IOS command for enabling re-authentication, for example, is as follows:

```
dot1x re-authentication
```

You may also find it useful to manually cause a supplicant to re-authenticate, such as when troubleshooting. Most authenticators allow you to do this. For example, the Cisco IOS command for prompting a manual re-authentication of a particular supplicant is as follows:

```
dot1x re-authenticate interface <interface-id>
```

Re-authentication Period Value

After enabling re-authentication, you should set the re-authentication period value, which is the amount of time that passes before the supplicants must re-authenticate. The Cisco IOS command for setting the re-authentication time-out value is as follows:

```
dot1x reauth-period <seconds>
```

The range for the re-authentication timeout value is usually 1 to 65,535 seconds (just over 18 hours), with 3,600 seconds (one hour) as the default value. In order to improve security, a smaller re-authentication period value would be ideal, but care must be taken not to overburden the network. If each supplicant must re-authenticate every few seconds, then there will be a lot of overhead traffic on the network. With many supplicants, this can overwhelm the available capacity of the network and significantly reduce performance for all users. Generally, the typical default value of one hour is sufficient to provide adequate levels of security.

> **NOTE** Instead of using the command-line interface (CLI), you can perform most configuration on authenticators via the web-based (port 80) administrative interface on the wired switch or wireless access point.

Configuring Wireless Access Points

Because of their security vulnerabilities, the majority of 802.1X port-based authentication systems make use of wireless access points. As a result, it's useful to understand how to best configure them. This section is not meant to be an exhaustive guide on setting up access points, but it provides enough details to point you in the right direction. It's important to also make use of other publications to fully understand the deployment of wireless networks.

For each of the following settings, you'll need to interface with the access point in some manner in order to issue configuration commands or view configuration screens. The section "Authenticator Administrative Interface" later in this chapter explains several different ways to access the configuration function of an access point.

IP Address

One of the first things you'll need to configure on an access point is its IP address. Some access points have a default IP address, such as 192.168.0.1, which allows you to interface with the access point over the wireless interface immediately after initially powering up the access point. Some access points, such as the Cisco 1240, don't have an IP address configured at the factory. As a result, you may need to configure the IP address, subnet mask, and default gateway before you're able to connect to the access point wirelessly or over the wired network for configuration purposes.

If no IP address is set by default, then you can sometimes connect the access point to a wired network that has a DHCP server, and the access point will receive an IP address automatically. This assumes that the access point is set by default to obtain an IP address through DHCP. Alternatively, you can generally connect to the access point via a serial cable and then configure the access point.

SSID

The SSID provides a name that wireless clients use when identifying a particular wireless LAN. The SSID can consist of up to 32 alphanumeric, case-sensitive characters, and it's configured in each access point. The SSID is what Microsoft Windows displays when a wireless network is found. For example, "linksys" and "default" are both SSIDs in the screenshot shown in Figure 7-12. In order to associate with an access point, the client radio must be configured with the SSID of the access point. Windows performs this configuration on the client radio automatically when the user chooses to connect to a particular wireless LAN (SSID) displayed in the Windows wireless configuration utility.

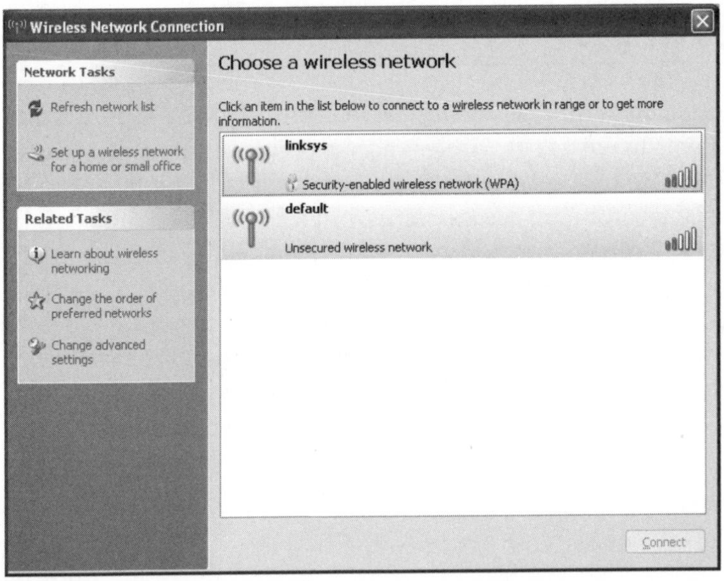

Figure 7-12: The SSID is displayed in the Microsoft Windows Wireless Network Configuration screen as an available wireless network.

The default SSID preconfigured in the access point will work for most access point models, but you should change the SSID to a different, unique value as part of the installation process. This prevents wireless users of neighboring networks from inadvertently connecting with your network (and vice versa). Generally, an enterprise will set the same SSID in each access point.

NOTE Some access points, such as the Cisco 1240, don't have a preconfigured SSID. As a result, you must configure the SSID in the access point before it will operate.

Most enterprise-grade access points allow the configuration of multiple SSIDs on each access point. Each SSID represents a separate virtual wireless LAN that can have its own unique configuration settings and connect to a specific VLAN on the wired side of the access point. Using multiple SSIDs enables you to establish different types of services. For example, one SSID may allow guests to connect to the network and have access to the Internet, whereas another SSID may be configured with encryption and make use of 802.1X port-based authentication for access to a protected network.

Some access points have a setting that disables the broadcasting of the SSID in beacon frames. If you disable beacon broadcasting, then Microsoft Windows will not find the network and display the SSID to users. As a result, in order to connect with a wireless LAN with SSID broadcasting disabled, you must configure the client radios with the applicable SSID. Previously, this was thought to be more secure than allowing the broadcasting of beacons, mainly because users can't readily find the SSID and associate with the network, but many wireless sniffing tools can still find the SSID of a network. If you want to hide your wireless LAN from casual eavesdroppers—for example, someone seeing the network in their Windows wireless configuration utility—then disabling SSID broadcasting may be beneficial; otherwise, disabling it may be more trouble than it's worth.

Radio Settings

There are several radio settings on an access point. Most of the default settings allow the access point to operate effectively, but you might consider changing them depending on requirements.

Transmit Power

The transmit power of the access point is generally set to the highest value. As a result, the access point will have maximum downlink range, which is the direction from the access point to the wireless client devices. As Chapter 1 explains, the highest transmit power setting of the access point is usually higher than client radios. As a result, it's not necessary to always use the highest transmit power setting on the access point. With networks that have relatively low utilization, it probably won't make much of a difference if you leave the access point set to the highest transmit power; but in some cases, such as when supporting voice applications, you should tune the transmit power of the access point to a level that optimizes performance. In this case, you should turn down the transmit power on the access point to a level equivalent to the transmit power of the client radios. This often significantly reduces the interference between access points set to the same channel, which increases the capacity of the wireless network.

When adjusting the transmit power of the access point, take into account the type of client devices that will be associating with the access point. Try to determine which ones will have the weakest transmit power, and adjust the transmit power of the access point to an equivalent value. Figure 7-13 illustrates this approach. To find the weakest client radio, you can associate the different client devices (lined up next to each other) with an access point, and log into the administrative interface of the access point to read their respective received signal strengths. After determining the associated client radio with the weakest received signal strength, use that one when adjusting the access point transmit power to match the weakest client radio. You can then use a signal measuring tool, such as NetStumbler or AirMagnet, on the client device to measure the access point's received signal strength at the client device. With this test setup, turn down the transmit power on the access point until the received signal strength of the client device at the access point (uplink) equals the received signal strength of the access point at the client device (downlink).

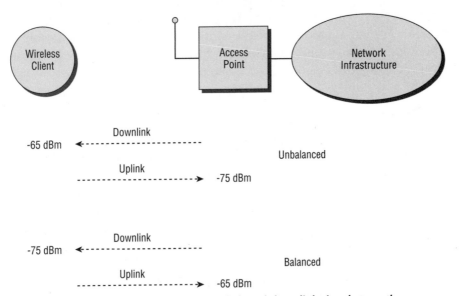

Figure 7-13: Balanced vs. unbalanced uplink and downlink signal strengths

Once you have the access point's transmit power set to balance the downlink with the uplink of the weakest client radio, you can perform an RF site survey using the access point configured with the balanced setting. The RF site survey will determine the optimum placement of access points throughout the facility. Measurements during the survey are taken from an access point placed at different locations within the facility. The received signal strength of the access point at a client device running site survey software will represent signal coverage. It's important to balance the downlink and uplink signals as explained above before performing the survey. This ensures that the measured signals do indeed represent signal coverage for the weakest client radios.

NOTE Some access points implement automatic transmit power control. If this is the case, then there may be no need to set the transmit power of the access point.

RF Channel

In most cases, the access point is set to a static RF channel. The client radios in the user devices will scan all channels for available access points and then tune to the RF channel of the access point as part of the connection process with the access point. The 802.11 standard defines up to 14 different RF channels for access points operating in the 2.4GHz band. In the U.S., the FCC allows operation in only the first 11 channels. Other countries may use more or fewer of the channels, depending on their regulations. The RF channels of access points, however, overlap significantly, leaving only channels 1, 6, and 11 that don't overlap. In most implementations, in order to maximize capacity and roaming capability, adjacent access points should be set to non-overlapping channels (1, 6, or 11) as shown in Figure 7-14. Keep in mind that in multi-floor facilities, the access points above and below each other will likely need to be set to non-overlapping channels as well.

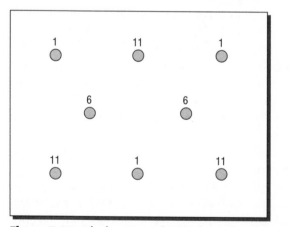

Figure 7-14: Ideal access point RF channel assignments

Some access points, such as the Cisco 1240, implement an optional automatic RF channel mode. With this configuration, the access point will automatically attempt to tune to an RF channel that has the least congestion. This may provide better performance because retransmission rates may be lower due to fewer collisions with RF interference and among client radios. If you're implementing voice applications, though, then the periodic changing of access point channels will force associated clients to re-associate, which can lead to voice calls that drop when the re-association occurs. Thus, it's advisable to not use automatic channel selection features when deploying voice applications.

Data Rates

The data rate settings on the access point apply to the data frames being sent from the access point to the client radios (downlink). The default setting is generally *auto*, which means that the access point will automatically shift to the optimum data rate. Usually, the data rate automatically selected is based on the signal strength of the client devices and retransmission rates. For example, a wireless client that is located within ten feet of an access point may warrant having the access point operate at the highest data rate. As the distance of the client devices from the access point increases, the signal strength will decrease and the retransmission rate will increase. Although shifting to a lower data rate may lower the data rate, the overall throughput may be higher because of fewer retransmissions.

In addition to the "auto" setting for data rates, most access points allow configuration of static data rates. In order to improve security, for example, it may be beneficial to set the access points to only operate at the highest data rate, such as 11 Mbps for 802.11b or 54 Mbps for 802.11g. Because of the requirements for operating at a relatively high data rate, client radios will only be able to associate with the access point at relatively short ranges from the access points. This can also significantly improve performance because all communication is done at very high data rates. In fact, some voice applications suggest configuring access point data rates at high static values. Of course, this means that you'd likely need to install many more access points to cover a specific area, but connecting to the wireless network from outside the facility would be very difficult.

Similarly, you can set the access point data rates to a fixed lower value, such as 1 Mbps for 802.11b or 6 Mbps for 802.11g. This configuration often maximizes the range compared to using the "auto" data rate setting because when using "auto," the access point may not shift down to the lowest data rate effectively. Forcing lower data rates ensures the maximum range based on the chosen data rate, but performance will likely be low. Using fixed low data rates could be a good choice for bar code applications, for which there is no huge need for high performance.

Preamble

The radio in the access point (and client radio) creates a frame for transmission over the air medium. At the beginning of this frame is a preamble, which synchronizes the receiver with the frame and designates the beginning of the frame. In the access point, you can set the radio preamble to long or short. The short preamble improves performance. Most vendor client radios and access points support short preambles. Some older client radios, however, only support long preambles. As a result, setting the preamble to long ensures compatibility for use with older devices. It pays to research each client radio that you plan to use on the network and determine whether there is a need to support long preambles. If there is no requirement for long preambles, then configure the access point for short preamble.

Beacon Period

As mentioned before, the access point periodically broadcasts a beacon, which is an 802.11 frame. The beacon also carries information about the network, such as the SSID and data rate capability. These beacons enable wireless adapters to identify the presence of the router. If more than one access point is part of the same network, then the wireless adapters use the signal strength of the received beacons to determine which one to associate with.

By default, the beacon period is 100 milliseconds, which is the amount of time between beacons. In most cases, you don't need to change the beacon interval. Perhaps the only reason you would adjust the beacon interval is if you want to extend battery life in the wireless client devices. If you increase the beacon interval to one or two seconds, then the wireless adapters will sleep longer and conserve more battery power; however, the longer beacon interval can cause throughput performance to decrease. In addition, longer beacon intervals may negatively affect roaming. Because beacons are occurring less often, a user roaming through a facility may cause the applicable client radio to not identify access points soon enough to accommodate roaming before losing connection with a particular access point.

Fragmentation

Access points allow you to activate an optional fragmentation process whereby each 802.11 data frame is broken up into small pieces (fragments) and sent as separate data frames, as Figure 7-15 shows. This can be effective when counteracting the damaging affects of RF interference. If interference hits a full-sized (unfragmented) data frame, then the access point must retransmit the entire frame, which takes time and adds considerable overhead to the network. With fragmentation, errors will likely occur in one of the fragments, which don't take nearly as long to retransmit.

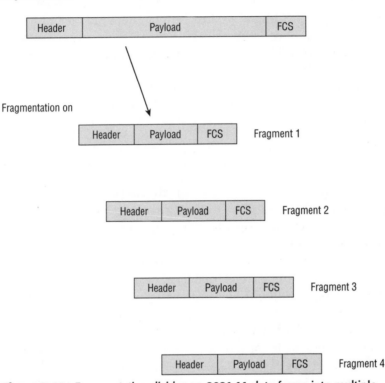

Figure 7-15: Fragmentation divides an 8021.11 data frame into multiple fragments.

If retransmission rates are relatively high (above 10 percent), consider activating fragmentation on the access point. If you're not suffering from poor performance, then it's not worth the hassle to activate and tune the fragmentation threshold settings. If you activate fragmentation, then always check performance levels on the wireless network and compare them to not using fragmentation. If the retransmission rate is higher or throughput is worse, then fragmentation is probably not going to help matters.

NOTE Refer to the section "Wireless Impairments" in Chapter 1 for details on wireless impairments.

Authenticator Management

Authenticators, which of course are wired switches or wireless access points, offer management functions, such as administrative interfaces and management information bases (MIBs). This section provides an overview of these topics as they relate to authenticators.

Authenticator Administrative Interface

In order to configure an authenticator, an administrator must interface with the wired switch or wireless access point using one of several different methods. The following sections briefly explain each way.

Terminal Connection

One way to interface with the authenticator is to connect a serial cable between a laptop and the authenticator and use terminal emulation software on the laptop to communicate with the authenticator. Figure 7-16 illustrates this method. After connecting the cable, the terminal emulation software will communicate with the administrative interface inside the switch or access point and provide a CLI for entering commands. This may be the only way to initially communicate with some access points, especially if they have no default IP address set. Some administrators, especially those who are well versed in the CLI commands for the particular equipment you're deploying, may prefer using the terminal connection for configuring the entire switch or access point.

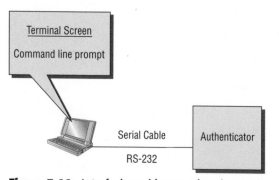

Figure 7-16: Interfacing with an authenticator via a terminal connection

Web Browser Interface

Wired switches and wireless access points also deploy a small web server within the hardware to display administrative support pages where you can configure most settings for the authenticator (see Figure 7-17). This is often preferred over using commands via a CLI because the web interface is more user-friendly. When using a web browser to perform the configurations, you must have a computer connected to the same network as the authenticator. With wireless access points, it's convenient to simply wirelessly associate the computer with the access point to establish a network connection. Keep in mind, however, that you need to set your computer's IP address and subnet mask to values that comply with the access point. You must set your computer to be in the same subnet and have an applicable IP address that doesn't conflict with another one in use. This is done automatically if the access point is automatically assigning IP addresses through DHCP. With wired switches, you need to connect both the switch and the computer to the Ethernet network in order to establish a network connection that allows the use of a web browser for configuring the authenticator. After connecting the computer to the same network, whether it is wireless or wired, type in the IP address of the authenticator as the URL in the web browser, and the browser should display the login page of the administrative interface on the switch or access point.

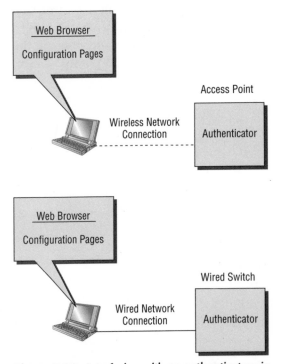

Figure 7-17: Interfacing with an authenticator via wireless and wired network connections

SNMP

Most enterprise-grade switches and access points include SNMP (Simple Network Management Protocol) for interfacing with management systems. This is important, especially for larger organizations, where it's beneficial to provide centralized and automated support. Via SNMP, management systems interface with the authenticator's MIB to configure and read statistics.

Administrator Access Control

To ensure that the access point is secure against someone attempting to reconfigure the access point to their advantage, such as disabling the need for 802.1X port-based authentication, ensure that you configure the username and password for the administrative interface to something different than the default values. This can generally be done when first interfacing with the access point through a web browser. If you don't configure the access control, then the system will be wide open to attack. Many of the default usernames and passwords for access points are well known throughout the industry.

Authenticator MIB

The 802.1X standard defines a MIB that includes many objects related to authenticators, such as configuring the quiet period and enabling re-authentication. The MIB also provides many different statistics that administrators can use to help troubleshoot problems. Some vendors also extend the 802.11X MIB with proprietary features.

NOTE Refer to the IEEE 802.1X standard for details on the 802.1X MIB.

CHAPTER 8

Configuring
Authentication Servers

In this chapter, we'll take a closer look at configuring authentication servers, with emphasis on RADIUS. This will provide you with some options when choosing RADIUS servers and a background on the parameters that generally require configuration.

Authentication Server Recap

As explained in Chapter 2, "Port-Based Authentication Concepts," an authentication server is a device that actually implements the authentication. The authentication server implements the specific EAP-Method that the client device is using. Client devices needing authentication utilize the EAP-Method to communicate with the authentication server. RADIUS protocols actually transport the EAP-Method data between the authenticator and the authentication server. Figure 8-1 illustrates how an authentication server interfaces with the other components of an 802.1X port-based authentication system.

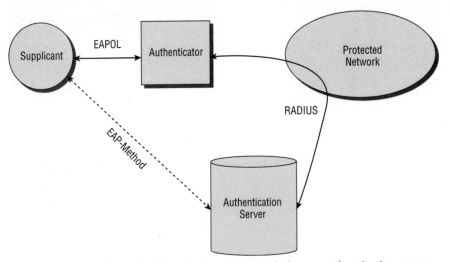

Figure 8-1: A port-based authentication system includes an authentication server, which verifies the identity of client devices.

Choosing RADIUS Servers

RADIUS is somewhat of a de facto standard for authentication servers. There are many different vendors, however, that make RADIUS server software, some of which is available as open source and some that is commercially available. RADIUS actually provides more than just support for 802.1X port-based authentication systems. RADIUS also offers authentication and accounting services in addition to authentication. Authorization determines whether a user is allowed on the network based on defined policies. Accounting functions record statistics for use in billing, troubleshooting, and management of resources.

> **NOTE** Consider evaluating various RADIUS server packages under a trial period before purchasing the software.

Commercial RADIUS Servers

In most cases, a fully supported commercial RADIUS product will be the best alternative because it saves time and includes support that may be crucial when problems arise. The following is a sample of common commercial RADIUS solutions:

- Aradial WiFi
- Bridgewater Wi-Fi AAA
- Cisco Secure Access Control Server
- Funk Odyssey
- IEA RadiusNT
- Infoblox RADIUS One Appliance
- Interlink Secure.XS
- LeapPoint AiroPoint Appliance
- Meetinghouse AEGIS
- Microsoft Internet Authentication Server
- OSC Radiator
- Vircom VOP Radius

Microsoft Internet Authentication Service (IAS) is likely the best solution if you have a Microsoft Windows 2000/2003 Server and users running Windows. You can find a lot of documentation on AIS, but you need a good background in Windows.

Open-Source RADIUS Servers

If you're inclined to working with source code and want to get by with less cost for software (and you're not a heavy Microsoft shop), then consider implementing a RADIUS server with an open-source solution. For example, FreeRADIUS is an 802.1X-capable open-source server that runs on Linux, OpenBSD, OSF/Unix, or Solaris. With this alternative, you need some previous experience working with Unix.

NOTE For more information about FreeRADIUS, visit www.freeradius.org.

There are other open-source RADIUS servers, but they are not actively maintained.

Outsourcing RADIUS Functionality

Another approach for establishing RADIUS server functionality is to pay someone else to do it through outsourcing, which Figure 8-2 illustrates. This is the best alternative if you don't have sufficient experience in Windows or Unix, which is required for the commercially available and open-source solutions. For example, the Wireless Security Corporation offers WSC Guard, a managed 802.1X service for less than $100 per user per year. A strong advantage of out-sourcing RADIUS functions is that it avoids the associated capital expenses and applicable implementation services. This can be great, especially for companies that plan to start with relatively few RADIUS users and then grow to larger numbers in the future.

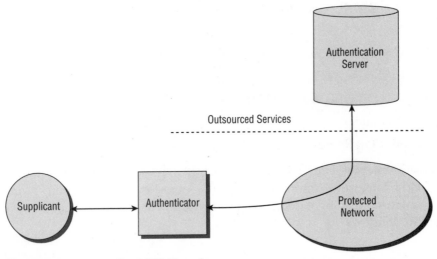

Figure 8-2: Outsourcing RADIUS services

Installing RADIUS Software

The following sections explain the primary tasks that you need to accomplish when installing RADIUS software. The information provided here gives you a general overview, primarily to underscore what to expect and to help provide a basis for deciding whether it's best to implement the solution yourself or use outsourcing. For details, be sure to carefully study and follow the instructions provided by the RADIUS solution provider you've chosen.

Review Release Notes

As with any software installation, *always* review release notes in order to learn of any late-breaking information, such as known software problems and doc-umentation corrections. In many cases, the release notes serve as an errata sheet. You'll find these notes either on the software installation CD or as a piece of paper slipped into the installation manual (or both).

Establish a Server

Of course, the RADIUS software will need to reside on a hardware server platform. The following sections present some things that you should take into consideration.

System Requirements

Review the system requirements for the RADIUS software that you've chosen and then select a server that meets those requirements. This may seem obvious, but you'd be surprised by how many people skip this step and later find themselves upgrading the server or finding a different one in order for the RADIUS software to run properly. Most RADIUS server software requires a host with at least 512MB of working memory and 40MB of disk space. The RADIUS administrator software will likely require another chunk of disk space. Check the specifics of your RADIUS software before getting too far along in the installation process.

Physical Location

Think ahead about where you want the RADIUS server to reside. You should choose a location that offers physical security, such as a locked room. For larger companies, the "server room" will likely be the best installation location, as shown in Figure 8-3. To ensure security during a fire, make sure that the chosen room has fire protection.

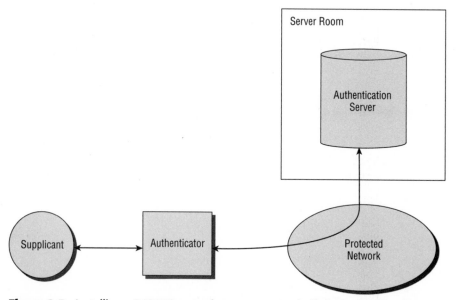

Figure 8-3: Installing a RADIUS server in a server room is likely the best location.

Verify Network Connections

Once you have selected a server and have it residing at the chosen location, verify the network connection. This is necessary to ensure that the server will be able to communicate with other network components using TCP/IP. You can use the `ping` command from the command prompt of a laptop or PC connected to the same network to determine whether the server responds correctly. The following is an example of using the `ping` command to verify a server with an IP address of 192.168.3.50:

```
C:\>ping 192.168.3.50

Reply from 192.168.3.50: bytes=32 time=8ms TTL=255
Reply from 192.168.3.50: bytes=32 time=6ms TTL=255
Reply from 192.168.3.50: bytes=32 time=7ms TTL=255
Reply from 192.168.3.50: bytes=32 time=8ms TTL=255
```

In this case, the ping test passed, indicating that the server is indeed connected properly to the network. If the ping test fails, then verify that the server is configured with the correct IP address.

In addition to verifying that the IP address is reachable, also ensure that the server has a stable resolvable hostname. You can do this via `ping` as follows for a server with the hostname of `radius.net`:

```
C:\>ping radius.net

Reply from 192.168.3.50: bytes=32 time=7ms TTL=255
Reply from 192.168.3.50: bytes=32 time=6ms TTL=255
Reply from 192.168.3.50: bytes=32 time=9ms TTL=255
Reply from 192.168.3.50: bytes=32 time=7ms TTL=255
```

NOTE To improve security, the RADIUS server should have no user accounts.

Configure Administrator Account Access

In order to configure the RADIUS server, you'll likely need administrator account access, as shown in Figure 8-4. Verify whether the administrator has this level of access. If not, then configure the access before installing the RADIUS software.

Administrative Access
Authentication Server

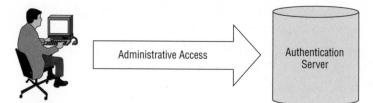

Figure 8-4: Administrative access is often needed to manage RADIUS servers.

With Windows, for example, you need to configure *root* administrative access. The following steps explain how to do this with Windows XP (other operating systems are similar):

1. Click Start and select the Control Panel.
2. Select Administrative Tools.
3. Select Computer Management. The window shown in Figure 8-5 will appear.

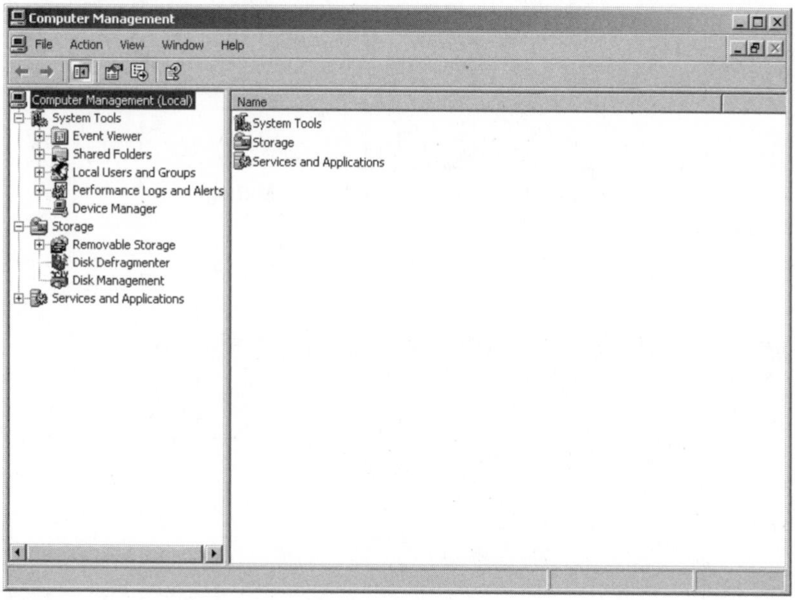

Computer Management
File Action View Window Help
Computer Management (Local)
System Tools
Event Viewer
Shared Folders
Local Users and Groups
Performance Logs and Alerts
Device Manager
Storage
Removable Storage
Disk Defragmenter
Disk Management
Services and Applications
Name
System Tools
Storage
Services and Applications

Figure 8-5: Microsoft Windows XP Computer Management window

4. In the Computer Management window, select Local Users and Groups. The window shown in Figure 8-6 will appear.

5. Select Users, right-click, and select New User from the drop-down menu, as shown in Figure 8-7. The New User dialog shown in Figure 8-8 appears.

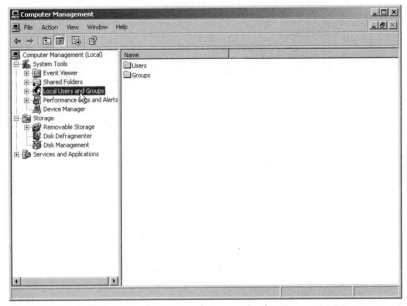

Figure 8-6: Selecting Local Users and Groups in the Computer Management window of Microsoft Windows XP

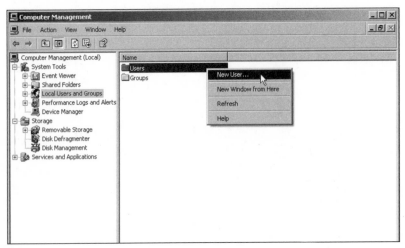

Figure 8-7: Selecting the New User function in Microsoft Windows XP

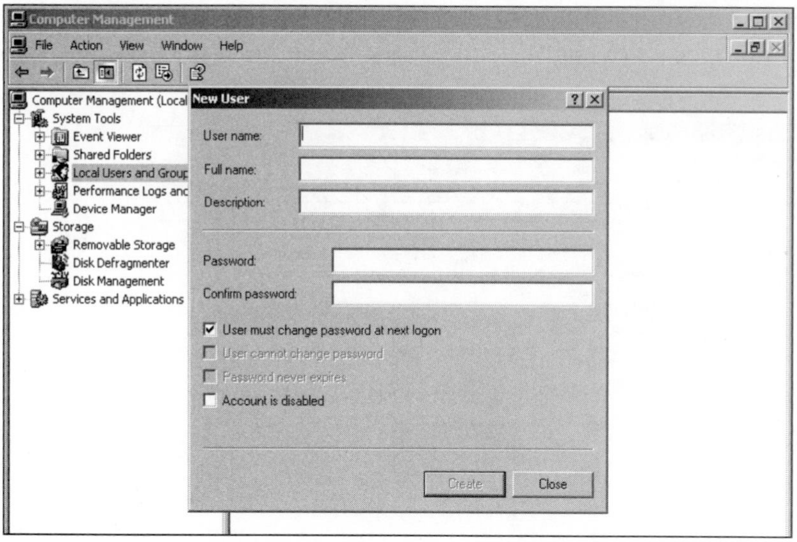

Figure 8-8: The New User dialog in Microsoft Windows XP

6. Configure the New User dialog with root as the user and create and confirm a password. It's probably not necessary to change the password on the next login, so you can uncheck "User must change password at next login." If you want the password to never expire, then check "Password never expires." Figure 8-9 illustrates these settings. After you've made your selections for these settings, click Create. The Computer Management window will appear (refer to Figure 8-6).

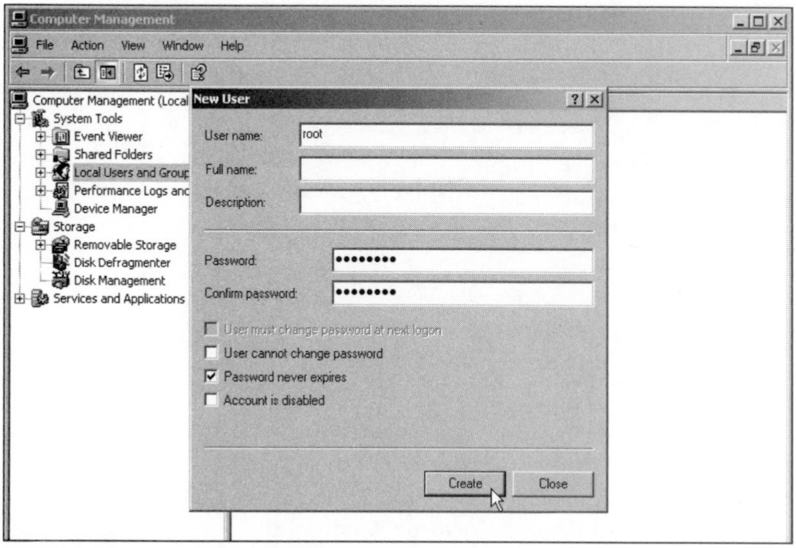

Figure 8-9: Example configuration for establishing a root user in Microsoft Windows XP

7. Select Users, right-click on root, and select Properties (see Figure 8-10). The root Properties dialog will appear, as shown in Figure 8-11.

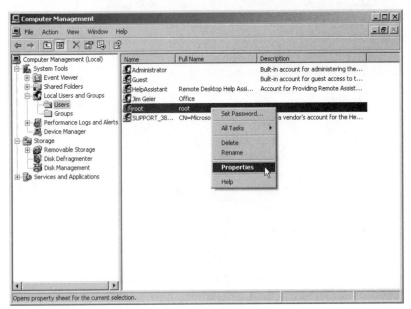

Figure 8-10: Selecting Properties when configuring the root user

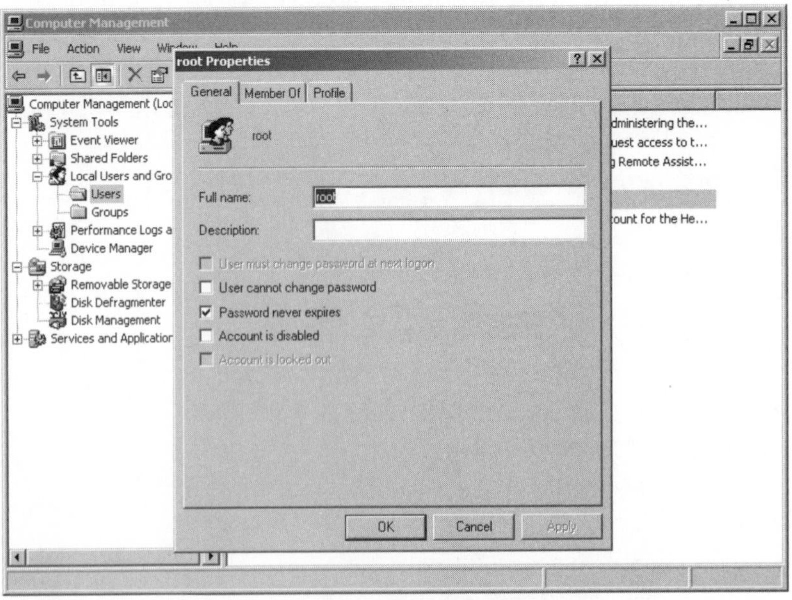

Figure 8-11: The root Properties dialog in Microsoft Windows XP

8. Select the Member Of tab and click Add, as shown in Figure 8-12. The Select Groups dialog shown in Figure 8-13 will appear.

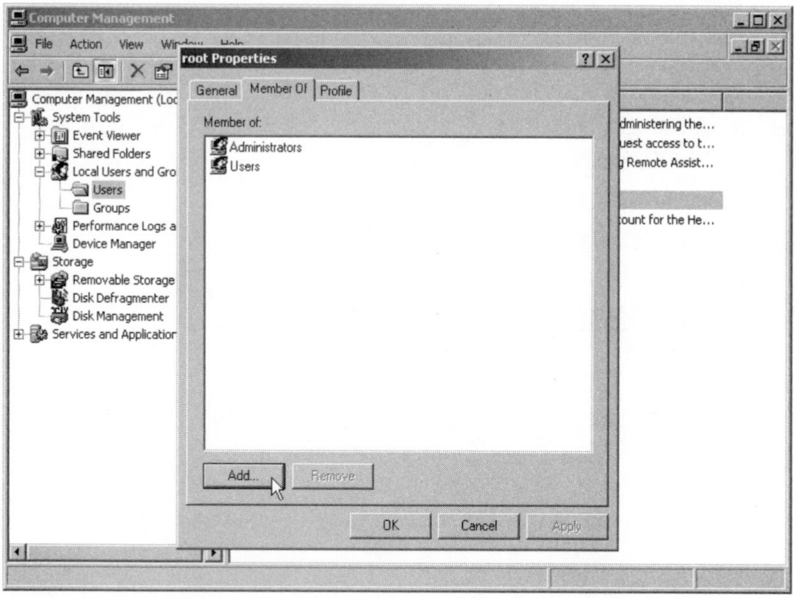

Figure 8-12: The Member Of tab of the root Properties dialog.

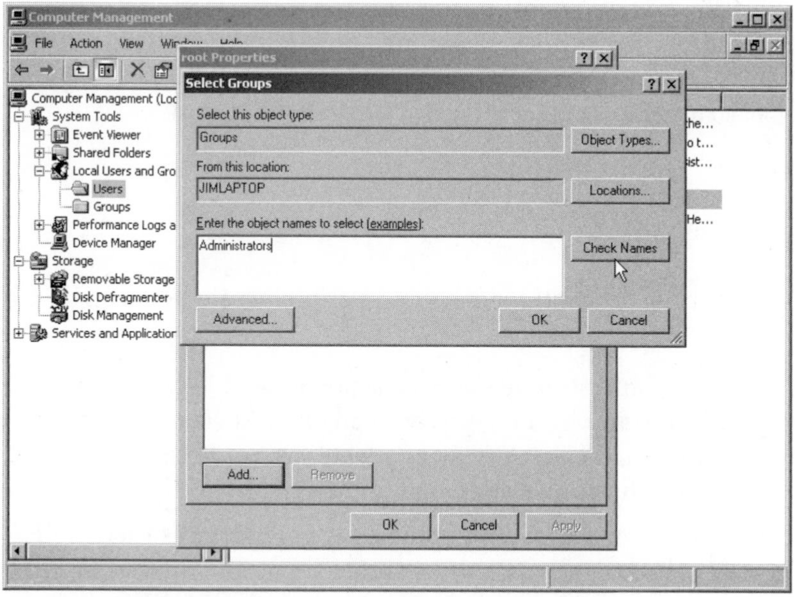

Figure 8-13: The Select Groups dialog in Microsoft Windows XP.

9. In the "Enter the object names to select" box, type **Administrators** and click Check Names. The system will display the Administrator group in the box labeled "Enter the object names to select."

10. Click OK. The root Properties dialog will indicate that root is a member of the Users and Administrators groups, as shown in Figure 8-14, and the root user will now have Windows Administrator privileges. As mentioned before, this step is generally necessary before you can configure a RADIUS server.

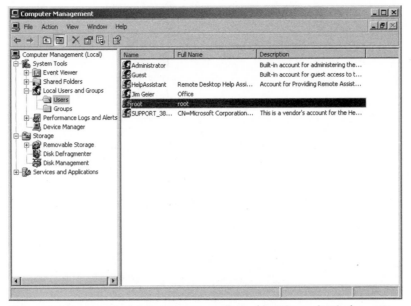

Figure 8-14: root administrative user configured in Microsoft Windows XP

Security Tips

The following are security tips that you should implement when installing a RADIUS server:

- ▪ Ensure that the administrative interface is not accessible from outside the network. For example, if the server interconnects via more than one network connection, then ensure that the network connection used for administration is physically separate from other networks.

- ▪ Ensure that the server does not run public network services such as FTP or HTTP, as this makes the server vulnerable to malicious attacks. In addition, it could negatively impact the performance of the RADIUS server.

- Assign a strong shared secret. (Shared secrets are described in the section "Shared Secret" later in this chapter.) You'll need to assign a shared secret to the RADIUS server. Make sure that you use long and random shared secrets to reduce the chances of someone determining the secret and compromising the system. For the same reason, avoid using the same shared secret on other servers. Some commercially available RADIUS servers include additional safeguards for producing secure secrets. For example, Juniper Network's free Password Amplifier utility takes an ordinary shared secret and hashes it repeatedly to produce a 16-character amplified secret, which you can configure in the server.

- Limit permissions related to the RADIUS server. With some servers, you can set file permissions to limit the ability of unauthorized people to access configuration, accounting, and log files. For example, with Steel-Belted Radius you can configure default file permissions in the `sbrd.conf` file.

NOTE If your business doesn't have much security risk, then consider deploying your wireless network using WPA with preshared keys. This avoids the need to set up a RADIUS server.

Install the Software

After completing the preceding steps, you should be ready to install the RADIUS software:

1. Be sure to carefully read the installation instructions supplied by the manufacturer of the RADIUS software that you've selected.

2. Log on to the Windows server as an administrator.

3. If you are upgrading an existing installation, then back up your root and server certificates, and verify that you know the password for your server certificate.

4. Perform the installation as directed in the vendor's installation instructions.

After installing the RADIUS software, wait for the instructions describing how to access the RADIUS administrative interface. For example, after installing Steel-Belted RADIUS, a window appears with the URL you need to point your browser to in order to access the administrative interface. Although the administrative manuals certainly explain how to access the interface, the installation window indicates the exact URL associated with your specific server that you must use. Figure 8-15 illustrates this helpful tip.

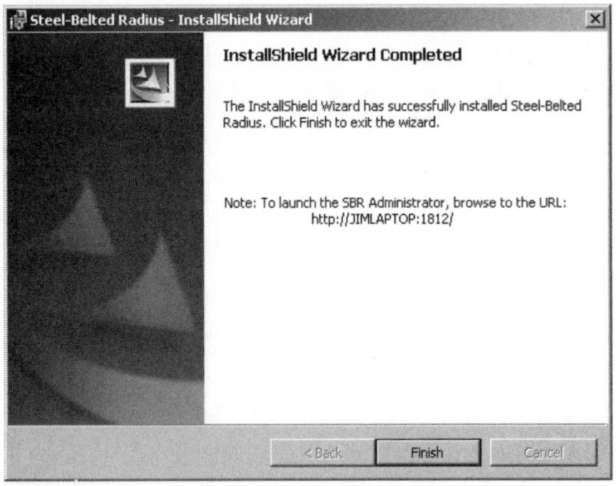

Figure 8-15: Installation splash screen identifying the URL for accessing the administrative interface for Steel-Belted Radius.

NOTE You must generally install RADIUS where you have root administrator access. In fact, the username and password necessary to boot the RADIUS configuration utility are often the root username and password.

Common RADIUS Configuration Parameters

This section discusses the common configuration parameters for RADIUS servers. In addition to helping you understand how these configuration parameters are used, it offers suggestions for how to decide among the various options.

Accessing RADIUS Configuration

Most RADIUS servers allow you to access RADIUS configuration via an applicable network connection and a web browser. For example, with Steel-Belted RADIUS, you start the SBR Administrator by opening a browser connection to the Steel-Belted RADIUS server you want to administer. If the Steel-Belted RADIUS server is running on a local host, enter `http://localhost:port/`, where *port* is the TCP port on which the server is listening for administration connections.

For example, if the local host is listening on port 1812, then place the following URL in your browser: `http://localhost:1813/`. If the Steel-Belted RADIUS server is running on a remote host, then enter `http://server:port/`, where *server* is the DNS name or IP address of the server. You can use the following URL if the Steel-Belted RADIUS server has an IP address of 192.168.24.15 on a remote host, and the host is listening on port 1812: `http://192.168.24.15:1812/`. With Steel-Belted RADIUS, the Administrator page opens, and you click the Launch link to download and start the SBR Administrator. Other RADIUS servers have similar methods to initiate administrative access for configuration purposes.

As with most other server-based applications, you need to log into the administrative interface. Figure 8-16 shows an example of logging into Steel-Belted RADIUS. You need to input the port number as directed by the administration manual and then insert your root admin User Name and Password.

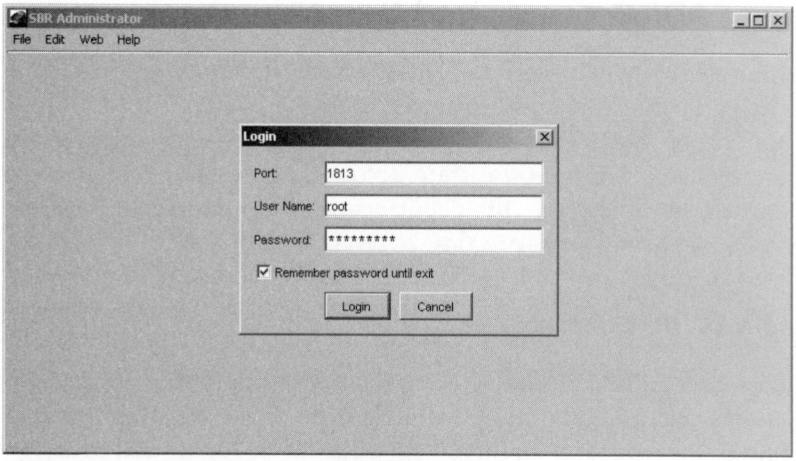

Figure 8-16: Logging into Steel-Belted RADIUS

After logging in, an administrative dialog will appear, such as the one shown in Figure 8-17 for Steel-Belted RADIUS. From this window, you're able to access all configuration functions for clients, users, and other components. At startup, the window also displays information about the configuration of the server.

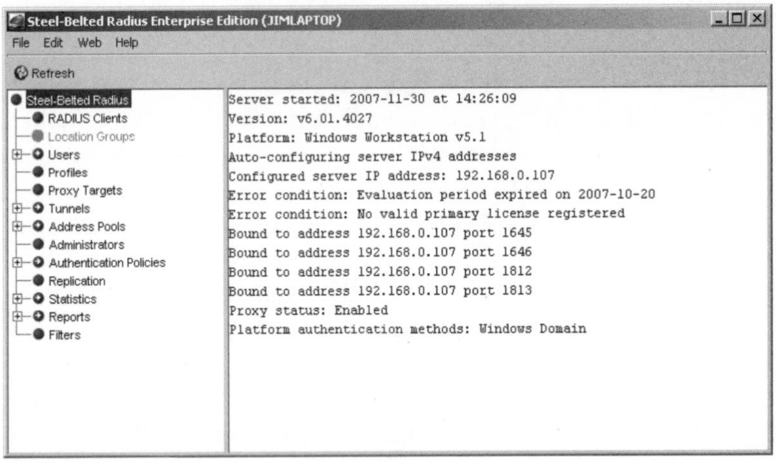

```
Steel-Belted Radius Enterprise Edition (JIMLAPTOP)                    _ □ ×
File   Edit   Web   Help

🕃 Refresh

● Steel-Belted Radius        Server started: 2007-11-30 at 14:26:09
  ── ● RADIUS Clients        Version: v6.01.4027
      ● Location Groups      Platform: Windows Workstation v5.1
  ⊞─ ● Users                 Auto-configuring server IPv4 addresses
  ── ● Profiles              Configured server IP address: 192.168.0.107
  ── ● Proxy Targets         Error condition: Evaluation period expired on 2007-10-20
  ⊞─ ● Tunnels               Error condition: No valid primary license registered
  ⊞─ ● Address Pools         Bound to address 192.168.0.107 port 1645
  ── ● Administrators        Bound to address 192.168.0.107 port 1646
  ⊞─ ● Authentication Policies Bound to address 192.168.0.107 port 1812
  ── ● Replication           Bound to address 192.168.0.107 port 1813
  ⊞─ ● Statistics            Proxy status: Enabled
  ⊞─ ● Reports               Platform authentication methods: Windows Domain
  ── ● Filters
```

Figure 8-17: Main administrative interface dialog for Steel-Belted RADIUS

Configuring RADIUS Clients and Users

Two primary things you need to configure on the RADIUS server are the clients and users. A *client* is a device that is connected to the network, such as a PC, or a software application that needs to contact the RADIUS server to perform authentication for users, whereas *users* are accounts representing the people using the network. In either case, the client needs to communicate with the RADIUS server when a user authenticates.

Configuring RADIUS Clients

In the RADIUS server administrative screens, choose the applicable function for configuring clients, and add all of the clients. Figure 8-18 shows an example of the client configuration function for Steel-Belted RADIUS. You'll need to assign a name and IP address to each client, as well as the shared secret associated with the RADIUS server. In most cases, you'll be able to define a group for clients that have common characteristics. For example, if some of the RADIUS clients have the same RADIUS attributes and have contiguous IP addresses, then consider defining a client group for these clients.

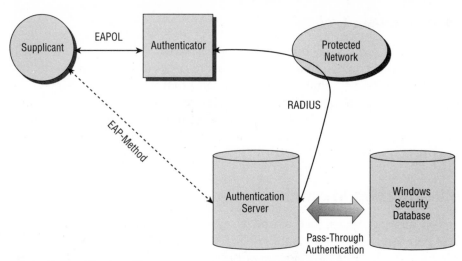

Figure 8-18: Client configuration screen for Steel-Belted RADIUS

Configuring RADIUS Users

After configuring the RADIUS clients, choose the applicable function for configuring users, and add all of the users. Figure 8-19 shows the Add Native User dialog box with an example of the user configuration function for Steel-Belted RADIUS. Add all of the users, which includes usernames, passwords, and authentication rules.

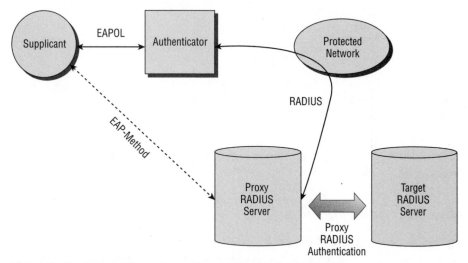

Figure 8-19: User configuration screen for Steel-Belted RADIUS

Configuring User Profiles

Some RADIUS servers, such as Steel-Belted RADIUS, allow you to establish default configuration templates for assigning to users. You can simply identify a user profile for a user that you're adding and that user will be assigned the configuration defined in the profile. This saves considerable time when adding users. Generally, you can also change one or more of the configuration values for a user after assigning a specific profile, and these changes will only affect that particular user.

Authentication Methods

RADIUS servers are designed to utilize several different authentication methods. If you choose to implement EAP-TLS, for example, you'll need to enable it. Figure 8-20 illustrates the enabling of EAP-TLS with Steel-Belted RADIUS.

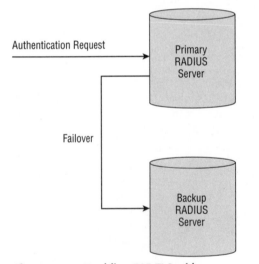

Figure 8-20: Enabling EAP-TLS with Steel-Belted RADIUS

The following sections describe several of the method configurations available on most RADIUS servers.

Native User Authentication

With native user authentication, the RADIUS server receives an authentication request, searches its database to find an entry matching the same username as the user requesting the authentication, and then validates the associated password. If native user authentication fails, then the RADIUS server may try another authentication method as defined in the user's configuration.

Pass-Through Authentication

A pass-through authentication method enables the RADIUS server to confer with another entity, such as a Windows security database, to validate the user's username and password. Figure 8-21 illustrates pass-through authentication.

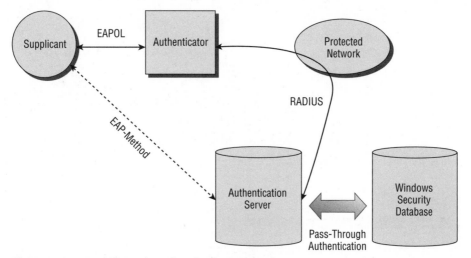

Figure 8-21: Pass-through authentication method

Proxy RADIUS Authentication

A RADIUS server may implement proxy RADIUS authentication, often referred to as proxy RADIUS. In this case, the primary (proxy) RADIUS server corresponds with a secondary (target) RADIUS server, as shown in Figure 8-22. The target RADIUS server then passes the authentication result to the proxy server. Proxy RADIUS authentication is valuable in scenarios that include a centralized database of usernames and passwords. The proxies avoid the need for replicating the information in all RADIUS servers, which is a strong advantage for supporting roaming in wireless systems.

Concurrent Connections

Most RADIUS servers enable you to limit the number of active connections for each user. This configuration is done when adding the user. It's often possible to set maximum concurrent connections on a per-user or per-group basis. If applied to a group, then all users within the applicable group will have the same maximum concurrent connections. Figure 8-23 shows an example configuration for the number of concurrent connections for a particular user. You need to enable the feature by selecting "Maximum concurrent connections," and then type in the number of allowable concurrent connections.

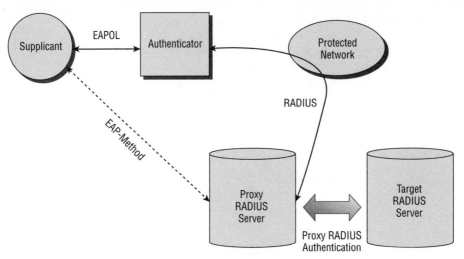

Figure 8-22: Proxy RADIUS authentication method

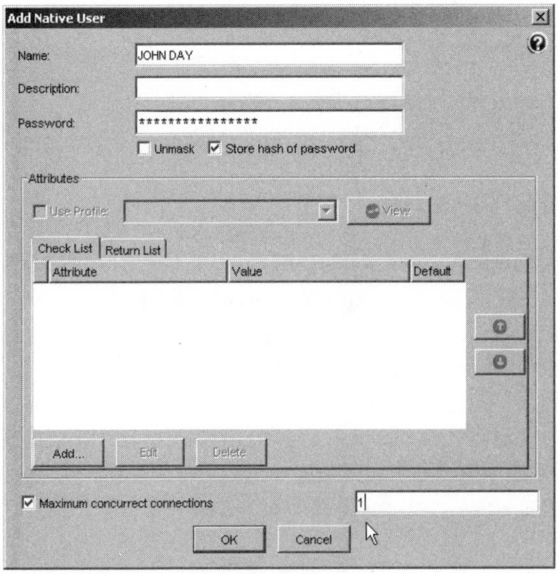

Figure 8-23: Configuring concurrent connections for a user in Steel-Belted RADIUS

Shared Secret

At some point, you'll need to enter the *shared secret*, which is a case-sensitive password that validates communications between the client and the RADIUS server. Steel-Belted RADIUS, for example, allows shared secrets of up to 127 alphanumeric characters, including spaces and special characters. Figure 8-24 shows an example of configuring the shared secret for a particular client.

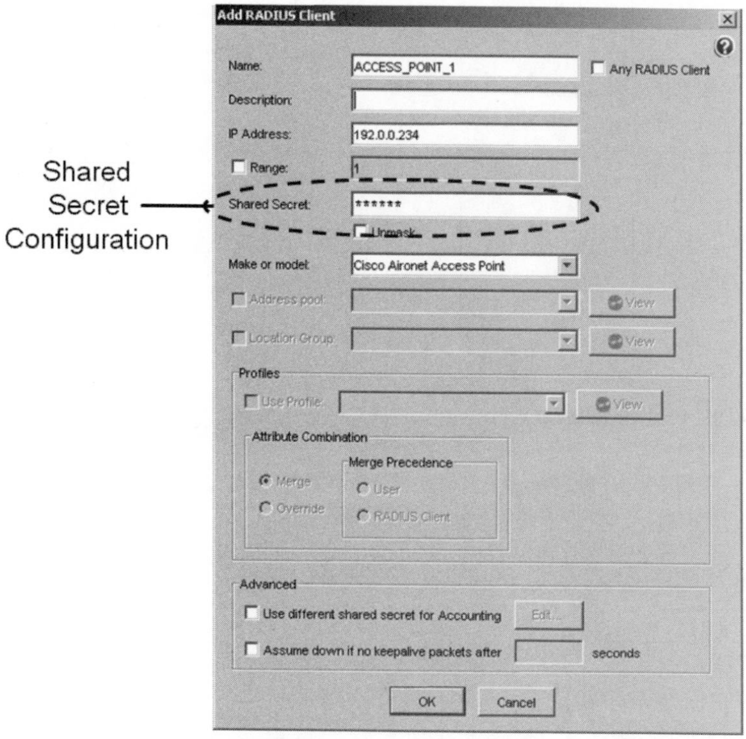

Figure 8-24: Configuring the shared secret for a client

Replication

Replication is a function that copies authentication data from one RADIUS server to another. As an example, Steel-Belted RADIUS supports replication from a primary server to up to ten other servers. The replication servers help ensure that authentication services will continue if the primary servers become inoperative. In addition, the replication servers can allow distribution of the authentication load. Figure 8-25 illustrates how a request for authentication servers of a primary server will failover to one of the replication servers.

Here, the authentication request arrives at the primary RADIUS server. If the server is down or too busy to handle the request, the authentication request will failover to the backup RADIUS server. Through replication processes, the backup RADIUS server will have the same authentication database as the primary server, allowing it to efficiently handle the request. The configuration of a replication server is fairly straightforward. Figure 8-26 shows the Add Server configuration dialog for adding a replication server.

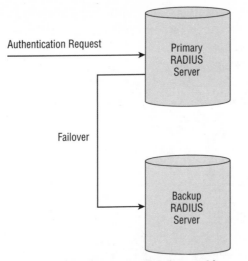

Figure 8-25: RADIUS server failover with replication servers

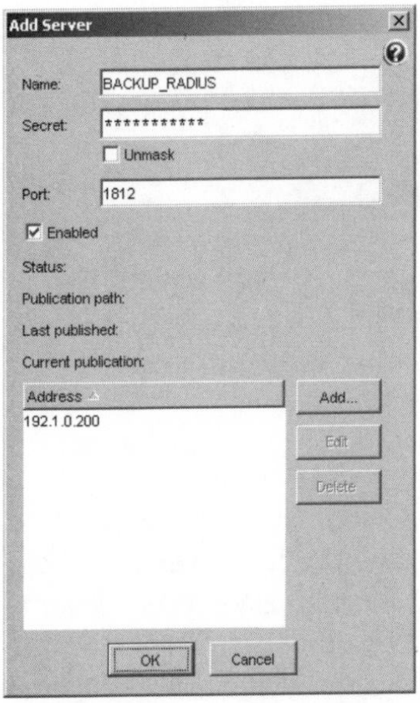

Figure 8-26: Setting up a replication server with Steel-Belted RADIUS

You need to include the name of the replication server, the shared secret for the server, the port address, and the IP address. In addition, don't forget to enable the replication server that you've configured.

CHAPTER 9

Troubleshooting

In this chapter, we'll dive into some of the common issues with 802.1X port-based authentication systems and explain how to resolve the underlying problems. Before you can be successful at troubleshooting 802.1X systems, however, you should have a thorough understanding of how 802.1X port-based authentication works. Be sure to review the previous chapters in this book, which cover the operation and configuration of 802.1X systems.

Troubleshooting Approaches

The most common problem you'll likely need to troubleshoot is when you have a client device attached to the network that can't authenticate. In most cases, these clients will be placed in the guest VLAN (if available) instead of the protected side of the network. You'll often hear related complaints finding their way to the help desk. As a result, you must be ready to identify and resolve the underlying problems.

Gather Information

Start by gathering information about the problem by getting answers to the following questions:

1. Is there an active supplicant on the client devices? The user may be a visitor or a new hire who has not been set up for accessing the protected network. If this is the case, then the 802.1X system is doing the right thing by not allowing the client device on the network.

2. Is the client device on the guest network? If you can browse the Internet but not reach protected corporate applications, then the device is likely on the guest network. Check the RADIUS logs, however, to be sure.

3. How long does it take for the client device to be placed onto the guest network or a protected VLAN? The user may be able to tell you this, but be sure to get realistic numbers. Some frustrated users may say "It took an hour to get connected!" although the actual time was only three minutes. As we'll discuss later in this chapter, the unavailability of a primary authentication server often causes significant delays (several minutes) during authentication. A delay can also result from a network infrastructure having problems that slowed down packet delivery.

4. Was the client device able to access the guest network but then, without any changes to the client device, was not able to access anything? Sometimes, the addition of a hub can cause problems such as this, and we'll look at this scenario in more detail later in this chapter.

5. How are the 802.1X port-based authentication protocols operating? View the system logs and run some 802.1X debug processes to understand what, when, and how packets are being sent. In addition, identify the state of various components. In order to accomplish this, you might need to attempt authenticating the client device to the network yourself.

6. In the case of mobile applications, where in the facility do the authentication issues occur? This could pinpoint where there might be signal coverage holes or strong RF interference that's limiting or even blocking communications from occurring between the supplicant and the authenticator.

7. Were any changes made to the system or network prior to when the authentication problems began appearing? If so, consider whether these changes could have caused the problem, and correct them as appropriate.

Spend some time getting answers to these questions and any others you feel are pertinent based on your experience. Try to avoid solving what appears to be the problem too early. You might go down the wrong path and leave underlying problems present before learning all of the issues.

Find the Root Problem (and Fix It)

Once you have sufficient data to work with, apply classic system troubleshooting principals: analyze information you know about the system and figure out where it broke. It's often best to start from the beginning of the authentication process, such as when the client device first connects to the network, and then follow through the process to the end. You'll find that it breaks somewhere.

Be certain to fully diagnose the system in order to find the root of the problem. For example, suppose a user is experiencing delays when authenticating with the primary server. As a fix, you might replace an old 10 Mbps Ethernet card in the server with a newer 100 Mbps card. The time to authenticate improves slightly, but the bigger problem is that the authentication process spans a wide area network that introduces significant delays. Often, difficulty solving a problem other than the root problem is caused by not having sufficient data regarding the issues you're trying to resolve. That is why it's so important to do some probing and collect as much data as possible (and practical)!

NOTE Be aware that the root problem causing issues with authentication may not be associated with the 802.1X port-based authentication protocols. For example, significant delays during authentication over a wireless network may result from significant RF interference or a coverage hole.

Test Tools

When troubleshooting 802.1X systems, you need the right tools in order to display information regarding the processes taking place and the state of various components.

Viewing System Configuration

As part of your information gathering, you should verify the configuration of each component. The system only does what you tell it to do through configuration. You might discover that a simple configuration setting is not right, enabling you to immediately fix the problem.

More likely, however, you'll need the configuration details to help you understand why certain things are happening the way they are. For example, you may wonder why only two retransmissions occur. After looking at the configuration, you discover that the setting for maximum retransmissions is set to "2." It may have been a while since you set up the system and you've forgotten the settings, or you may be totally unfamiliar with how the system was originally configured. In short, take a look at the system configuration before getting too far with your troubleshooting.

For most implementations, you can use the following command to view global system configurations:

```
show dot1x
```

The actual information that this commands displays varies according to the version of 802.1X you're implementing and the specific 802.1X equipment in use, but the following is a sample:

```
PAE capability                     Authenticator only
Maximum retransmissions            2
Quiet period                       60 seconds
Re-authentication period           3600 seconds
Server timeout                     30 seconds
Shutdown timeout                   0 seconds
Supplicant timeout                 30 seconds
Supplicant allowed in guest VLAN   yes
```

In most cases, you'll be able to display information for a particular port. The following IOS command is an example:

```
show dot1x interface <interface>
```

The preceding command will return the following information:

- MAC address of the supplicant (if applicable)
- Authorization state
- Port status
- Maximum retries
- Quiet period
- Re-authentication enablement
- Re-authentication period
- Sever timeout
- Supplicant timeout
- Guest VLAN

Viewing System Statistics

The configuration information doesn't tell the whole story about what's happening. In addition, you should gather some statistics for the system and components. It's helpful to see the overall picture (system statistics) and then focus on the components where you think the problem might be occurring.

The following IOS command, for example, will display 802.1X statistics:

```
show dot1x statistics interface <interface>
```

This will provide valuable information, such as the number of transmit requests, received starts, last received MAC address, and so on.

Debugging Processes

In addition to the system configuration information and statistics, you might also need to run some debugging processes to best diagnose the problem. For example, the following IOS command, used with specific modifiers, provides a list of events that have occurred:

```
debug dot1x <modifier>
```

Most implementations have `all` as a modifier, which shows all details regarding the communications process. You can also pare it down to only include errors, state changes, and so on. Refer to the documentation for your 802.1X components for specific modifier values, as they vary widely from one vendor to another. The effective use of built-in debugging tools precludes the needs for a third-party packet analyzer. The debug processes do a great job of identifying exactly when specific events occurred and the resulting state of the components.

NOTE Even before you have any need to troubleshoot an 802.1X port-based authentication system, learn how to view related configurations and statistics and utilize debugging tools. Practice using these tools so that when you actually need them, troubleshooting is easy.

Viewing Wireless Communications

If you're implementing 802.1X over a wireless network, then you may need to view wireless communications to determine whether the wireless network is causing the problem. In this case, you'll need specific tools that "sniff" the environment and provide information about what's going on.

Signal Tester

This device measures the strength of data signals. The strength of the data signal, for example, aids you in determining whether a coverage hole is causing the problem. With Wi-Fi networks, for example, the minimum data signal level is generally around –75 dBm for good performance. If the data signal falls below this value, then significant delays or complete disruption in communications may occur.

Most signal testers also identify average noise, sometimes referred to as the *noise floor,* which represents the combination of all interfering sources as an average value. If the average noise is below -95 dBm, then RF interference is likely not causing any problems. If the average noise is higher, then RF interference could be causing delays when communicating over the wireless network.

Figure 9-1 shows a screen shot of the signal strength panel of AirMagnet Survey, a typical wireless LAN test tool. For this network, the tool reports a D-Link access point on channel 1 with a signal level of –55 dBm and noise level of –96 dBm at the location of the test tool. This indicates acceptable signal coverage. Some tools also enable you to generate signal coverage maps. Figure 9-2 shows an example of a signal coverage diagram, often referred to as a "heat map," generated by AirMagnet Survey.

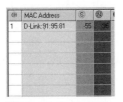

Figure 9-1: Typical signal strength panel

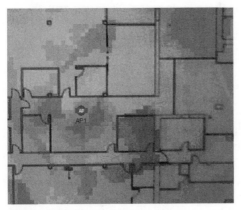

Figure 9-2: Signal coverage map

Spectrum Analyzer

A spectrum analyzer displays the specific amplitude of signals (data and noise) in various parts of the frequency spectrum. This enables you to identify the sources of RF interference and determine whether it is within a part of the frequency spectrum where it will result in problems. For example, a spectrum analyzer may indicate strong RF interference in the top portion of the 2.4 GHz band. Any access points tuned to channels in this part of the band will experience sluggish performance, whereas access points tuned to the lower channels within this band will not experience slowness due to the interfering signals.

Thus, if the access point with which the 802.1X client device is associating is set to a high channel, such as channel 11, then RF interference is probably causing slowness. However, if the 802.1X client device is associating with a lower channel, such as channel 1, then RF interference is probably not the problem. As you can see, a spectrum analyzer aids in diagnosing this type of problem.

Figure 9-3 shows a spectrum analyzer image of the 2.4 GHz band using a Bantam Instruments spectrum analyzer. As shown in the diagram, significant RF interference is present in the lower portion of the 2.4 GHz band, which would likely cause sluggish authentication processes if the access points are tuned to applicable RF channels.

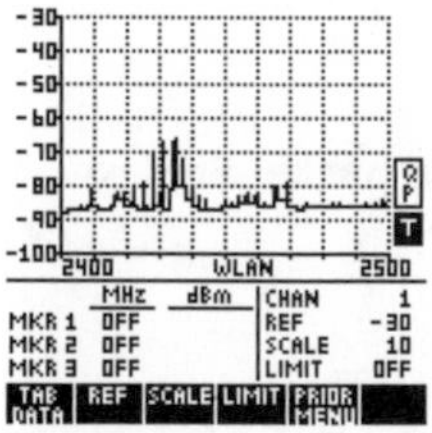

Figure 9-3: Spectrum analyzer image of the 2.4 GHz band

Packet Analyzer

The debug processes that are part of 802.1X systems only display 802.1X-specific events and packets. In order to dig deeper and determine whether or not the wireless network infrastructure is causing the problem, you probably need to use a packet analyzer to observe events and packets occurring within the wireless network infrastructure, which operates at a lower level than 802.1X. The packet analyzer shows specific packets that have been sent in time, as shown in Figure 9-4. Most packet analyzers also display the state of various wireless components (access points and client radios).

No	Delta	CH	Length	●	Source	Destination	BSSID	Summary
16256	0.000000	1	232	1	D-Link:91:95:81	01:00:5E:04:02:03	D-Link:91:95:81	UDP port:8012 -> port:8010
16257	0.012308	1	87	1	D-Link:91:95:81	FF:FF:FF:FF:FF:FF	D-Link:91:95:81	802.11 beacon
16258	0.014175	1	24	36	00:15:70:14:26:C1	D-Link:91:95:81	D-Link:91:95:81	802.11 null-function
16259	0.016190	1	55	1	00:15:70:14:26:C1	FF:FF:FF:FF:FF:FF	FF:FF:FF:FF:FF:FF	802.11 probe request
16260	0.017445	1	81	1	D-Link:91:95:81	00:15:70:14:26:C1	D-Link:91:95:81	802.11 probe response
16261	0.017767	1	10	1		D-Link:91:95:81		802.11 acknowledgement
16262	0.114212	1	87	1	D-Link:91:95:81	FF:FF:FF:FF:FF:FF	D-Link:91:95:81	802.11 beacon
16263	0.117194	1	55	1	00:15:70:14:26:C1	FF:FF:FF:FF:FF:FF	FF:FF:FF:FF:FF:FF	802.11 probe request
16264	0.216623	1	87	1	D-Link:91:95:81	FF:FF:FF:FF:FF:FF	D-Link:91:95:81	802.11 beacon
16265	0.245158	1	55	1	00:15:70:14:26:C1	FF:FF:FF:FF:FF:FF	FF:FF:FF:FF:FF:FF	802.11 probe request
16266	0.277975	1	55	1	00:15:70:14:26:C1	FF:FF:FF:FF:FF:FF	FF:FF:FF:FF:FF:FF	802.11 probe request
16267	0.310732	1	55	1	00:15:70:14:26:C1	FF:FF:FF:FF:FF:FF	FF:FF:FF:FF:FF:FF	802.11 probe request
16268	0.318957	1	87	1	D-Link:91:95:81	FF:FF:FF:FF:FF:FF	D-Link:91:95:81	802.11 beacon
16269	0.376211	1	232	36	00:15:70:14:26:C1	D-Link:91:95:81	D-Link:91:95:81	UDP port:8012 -> port:8010
16270	0.376308	1	232	36	00:15:70:14:26:C1	D-Link:91:95:81	D-Link:91:95:81	UDP port:8012 -> port:8010
16271	0.378601	1	232	1	D-Link:91:95:81	01:00:5E:04:02:03	D-Link:91:95:81	UDP port:8012 -> port:8010
16272	0.378963	1	232	36	00:15:70:14:26:C1	D-Link:91:95:81	D-Link:91:95:81	UDP port:8012 -> port:8010

Figure 9-4: Packet trace of a wireless network

NOTE When monitoring the communications between the authenticator and the authentication server with a packet analyzer, you won't be able to decode the actual EAP-Method data because this data is encrypted.

NOTE Sometimes a single tool includes both signal testing and packet analysis functions.

Network Connectivity Issues

A good place to start when troubleshooting 802.1X authentication problems is to rule out network connectivity issues. As mentioned earlier, network connectivity could be the root problem of 802.1X authentication issues. The network infrastructure itself could be keeping the 802.1X communications process from completing properly.

Network Interface Problems

Network interface problems can result in the user not being able to authenticate or being placed in a guest network, or experiencing significant delays when trying to do so. This is typically the result of faulty client hardware, wireless coverage holes, or RF interference.

Faulty Client Cards

Sometimes the client radio, for users connecting via a wireless network, or the Ethernet card, for users connecting to a wired network, ends up in a faulty condition. In most cases, this causes the authentication process to not work at all. In fact, the supplicant and authenticator will not be able to communicate, resulting in the 802.11X communications not beginning.

The following list describes some causes of client card failures:

- **Corrupted driver:** The driver for the card may somehow become corrupted. This can happen sometimes when memory problems occur or after the driver has been updated. The symptom is that the card will not connect at all to the network. In most cases, the client operating system will indicate an error associated with the driver. To resolve this situation, reinstall the driver. If that doesn't work, try rolling the driver back to an earlier version, especially if the problem started after updating the driver.

- **Corrupted firmware:** If the card stops operating correctly, it may have encountered a hiccup in the software, due to a programming error. You may see this happen soon after installing an update to the driver. That's why it's always best to read the notes associated with the driver update before installing it to determine whether you might experience any known errors. Try disabling and reenabling the client card to fix the problem. This will be a temporary fix, so consider rolling the driver back to the earlier version (if applicable) or track down any known errors in the firmware, and relevant fixes, through the vendor.

- **Physical damage:** Physical damage to the card is less common than other problems that cause faults, but it doesn't hurt to verify that the card appears to be in good condition. Users have been known to drop their computer or smash something into the card, causing it to become inoperative. You'll generally see actual damage to the card, however, if this is the problem.

- **Missing or misaligned antenna:** With wireless networks, confirm that the antenna on the client device is intact and aligned properly. Sometimes, especially with desktop PCs, users push their computer too close to a wall and the antenna breaks loose from the card. The antenna may still be partly attached, however, so be sure to move the antenna around a bit to verify that it still feels solidly connected to the card. If the antenna appears to be broken, then you may be able to replace it if the card allows antenna replacement (some do and some don't).

In order to troubleshoot these problems, check whether the client radio or Ethernet card is associating with the network by reviewing access point or switch

logs or by running a ping test between the client device and another component on the network.

Wireless Coverage Holes

Wireless networks commonly have areas of the facility where signal strength is
below the level required for reliable connectivity. This problem often crops up
when the application is mobile. In this case, the user may encounter connectivity issues periodically, but generally associated with certain locations. Thus,
coverage holes often provide intermittent issues with 802.1X authentication. In
the most severe cases, a coverage hole precludes the wireless client device
from associating with the access point.

The following list describes some causes of coverage holes:

- **Obstacles blocking the signal:** After a wireless network has been up
  and running for a while, a company may change the facility in a way
  that introduces obstacles that cause relatively high degrees of attenuation to the radio signals. For example, a company may segment a large
  room to create individual offices. The walls add a source of attenuation
  that might cause portions of the facility, especially the new rooms, to not
  have adequate signal strength. Similarly, an office might install a long
  row of high filing cabinets that highly attenuate the signals. If any new
  obstacles have been introduced to the facility that create coverage holes,
  you'll need to redesign the wireless network to accommodate the corresponding attenuation by moving or installing additional access points.

- **Transmit power too low:** The client device may have a new lower-
  powered radio card, or the user might have changed the transmit
  power settings on the card to a lower value. These situations may
  result in the client device not being able to connect with the network
  as well as it did before. Therefore, confirm that the client radio is set
  to the highest transmit power.

- **Too far from an access point:** If the design of the wireless network was
  not very good, then there may not be enough access points to cover all
  areas of the facility. Or, if the verification testing that was performed after
  installing the wireless network was not adequate, there may be places
  throughout the facility where coverage holes exist. To resolve this situation, consider redesigning the wireless network and either moving (or
  adding more) access points to provide good coverage throughout the
  entire facility.

RF Interference

RF interference can cause a significant retransmission rate, which results in delays and intermittent connectivity while the RF interference lasts. The following are examples of sources of RF interference:

- **Microwave ovens:** Microwave oven interference can significantly degrade a wireless network connection, but it only occurs when the microwave oven is operating. You may receive complaints from users near break rooms containing a microwave oven. If a wireless user is close to (within twenty feet or so) an operating microwave oven, then the oven is likely the source of the problem. That's easy to troubleshoot if the problem goes away when the oven is not in operation.

- **Cordless phones:** Cordless phones that operate on the same frequency band as the wireless network (e.g., 2.4 GHz) may offer significant RF interference that results in slow performance during the authentication process. Keep in mind that some cordless phones cause interference even when they are not actively in use (i.e., a call is taking place). If you suspect that cordless phones may be causing problems with 802.1X authentication, then you'll probably need to redesign the wireless network by adding more access points. This is necessary in order to boost the signal strength of the wireless network to better compete with the cordless phones. Alternatively, you could eliminate the use of cordless phones or use phones that operate on a different frequency (e.g., 900 MHz or 5 GHz).

Infrastructure Problems

In addition to network interfaces, consider the network infrastructure as the possible root of the problem. Changes made to the infrastructure, such as downed routers or switching to slower communications links between facilities, may cause problems with 802.1X authentication. Run network diagnostic tools, and ensure that TCP/IP connectivity exists throughout the entire path between the client device and the authentication server. Figure 9-5 illustrates this problem.

NOTE When adding a new switch to a network that supports 802.1X, disable 802.1X on the port where you're connecting the switch and make the new switch an authenticator.

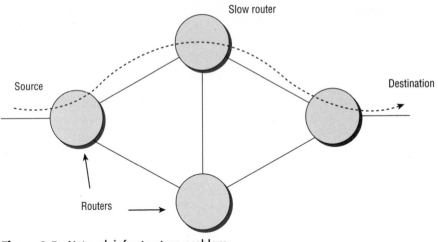

Figure 9-5: Network infrastructure problem

Supplicant Issues

With an 802.1X system that has been up and running successfully for some time, a common source of authentication problems are issues related to the supplicant. After ruling out network access and infrastructure issues, a good place to start within the realm of 802.1X is the supplicant.

Missing Supplicant

If a user complains that he or she can't access a particular server on the corporate network, determine whether the user has a valid supplicant. The user may have brought in a laptop from home for use on the corporate network, unaware that an 802.1X supplicant is required. In this case, the user may be granted access to the public network, including access to the Internet, but without access to the rest of the corporate systems. Of course, with these situations, you need to equip the user with a valid supplicant if they are so authorized.

NOTE The most frequent reason for placing a client device in a guest VLAN is lack of supplicant software or a supplicant that is not functioning correctly.

Missing Supplicant Behavior

The following steps describe the flow of packets and tasks that occur in a debug routine when there is a missing or disabled supplicant (see Figure 9-6):

1. The port on the authenticator is made active with an unauthorized state.

2. The authenticator sends an EAP Failure packet.

3. The authenticator sends an EAP Request Identity packet.

4. After 30 seconds (the default timeout), the authenticator sends a second EAP Request Identity packet.

5. After another 30 seconds, the authenticator gives up because the maximum number of attempts (the default of 2) has been exceeded.

6. The authenticator determines whether a guest VLAN has been configured.

7. If a guest VLAN is available, then the authenticator authorizes the port for the guest VLAN number configured in the authenticator (if implemented), and the client device has access to services available on the VLAN. This is generally only Internet connectivity outside the firewall of the company. Figure 9-7 illustrates this conclusion.

8. If a guest VLAN is not configured, then the authenticator leaves the port status in the unauthorized state, and the client device has no access to anything beyond the authenticator.

With this process, there is no need for the authenticator to communicate with the authentication server. Thus, the authenticator is the decision-maker when it comes to supplicants that are either missing or not enabled. The process is fairly automatic from the perspective of users. They don't have to input a username and password, but they will experience a connection time that often exceeds 60 seconds. Of course, this will be annoying to most users, prompting them to contact the help desk. Therefore, if you receive trouble calls indicating delays of a minute or so when user devices are authenticating, ensure that the supplicant is present and enabled on the client device. That is often the reason for this problem.

NOTE Sometimes in the case of a missing or disabled supplicant, when an authentication is not successful, debugging might indicate that the port is assigned to a correct VLAN, but the port is not active. This can be confusing when found, but keep in mind that the client still doesn't have access to the protected side of the network.

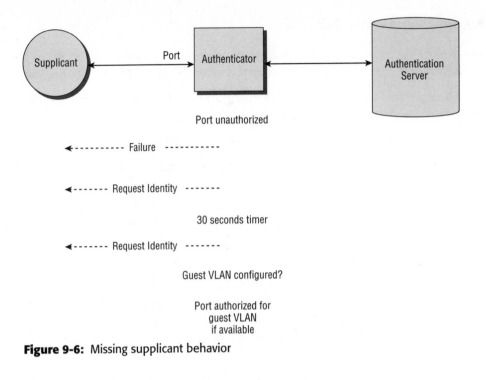

Figure 9-6: Missing supplicant behavior

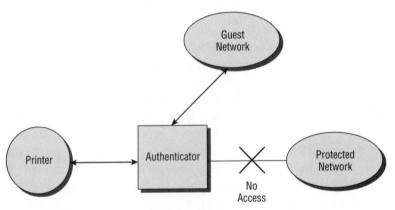

Figure 9-7: Client device authorized for the guest VLAN

Peripheral Devices

Many peripheral devices, such as printers, do not have supplicants. This poses a major problem when you need to include them in an 802.1X port-based authentication system. If you simply plug a printer without a valid supplicant into an existing 802.1X network, for example, the communications among the supplicant, authenticator, and the authentication server will be similar to that described for the missing supplicant. If guest access is available, then the printer will be placed into the guest VLAN (refer to Figure 9-7). The problem now, however, is that none of the client devices on the protected side of the network can access the printer (see Figure 9-8).

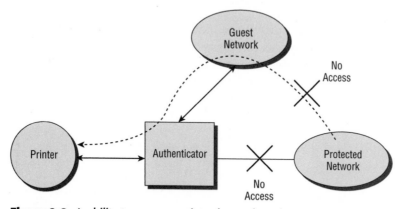

Figure 9-8: Inability to access a printer located on the guest network

In this case, you may be able to set up access lists in a way that allows printing across VLANs, but this may introduce security issues. Instead, you could connect the printer to a switch port mapped to an applicable VLAN on the protected side of the network, deactivate 802.1X on the port, and implement MAC address filtering that restricts access to the port to the MAC address of the printer. This offers some protection, but not nearly as much as a fully compliant 802.1X system.

Ideally, choose printers and other peripherals that implement a supplicant with the appropriate EAP-Method for your system. This requires some planning during the design and rollout of the system. You likely won't be able to utilize existing printers in this manner, though, because they probably won't have the capability to support supplicants.

NOTE In order to connect printers to an 802.1X port-based authentication system, consider using a print server that implements 802.1X, such as the HP Jetdirect print servers. Include the print server as a user in the authentication server.

Hubs

Hubs don't work very well with 802.1X systems. Most hubs do not implement supplicants, resulting in the hub being unauthenticated and placed in the guest VLAN. Client devices attaching to the hub also have access to the guest

VLAN and can communicate with each other through the hub. If guest access is not supported, then a hub will not be authorized to connect to the network.

> **NOTE** By default, 802.1X allows only a single MAC address to be active on a given port.

A hub does not have a MAC address, so the authenticator will not associate any MAC address with the applicable port to which the hub is connecting. This shows up in the statistics of the applicable port as a last received MAC address of "0000.0000.0000." Client devices connecting to the hub have access to the guest network, as shown in Figure 9-9.

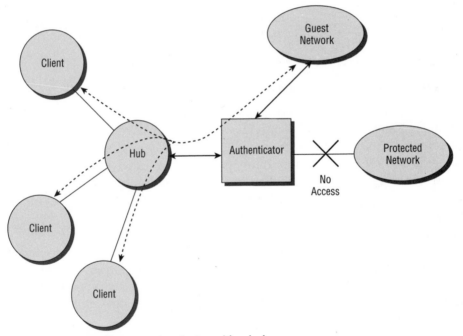

Figure 9-9: Extending an authenticator with a hub

Because no MAC address is associated with the port, another client device attaching to the hub can restart the authentication process. This is where problems arise. If this authentication is successful, then the authenticator assigns the port to the applicable VLAN, which may be something other than the guest VLAN. In fact, as soon as the authenticator sends the EAPOL-Start to the supplicant to start the authentication process, the port is switched to an unauthorized state. As a result, any communications taking place between other client devices connecting to the hub with applications on the network will halt, as shown in Figure 9-10.

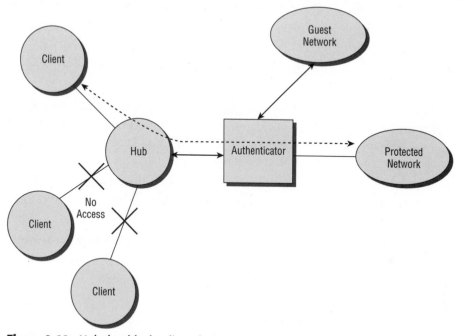

Figure 9-10: Hub that blocks client devices from accessing the network

To avoid this situation, you could enable the port to operate with multiple MAC addresses, such as four MAC addresses if the hub allows four connections. This will keep other client devices (due to different MAC addresses) from communicating on the network even if the other client devices have valid supplicants. In other words, adding hubs without proper planning will result in problems that are often difficult to diagnose. Therefore, identify any hubs attached in this manner and redesign the architecture accordingly.

Bad Credentials

It's common for passwords to be reset, which leads to bad credentials being sent from the supplicant to the authentication server during the authentication process. This sometimes causes users to become frustrated and call the help desk. The common symptom, similar to other supplicant problems, is that the client device ends up on the guest VLAN instead of the protected side of the network.

Bad Credentials Behavior

The following steps describe the flow of packets and tasks that are displayed in a debug routine when an active supplicant has bad credentials (see Figure 9-11):

1. The supplicant has a successful exchange of EAP/EAPOL packets with the authenticator.

2. The authenticator establishes communications with the authentication server.

3. Supplicant and authentication server exchange EAP-Method data via the authenticator, which packages the EAP-Method data into EAPOL or RADIUS packets, depending on whether the data is being delivered to the supplicant or the authentication server.

4. After several packet exchanges between the supplicant and the authentication server, the authentication server sends an Access-Reject packet to the authenticator.

5. The authenticator notifies the supplicant via an EAP-Failure packet and keeps the port in an unauthorized state.

6. If the system supports guest access, then the authenticator should place the client on the guest VLAN.

7. After the quiet period timer expires, the authenticator initiates the authentication process again.

The key to diagnosing the problem as bad credentials is identifying the EAP-Failure packet sent from the authenticator to the supplicant. If the system supports guest access, then the symptom is generally that a user with an active supplicant is always placed into the guest network and not allowed access to the protected side of the network. If this happens, then consider bad credentials as the culprit, especially if the debug shows EAP-Failure packets. The RADIUS logs should also indicate the reason for the failure as bad credentials.

NOTE Some authentication servers will alert the user that the credentials supplied during the authentication process were bad, which gives the user an opportunity to fix the problem.

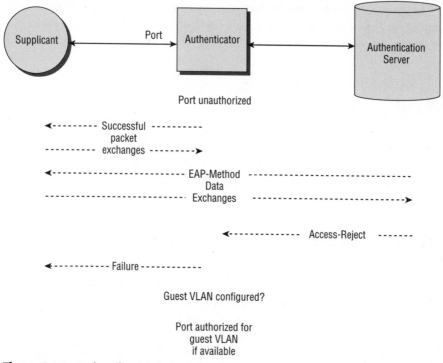

Figure 9-11: Bad credentials behavior

Incorrect EAP-Method

If the supplicant on the client device is configured with the wrong EAP-Method, then the flow of packets among the supplicant, authenticator and the authentication server will be similar to that described above for bad credentials. RADIUS logs, though, should clarify whether the problem is actually bad credentials or an incorrect EAP-Method as the cause of authentication failure. The solution for this problem may be to simply reconfigure the client device. Keep in mind, however, that an EAP-Method mismatch may be resulting because the client device belongs to a visitor, such as a contractor or customer. In this case, the system is operating OK because the visitor is being placed appropriately in the guest VLAN and not a VLAN on the protected side of the network.

NOTE As part of the troubleshooting process, refer to Chapter 6, "Configuring Supplicants," and the supplicant vendor's configuration guide to ensure that the suppliant is configured properly.

Authenticator Issues

Sometimes the 802.1X authentication problems are within the authenticator. If the supplicant seems to be okay, then take a closer look at the authenticator. The following sections cover some problems that commonly occur with authenticators.

No 802.1X Support

Of course, if the switch that the supplicant is attempting to authenticate through doesn't support 802.1X, then the switch is not an authenticator, and the authentication process will not work. If the switch is not really an authenticator, then 802.1X can't be started. If debugging shows that the authenticator never sends an EAP Failure packet to start the process or the authenticator doesn't respond to attempts of the supplicant starting the process, then the authenticator is likely not present or operating correctly. Don't take it for granted that the switch actually supports 802.1X. This is actually a fairly common problem, especially in large networks where someone may have installed a new switch without coordinating with those responsible for configuration management. Therefore, if the debug shows that the 802.1X process isn't starting, begin your troubleshooting by ensuring that you're actually dealing with a valid authenticator.

802.1X Not Enabled

For some reason, the authenticator (that actually supports 802.1X) may have 802.1X disabled. This may occur as the result of someone installing a new switch or making configuration changes without adequately thinking through the repercussions. If the authenticator is not kicking off the authentication process or responding to supplicants that want to authenticate, then verify that the system and port are enabled for 802.1X.

RADIUS Server Address Incorrect

Another authenticator configuration parameter that may go astray is the RADIUS server address. An administrator may change the address to accommodate a new network configuration, and the address may no longer point to the RADIUS server. As a result, the supplicant will successfully communicate and connect to the authenticator, but the remainder of the authentication process will continue as described in the preceding section for the missing authentication server. If system status shows the authentication server is active, then ensure that the RADIUS server address is correctly configured.

EAP-Method Not Supported

If the EAP-Method that the supplicants and authentication server implement are not supported by the authenticator, then the system will respond in various ways depending on the implementation. In most cases, the authenticator will treat the supplicant as if it has bad credentials. This results in the supplicant being placed on the guest VLAN if one exists.

> **NOTE** As part of the troubleshooting process, refer to Chapter 7, "Configuring Authenticators," and the vendor's authenticator configuration guide to ensure that the authenticator is configured properly.

Authentication Server Issues

The authentication server could cause authentication problems. The following sections cover the most common problems that occur.

Missing Authentication Server

If there is no authentication server, then the authenticator won't activate the 802.1X port for any VLAN, including the guest VLAN. If debugging indicates this, then consider the scenario in which the authentication is missing in some way.

Missing Authentication Server Behavior

The following steps outline a sequence of packets and tasks that occur when there is a missing authentication server (see Figure 9-12):

1. The supplicant has a successful exchange of EAP/EAPOL packets with the authenticator.

2. The authenticator continually retransmits RADIUS packets to the authentication server and eventually gives up. By default, this takes about 20 seconds.

3. The authenticator attempts to communicate with alternate authentication

servers (in a predetermined sequence as configured) if configured in the system. By default, this takes about 20 seconds per authentication server.

4. If an alternative authentication server is found, then the remaining authentication process is completed successfully.

5. If no alternative authentication server is found, then the port assigned for that suppliant is placed in an unauthorized state.

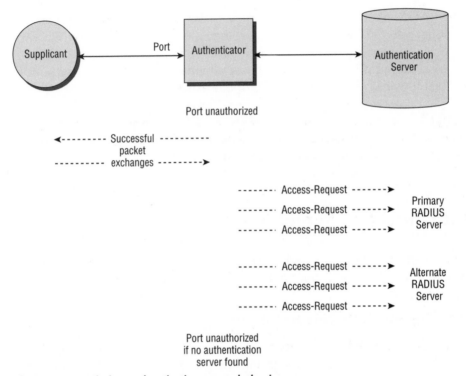

Figure 9-12: Missing authentication server behavior

Thus, a user needs to wait a considerable amount of time, roughly 20 seconds, to authenticate with the network if a backup authentication server is available. This is certainly better than not authenticating at all, so be sure to implement backup authentication servers if possible.

The problem is that, with most 802.1X implementations, the authenticator will attempt to reach the primary authentication server every time the supplicant sends something to the authentication server. EAP-Methods require several packets back and forth. This can result in several minutes before the client device is actually authenticated with the network. Users will surely contact the help desk within this period of time. If you suspect that the primary authentication server is down, then configure it as dead in the RADIUS configuration.

This will keep the authenticator from attempting to authenticate with it and significantly reduce delays when supplicants authenticate.

NOTE Most problems with authentication occur after a change is made to the network or system, so be sure to consider any changes that were made just prior to when authentication problems began to appear. This could lead you directly to what needs to be fixed.

Verifying the Authentication Server

If you suspect that the authentication server is missing, verify that

- The authentication server is not crashed and is running normally. Log into the administration port of the server and ensure that the server is operating OK.

- The connection to the authentication server is available. Ping the server from the location of the client device, and ensure that the result indicates a TCP/IP connection.

- The authentication server is configured correctly. Make sure that the configuration settings are not disabling the RADIUS services in any way.

NOTE As part of the troubleshooting process, refer to Chapter 8, "Configuring Authentication Servers," and the vendor's authentication server configuration guide to ensure that the authenticator is configured properly.

Guest Access Issues

In most cases, you'll want to allow guest access to the network. This can invite a host of problems, however, that you must be ready to handle.

Local Visitor Problems

Local visitors are users who are not authorized to access the protected side of the network and can benefit by accessing unprotected applications, such as access to the company website or, more broadly, the Internet. These users may be company personnel who haven't yet been granted authorization, possibly because they're waiting for a background investigation to be completed, or they might be contractors or customers visiting the facility.

Visitor with No Supplicant

If you implement 802.1X on your network, then assume a visitor without 802.1X may attempt to connect to the system. In this case, the visitor's client device has no supplicant, and the client device is placed onto the guest VLAN, as explained earlier for a missing supplicant. This is exactly how the system should operate and isn't really a problem, but it's worth explaining to be complete.

Visitor with Active Supplicant

Things get interesting when the visitor has 802.1X implemented on his or her client device, which means they have a supplicant, possibly because the visitor's home network implements 802.1X authentication or the supplicant was left on the client device from a previous employer. This creates a situation in which the client device gets through part of the authentication process, but problems arise that vary depending on the situation.

With newer 802.1X implementations (based on the 2004 version of the 802.1X specification), a client device in this condition will be placed on the guest VLAN if available. In earlier implementations (such as the 2001 version of the 802.1X specification), the client device is not placed into a guest VLAN (even if configured), and the port remains in an unauthorized state, as shown in Figure 9-13. If you determine that this is the case, then the only practical way to fix the problem is to disable or remove the supplicant from the visiting client device, which allows the client device to connect more easily to the guest network. This is probably OK for a new hire who has a supplicant left on their device from a previous employer, but it's not generally practical for customers who have a supplicant because they require 802.1X authentication on their home network.

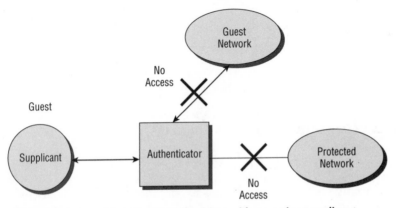

Figure 9-13: Possible outcome of a visitor with an active supplicant

Visitor with Active Supplicant Behavior

The following steps outline the flow of packets and tasks that are displayed in a debug routine when a visitor has an active supplicant and attempts to connect to the network (see Figure 9-14):

1. The supplicant has a successful exchange of EAP/EAPOL packets with the authenticator.

2. The authenticator establishes communications with the authentication server.

3. The supplicant and authentication server exchange EAP-Method data via the authenticator, which packages the EAP-Method data into EAPOL or RADIUS packets depending on whether it's delivering the data to the supplicant or the authentication server.

4. After several packet exchanges between the supplicant and the authentication server, the authentication server sends an Access-Reject packet to the authenticator.

5. The authenticator notifies the supplicant via an EAP-Failure packet and keeps the port in an unauthorized state.

6. If the system supports guest access, then the authenticator should automatically place the visitor in the guest VLAN if supported by newer versions (2004 or later) of the 802.1X specification. Otherwise, the visiting user will not be authorized to access any of the network.

7. After the quiet period timer expires, the authenticator will initiate the authentication process again.

A wireless LAN implementing multiple SSIDs alleviates the issues of visitors with active supplicants attempting to authenticate with authenticators and ending up not being allowed on the network at all. In fact, it's probably most likely that a visitor will have an opportunity to connect if a wireless LAN is present. A visitor SSID is configured on the authenticator for visitors to associate with, which connects the visitors directly to the guest VLAN. Figure 9-15 illustrates this configuration. In this case, the visitors can make a conscious decision to connect to the guest SSID. Either this would be obvious, such as an SSID of "Guest," or they would need to be told what SSID to associate with for the guest network. Authorized users would be instructed to connect with the SSID pertaining to the 802.1X-enabled network, such as "Company" (refer to Figure 9-15). Thus, if your wireless LAN is not configured with a separate SSID for the guest VLAN, consider doing so.

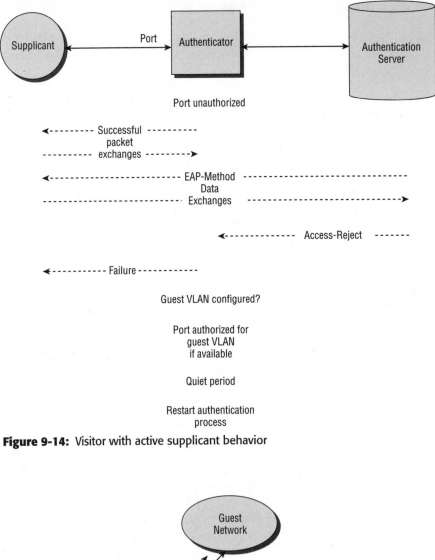

Figure 9-14: Visitor with active supplicant behavior

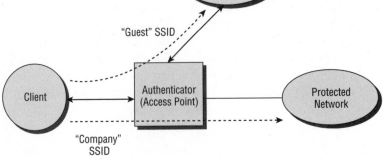

Figure 9-15: Use of separate SSIDs for protected and guest networks

NOTE It's possible for a client device to be associated with a wireless access point but not actually authenticated with the authentication server. This is the case when a client device's supplicant has been placed on the guest VLAN of the network.

Remote Visitor Problems

When one of your users has an active supplicant and attempts to connect to a remote network, such as a customer site, they will experience the same situation as described earlier for the visitor with an active supplicant. They may be placed into the guest VLAN if configured, or they may not be given any access at all. If you receive a call from a user in this situation, then ask them to disable the supplicant on their client device and try reconnecting.

RFC 3748: Extensible Authentication Protocol (EAP)

Network Working Group

Request for Comments: 3748

Obsoletes: 2284

Category: Standards Track

B. Aboba

   Microsoft

L. Blunk

   Merit Network, Inc

J. Vollbrecht

   Vollbrecht Consulting LLC

J. Carlson

   Sun

H. Levkowetz, Ed.

   ipUnplugged

June 2004

Extensible Authentication Protocol (EAP)

Status of this Memo

This document specifies an Internet standards track protocol for the Internet community, and requests discussion and suggestions for improvements. Please refer to the current edition of the "Internet Official Protocol Standards" (STD 1) for the standardization state and status of this protocol. Distribution of this memo is unlimited.

Copyright Notice

Abstract

This document defines the Extensible Authentication Protocol (EAP), an authentication framework which supports multiple authentication methods. EAP typically runs directly over data link layers such as Point-to-Point Protocol (PPP) or IEEE 802, without requiring IP. EAP provides its own support for duplicate elimination and retransmission, but is reliant on lower layer ordering guarantees. Fragmentation is not supported within EAP itself; however, individual EAP methods may support this.

This document obsoletes RFC 2284. A summary of the changes between this document and RFC 2284 is available in Appendix A.

Table of Contents

1. Introduction

This document defines the Extensible Authentication Protocol (EAP), an authentication framework which supports multiple authentication methods. EAP typically runs directly over data link layers such as Point-to-Point Protocol (PPP) or IEEE 802, without requiring IP. EAP provides its own support for duplicate elimination and retransmission, but is reliant on lower layer ordering guarantees. Fragmentation is not supported within EAP itself; however, individual EAP methods may support this.

EAP may be used on dedicated links, as well as switched circuits, and wired as well as wireless links. To date, EAP has been implemented with hosts and routers that connect via switched circuits or dial-up lines using PPP [RFC1661]. It has also been implemented with switches and access points using IEEE 802 [IEEE-802]. EAP encapsulation on IEEE 802 wired media is described in [IEEE-802.1X], and encapsulation on IEEE wireless LANs in [IEEE-802.11i].

One of the advantages of the EAP architecture is its flexibility. EAP is used to select a specific authentication mechanism, typically after the authenticator requests more information in order to determine the specific authentication method to be used. Rather than requiring the authenticator to be updated to support each new authentication method, EAP permits the use of a backend authentication server, which may implement some or all authentication methods, with the authenticator acting as a pass-through for some or all methods and peers.

Within this document, authenticator requirements apply regardless of whether the authenticator is operating as a pass-through or not. Where the requirement is meant to apply to either the authenticator or backend authentication server, depending on where the EAP authentication is terminated, the term "EAP server" will be used.

1.1. Specification of Requirements

In this document, several words are used to signify the requirements of the specification. The key words "MUST", "MUST NOT", "REQUIRED", "SHALL", "SHALL NOT", "SHOULD", "SHOULD NOT", "RECOMMENDED", "MAY", and "OPTIONAL" in this document are to be interpreted as described in [RFC2119].

1.2. Terminology

This document frequently uses the following terms:

- **authenticator:** The end of the link initiating EAP authentication. The term authenticator is used in [IEEE-802.1X], and has the same meaning in this document.

- **peer:** The end of the link that responds to the authenticator. In [IEEE-802.1X], this end is known as the Supplicant.

- **Supplicant:** The end of the link that responds to the authenticator in [IEEE-802.1X]. In this document, this end of the link is called the peer.

- **backend authentication server:** A backend authentication server is an entity that provides an authentication service to an authenticator. When used, this server typically executes EAP methods for the authenticator. This terminology is also used in [IEEE-802.1X].

- **AAA (Authentication, Authorization, and Accounting):** AAA protocols with EAP support include RADIUS [RFC3579] and Diameter [DIAM-EAP]. In this document, the terms "AAA server" and "backend authentication server" are used interchangeably.

- **Displayable Message:** This is interpreted to be a human readable string of characters. The message encoding MUST follow the UTF-8 transformation format [RFC2279].

- **EAP server:** The entity that terminates the EAP authentication method with the peer. In the case where no backend authentication server is used, the EAP server is part of the authenticator. In the case where the authenticator operates in pass-through mode, the EAP server is located on the backend authentication server.

- **Silently Discard:** This means the implementation discards the packet without further processing. The implementation SHOULD provide the capability of logging the event, including the contents of the silently discarded packet, and SHOULD record the event in a statistics counter.

- **Successful Authentication:** In the context of this document, "successful authentication" is an exchange of EAP messages, as a result of which the authenticator decides to allow access by the peer, and the peer decides to use this access. The authenticator's decision typically involves both authentication and authorization aspects; the peer may successfully authenticate to the authenticator, but access may be denied by the authenticator due to policy reasons.

- **Message Integrity Check (MIC):** A keyed hash function used for authentication and integrity protection of data. This is usually called a Message Authentication Code (MAC), but IEEE 802 specifications (and this document) use the acronym MIC to avoid confusion with Medium Access Control.

- **Cryptographic Separation:** Two keys (x and y) are "cryptographically separate" if an adversary that knows all messages exchanged in the protocol cannot compute x from y or y from x without "breaking" some cryptographic assumption. In particular, this definition allows that the adversary has the knowledge of all nonces sent in cleartext, as well as all predictable counter values used in the protocol. Breaking a cryptographic assumption would typically require inverting a one-way function or predicting the outcome of a cryptographic pseudo-random number generator without knowledge of the secret state. In other words, if the keys are cryptographically separate, there is no shortcut to compute x from y or y from x, but the work an adversary must do to perform this computation is equivalent to performing an exhaustive search for the secret state value.

- **Master Session Key (MSK):** Keying material that is derived between the EAP peer and server and exported by the EAP method. The MSK is at least 64 octets in length. In existing implementations, a AAA server acting as an EAP server transports the MSK to the authenticator.

- **Extended Master Session Key (EMSK):** Additional keying material derived between the EAP client and server that is exported by the EAP method. The EMSK is at least 64 octets in length. The EMSK is not shared with the authenticator or any other third party. The EMSK is reserved for future uses that are not defined yet.

- **Result indications:** A method provides result indications if after the method's last message is sent and received:

  1. The peer is aware of whether it has authenticated the server, as well as whether the server has authenticated it.

  2. The server is aware of whether it has authenticated the peer, as well as whether the peer has authenticated it.

In the case where successful authentication is sufficient to authorize access, then the peer and authenticator will also know if the other party is willing to provide or accept access. This may not always be the case. An authenticated peer may be denied access due to lack of authorization (e.g., session limit) or other reasons. Since the EAP exchange is run between the peer and the server, other nodes (such as AAA proxies) may also affect the authorization decision. This is discussed in more detail in Section 7.16.

1.3. Applicability

EAP was designed for use in network access authentication, where IP layer connectivity may not be available. Use of EAP for other purposes, such as bulk data transport, is NOT RECOMMENDED.

Since EAP does not require IP connectivity, it provides just enough support for the reliable transport of authentication protocols, and no more.

EAP is a lock-step protocol which only supports a single packet in flight. As a result, EAP cannot efficiently transport bulk data, unlike transport protocols such as TCP [RFC793] or SCTP [RFC2960].

While EAP provides support for retransmission, it assumes ordering guarantees provided by the lower layer, so out of order reception is not supported.

Since EAP does not support fragmentation and reassembly, EAP authentication methods generating payloads larger than the minimum EAP MTU need
to provide fragmentation support.

While authentication methods such as EAP-TLS [RFC2716] provide support
for fragmentation and reassembly, the EAP methods defined in this document
do not. As a result, if the EAP packet size exceeds the EAP MTU of the link,
these methods will encounter difficulties.

EAP authentication is initiated by the server (authenticator), whereas many
authentication protocols are initiated by the client (peer). As a result, it may be
necessary for an authentication algorithm to add one or two additional messages (at most one roundtrip) in order to run over EAP.

Where certificate-based authentication is supported, the number of additional roundtrips may be much larger due to fragmentation of certificate
chains. In general, a fragmented EAP packet will require as many round-trips
to send as there are fragments. For example, a certificate chain 14960 octets in
size would require ten round-trips to send with a 1496 octet EAP MTU.

Where EAP runs over a lower layer in which significant packet loss is experienced, or where the connection between the authenticator and authentication server experiences significant packet loss, EAP methods requiring many
round-trips can experience difficulties. In these situations, use of EAP methods
with fewer roundtrips is advisable.

2. Extensible Authentication Protocol (EAP)

The EAP authentication exchange proceeds as follows:

1. The authenticator sends a Request to authenticate the peer. The Request
    has a Type field to indicate what is being requested. Examples of Request
    Types include Identity, MD5-challenge, etc. The MD5-challenge Type cor-
    responds closely to the CHAP authentication protocol [RFC1994]. Typi-
    cally, the authenticator will send an initial Identity Request; however, an
    initial Identity Request is not required, and MAY be bypassed. For exam-
    ple, the identity may not be required where it is determined by the port
    to which the peer has connected (leased lines, dedicated switch or dial-up
    ports), or where the identity is obtained in another fashion (via calling
    station identity or MAC address, in the Name field of the MD5-Challenge
    Response, etc.).

2. The peer sends a Response packet in reply to a valid Request. As with
    the Request packet, the Response packet contains a Type field, which
    corresponds to the Type field of the Request.

3. The authenticator sends an additional Request packet, and the peer replies with a Response. The sequence of Requests and Responses continues as long as needed. EAP is a 'lock step' protocol, so that other than the initial Request, a new Request cannot be sent prior to receiving a valid Response. The authenticator is responsible for retransmitting requests as described in Section 4.1. After a suitable number of retransmissions, the authenticator SHOULD end the EAP conversation. The authenticator MUST NOT send a Success or Failure packet when retransmitting or when it fails to get a response from the peer.

4. The conversation continues until the authenticator cannot authenticate the peer (unacceptable Responses to one or more Requests), in which case the authenticator implementation MUST transmit an EAP Failure (Code 4). Alternatively, the authentication conversation can continue until the authenticator determines that successful authentication has occurred, in which case the authenticator MUST transmit an EAP Success (Code 3).

Advantages:

- The EAP protocol can support multiple authentication mechanisms without having to pre-negotiate a particular one.

- Network Access Server (NAS) devices (e.g., a switch or access point) do not have to understand each authentication method and MAY act as a pass-through agent for a backend authentication server. Support for pass-through is optional. An authenticator MAY authenticate local peers, while at the same time acting as a pass-through for non-local peers and authentication methods it does not implement locally.

- Separation of the authenticator from the backend authentication server simplifies credentials management and policy decision making.

Disadvantages:

- For use in PPP, EAP requires the addition of a new authentication Type to PPP LCP and thus PPP implementations will need to be modified to use it. It also strays from the previous PPP authentication model of negotiating a specific authentication mechanism during LCP. Similarly, switch or access point implementations need to support [IEEE-802.1X] in order to use EAP.

- Where the authenticator is separate from the backend authentication server, this complicates the security analysis and, if needed, key distribution.

2.1. Support for Sequences

An EAP conversation MAY utilize a sequence of methods. A common example of this is an Identity request followed by a single EAP authentication method such as an MD5-Challenge. However, the peer and authenticator MUST utilize only one authentication method (Type 4 or greater) within an EAP conversation, after which the authenticator MUST send a Success or Failure packet.

Once a peer has sent a Response of the same Type as the initial Request, an authenticator MUST NOT send a Request of a different Type prior to completion of the final round of a given method (with the exception of a Notification-Request) and MUST NOT send a Request for an additional method of any Type after completion of the initial authentication method; a peer receiving such Requests MUST treat them as invalid, and silently discard them. As a result, Identity Requery is not supported.

A peer MUST NOT send a Nak (legacy or expanded) in reply to a Request after an initial non-Nak Response has been sent. Since spoofed EAP Request packets may be sent by an attacker, an authenticator receiving an unexpected Nak SHOULD discard it and log the event.

Multiple authentication methods within an EAP conversation are not supported due to their vulnerability to man-in-the-middle attacks (see Section 7.4) and incompatibility with existing implementations.

Where a single EAP authentication method is utilized, but other methods are run within it (a "tunneled" method), the prohibition against multiple authentication methods does not apply. Such "tunneled" methods appear as a single authentication method to EAP. Backward compatibility can be provided, since a peer not supporting a "tunneled" method can reply to the initial EAP-Request with a Nak (legacy or expanded). To address security vulnerabilities, "tunneled" methods MUST support protection against man-in-the-middle attacks.

2.2. EAP Multiplexing Model

Conceptually, EAP implementations consist of the following components:

a **Lower layer:** The lower layer is responsible for transmitting and receiving EAP frames between the peer and authenticator. EAP has been run over a variety of lower layers including PPP, wired IEEE 802 LANs [IEEE-802.1X], IEEE 802.11 wireless LANs [IEEE-802.11], UDP (L2TP [RFC2661] and IKEv2 [IKEv2]), and TCP [PIC]. Lower layer behavior is discussed in Section 3.

b **EAP layer:** The EAP layer receives and transmits EAP packets via the lower layer, implements duplicate detection and retransmission, and delivers and receives EAP messages to and from the EAP peer and authenticator layers.

c **EAP peer and authenticator layers:** Based on the Code field, the EAP layer demultiplexes incoming EAP packets to the EAP peer and authenticator layers. Typically, an EAP implementation on a given host will support either peer or authenticator functionality, but it is possible for a host to act as both an EAP peer and authenticator. In such an implementation both EAP peer and authenticator layers will be present.

d **EAP method layers:** EAP methods implement the authentication algorithms and receive and transmit EAP messages via the EAP peer and authenticator layers. Since fragmentation support is not provided by EAP itself, this is the responsibility of EAP methods, which are discussed in Section 5.

The EAP multiplexing model is illustrated in Figure 1 below. Note that there is no requirement that an implementation conform to this model, as long as the on-the-wire behavior is consistent with it.

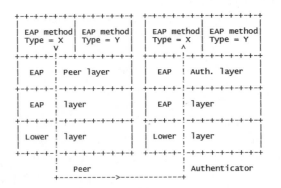

Figure 1: EAP Multiplexing Model

Within EAP, the Code field functions much like a protocol number in IP. It is assumed that the EAP layer demultiplexes incoming EAP packets according to the Code field. Received EAP packets with Code=1 (Request), 3 (Success), and 4 (Failure) are delivered by the EAP layer to the EAP peer layer, if implemented. EAP packets with Code=2 (Response) are delivered to the EAP authenticator layer, if implemented.

Within EAP, the Type field functions much like a port number in UDP or TCP. It is assumed that the EAP peer and authenticator layers demultiplex incoming EAP packets according to their Type, and deliver them only to the EAP method corresponding to that Type. An EAP method implementation on a host may register to receive packets from the peer or authenticator layers, or both, depending on which role(s) it supports.

Since EAP authentication methods may wish to access the Identity, implementations SHOULD make the Identity Request and Response accessible to authentication methods (Types 4 or greater), in addition to the Identity method. The Identity Type is discussed in Section 5.1.

A Notification Response is only used as confirmation that the peer received the Notification Request, not that it has processed it, or displayed the message to the user. It cannot be assumed that the contents of the Notification Request or Response are available to another method. The Notification Type is discussed in Section 5.2.

Nak (Type 3) or Expanded Nak (Type 254) are utilized for the purposes of method negotiation. Peers respond to an initial EAP Request for an unacceptable Type with a Nak Response (Type 3) or Expanded Nak Response (Type 254). It cannot be assumed that the contents of the Nak Response(s) are available to another method. The Nak Type(s) are discussed in Section 5.3.

EAP packets with Codes of Success or Failure do not include a Type field, and are not delivered to an EAP method. Success and Failure are discussed in Section 4.2.

Given these considerations, the Success, Failure, Nak Response(s), and Notification Request/Response messages MUST NOT be used to carry data destined for delivery to other EAP methods.

2.3. Pass-Through Behavior

When operating as a "pass-through authenticator", an authenticator performs checks on the Code, Identifier, and Length fields as described in Section 4.1. It forwards EAP packets received from the peer and destined to its authenticator layer to the backend authentication server; packets received from the backend authentication server destined to the peer are forwarded to it.

A host receiving an EAP packet may only do one of three things with it: act on it, drop it, or forward it. The forwarding decision is typically based only on examination of the Code, Identifier, and Length fields. A pass-through authenticator implementation MUST be capable of forwarding EAP packets received from the peer with Code=2 (Response) to the backend authentication server. It also MUST be capable of receiving EAP packets from the backend authentication server and forwarding EAP packets of Code=1 (Request), Code=3 (Success), and Code=4 (Failure) to the peer.

Unless the authenticator implements one or more authentication methods locally which support the authenticator role, the EAP method layer header fields (Type, Type-Data) are not examined as part of the forwarding decision. Where the authenticator supports local authentication methods, it MAY examine the Type field to determine whether to act on the packet itself or forward it. Compliant pass-through authenticator implementations MUST by default forward EAP packets of any Type.

EAP packets received with Code=1 (Request), Code=3 (Success), and Code=4 (Failure) are demultiplexed by the EAP layer and delivered to the peer layer. Therefore, unless a host implements an EAP peer layer, these packets will be silently discarded. Similarly, EAP packets received with Code=2 (Response) are demultiplexed by the EAP layer and delivered to the authenticator layer. Therefore, unless a host implements an EAP authenticator layer, these packets will be silently discarded. The behavior of a "pass-through peer" is undefined within this specification, and is unsupported by AAA protocols such as RADIUS [RFC3579] and Diameter [DIAM-EAP].

The forwarding model is illustrated in Figure 2.

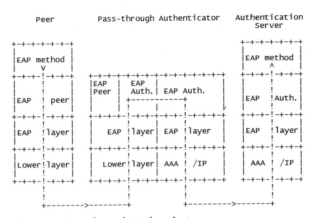

Figure 2: Pass-through Authenticator

For sessions in which the authenticator acts as a pass-through, it MUST determine the outcome of the authentication solely based on the Accept/Reject indication sent by the backend authentication server; the outcome MUST NOT be determined by the contents of an EAP packet sent along with the Accept/Reject indication, or the absence of such an encapsulated EAP packet.

2.4. Peer-to-Peer Operation

Since EAP is a peer-to-peer protocol, an independent and simultaneous authentication may take place in the reverse direction (depending on the capabilities of the lower layer). Both ends of the link may act as authenticators and peers at the same time. In this case, it is necessary for both ends to implement EAP authenticator and peer layers. In addition, the EAP method implementations on both peers must support both authenticator and peer functionality.

Although EAP supports peer-to-peer operation, some EAP implementations, methods, AAA protocols, and link layers may not support this. Some EAP methods may support asymmetric authentication, with one type of credential being required for the peer and another type for the authenticator.

Hosts supporting peer-to-peer operation with such a method would need to be provisioned with both types of credentials.

For example, EAP-TLS [RFC2716] is a client-server protocol in which distinct certificate profiles are typically utilized for the client and server. This implies that a host supporting peer-to-peer authentication with EAP-TLS would need to implement both the EAP peer and authenticator layers, support both peer and authenticator roles in the EAP-TLS implementation, and provision certificates appropriate for each role.

AAA protocols such as RADIUS/EAP [RFC3579] and Diameter EAP [DIAM-EAP] only support "pass-through authenticator" operation. As noted in [RFC3579] Section 2.6.2, a RADIUS server responds to an Access-Request encapsulating an EAP-Request, Success, or Failure packet with an Access-Reject. There is therefore no support for "pass-through peer" operation.

Even where a method is used which supports mutual authentication and result indications, several considerations may dictate that two EAP authentications (one in each direction) are required. These include:

1. **Support for bi-directional session key derivation in the lower layer:**
   Lower layers such as IEEE 802.11 may only support uni-directional
   derivation and transport of transient session keys. For example, the
   group-key handshake defined in [IEEE-802.11i] is uni-directional, since
   in IEEE 802.11 infrastructure mode, only the Access Point (AP) sends
   multicast/broadcast traffic. In IEEE 802.11 ad hoc mode, where either
   peer may send multicast/broadcast traffic, two uni-directional group-
   key exchanges are required. Due to limitations of the design, this also
   implies the need for unicast key derivations and EAP method
   exchanges to occur in each direction.

2. **Support for tie-breaking in the lower layer:** Lower layers such as IEEE
   802.11 ad hoc do not support "tie breaking" wherein two hosts initiating
   authentication with each other will only go forward with a single authentication. This implies that even if 802.11 were to support a bi-directional
   group-key handshake, then two authentications, one in each direction,
   might still occur.

3. **Peer policy satisfaction:** EAP methods may support result indications,
   enabling the peer to indicate to the EAP server within the method that
   it successfully authenticated the EAP server, as well as for the server
   to indicate that it has authenticated the peer. However, a pass-through
   authenticator will not be aware that the peer has accepted the credentials offered by the EAP server, unless this information is provided to
   the authenticator via the AAA protocol. The authenticator SHOULD
   interpret the receipt of a key attribute within an Accept packet as an
   indication that the peer has successfully authenticated the server.

However, it is possible that the EAP peer's access policy was not satisfied during the initial EAP exchange, even though mutual authentication occurred. For example, the EAP authenticator may not have demonstrated authorization to act in both peer and authenticator roles. As a result, the peer may require an additional authentication in the reverse direction, even if the peer provided an indication that the EAP server had successfully authenticated to it.

3. Lower Layer Behavior

3.1. Lower Layer Requirements

EAP makes the following assumptions about lower layers:

1. **Unreliable transport:** In EAP, the authenticator retransmits Requests that have not yet received Responses so that EAP does not assume that lower layers are reliable. Since EAP defines its own retransmission behavior, it is possible (though undesirable) for retransmission to occur both in the lower layer and the EAP layer when EAP is run over a reliable lower layer.

   NOTE Note that EAP Success and Failure packets are not retransmitted. Without a reliable lower layer, and with a non-negligible error rate, these packets can be lost, resulting in timeouts. It is therefore desirable for implementations to improve their resilience to loss of EAP Success or Failure packets, as described in Section 4.2.

2. **Lower layer error detection:** While EAP does not assume that the lower layer is reliable, it does rely on lower layer error detection (e.g., CRC, Checksum, MIC, etc.). EAP methods may not include a MIC, or if they do, it may not be computed over all the fields in the EAP packet, such as the Code, Identifier, Length, or Type fields. As a result, without lower layer error detection, undetected errors could creep into the EAP layer or EAP method layer header fields, resulting in authentication failures.

   For example, EAP TLS [RFC2716], which computes its MIC over the Type-Data field only, regards MIC validation failures as a fatal error. Without lower layer error detection, this method, and others like it, will not perform reliably.

3. **Lower layer security:** EAP does not require lower layers to provide security services such as per-packet confidentiality, authentication, integrity,

and replay protection. However, where these security services are available, EAP methods supporting Key Derivation (see Section 7.2.1) can be used to provide dynamic keying material. This makes it possible to bind the EAP authentication to subsequent data and protect against data modification, spoofing, or replay. See Section 7.1 for details.

4. **Minimum MTU:** EAP is capable of functioning on lower layers that provide an EAP MTU size of 1020 octets or greater.

   EAP does not support path MTU discovery, and fragmentation and reassembly is not supported by EAP, nor by the methods defined in this specification: Identity (1), Notification (2), Nak Response (3), MD5-Challenge (4), One Time Password (5), Generic Token Card (6), and expanded Nak Response (254) Types.

   Typically, the EAP peer obtains information on the EAP MTU from the lower layers and sets the EAP frame size to an appropriate value. Where the authenticator operates in pass-through mode, the authentication server does not have a direct way of determining the EAP MTU, and therefore relies on the authenticator to provide it with this information, such as via the Framed-MTU attribute, as described in [RFC3579], Section 2.4.

   While methods such as EAP-TLS [RFC2716] support fragmentation and reassembly, EAP methods originally designed for use within PPP where a 1500 octet MTU is guaranteed for control frames (see [RFC1661], Section 6.1) may lack fragmentation and reassembly features.

   EAP methods can assume a minimum EAP MTU of 1020 octets in the absence of other information. EAP methods SHOULD include support for fragmentation and reassembly if their payloads can be larger than this minimum EAP MTU.

   EAP is a lock-step protocol, which implies a certain inefficiency when handling fragmentation and reassembly. Therefore, if the lower layer supports fragmentation and reassembly (such as where EAP is transported over IP), it may be preferable for fragmentation and reassembly to occur in the lower layer rather than in EAP. This can be accomplished by providing an artificially large EAP MTU to EAP, causing fragmentation and reassembly to be handled within the lower layer.

5. **Possible duplication:** Where the lower layer is reliable, it will provide the EAP layer with a non-duplicated stream of packets. However, while it is desirable that lower layers provide for non-duplication, this is not a requirement. The Identifier field provides both the peer and authenticator with the ability to detect duplicates.

6. **Ordering guarantees:** EAP does not require the Identifier to be monotonically increasing, and so is reliant on lower layer ordering guarantees for correct operation. EAP was originally defined to run on PPP, and [RFC1661] Section 1 has an ordering requirement:

   ▪ "The Point-to-Point Protocol is designed for simple links which transport packets between two peers. These links provide full-duplex simultaneous bi-directional operation, and are assumed to deliver packets in order."

Lower layer transports for EAP MUST preserve ordering between a source and destination at a given priority level (the ordering guarantee provided by [IEEE-802]).

Reordering, if it occurs, will typically result in an EAP authentication failure, causing EAP authentication to be re-run. In an environment in which reordering is likely, it is therefore expected that EAP authentication failures will be common. It is RECOMMENDED that EAP only be run over lower layers that provide ordering guarantees; running EAP over raw IP or UDP transport is NOT RECOMMENDED. Encapsulation of EAP within RADIUS [RFC3579] satisfies ordering requirements, since RADIUS is a "lockstep" protocol that delivers packets in order.

3.2. EAP Usage Within PPP

In order to establish communications over a point-to-point link, each end of the PPP link first sends LCP packets to configure the data link during the Link Establishment phase. After the link has been established, PPP provides for an optional Authentication phase before proceeding to the Network-Layer Protocol phase.

By default, authentication is not mandatory. If authentication of the link is desired, an implementation MUST specify the Authentication Protocol Configuration Option during the Link Establishment phase.

If the identity of the peer has been established in the Authentication phase, the server can use that identity in the selection of options for the following network layer negotiations.

When implemented within PPP, EAP does not select a specific authentication mechanism at the PPP Link Control Phase, but rather postpones this until the Authentication Phase. This allows the authenticator to request more information before determining the specific authentication mechanism. This also permits the use of a "backend" server which actually implements the various mechanisms while the PPP authenticator merely passes through the authentication exchange. The PPP Link Establishment and Authentication phases, and the Authentication Protocol Configuration Option, are defined in The Point-to-Point Protocol (PPP) [RFC1661].

3.2.1. PPP Configuration Option Format

A summary of the PPP Authentication Protocol Configuration Option format to negotiate EAP follows. The fields are transmitted from left to right.

Exactly one EAP packet is encapsulated in the Information field of a PPP Data Link Layer frame where the protocol field indicates type hex C227 (PPP EAP).

```
 0                   1                   2                   3
 0 1 2 3 4 5 6 7 8 9 0 1 2 3 4 5 6 7 8 9 0 1 2 3 4 5 6 7 8 9 0 1
+-+-+-+-+-+-+-+-+-+-+-+-+-+-+-+-+-+-+-+-+-+-+-+-+-+-+-+-+-+-+-+-+
|     Type      |    Length     |    Authentication Protocol    |
+-+-+-+-+-+-+-+-+-+-+-+-+-+-+-+-+-+-+-+-+-+-+-+-+-+-+-+-+-+-+-+-+
```

Type

3

Length

4

Authentication Protocol

C227 (Hex) for Extensible Authentication Protocol (EAP)

3.3. EAP Usage Within IEEE 802

The encapsulation of EAP over IEEE 802 is defined in [IEEE-802.1X]. The IEEE 802 encapsulation of EAP does not involve PPP, and IEEE 802.1X does not include support for link or network layer negotiations. As a result, within IEEE 802.1X, it is not possible to negotiate non-EAP authentication mechanisms, such as PAP or CHAP [RFC1994].

3.4. Lower Layer Indications

The reliability and security of lower layer indications is dependent on the lower layer. Since EAP is media independent, the presence or absence of lower layer security is not taken into account in the processing of EAP messages.

To improve reliability, if a peer receives a lower layer success indication as defined in Section 7.2, it MAY conclude that a Success packet has been lost, and behave as if it had actually received a Success packet. This includes choosing to ignore the Success in some circumstances as described in Section 4.2.

A discussion of some reliability and security issues with lower layer indications in PPP, IEEE 802 wired networks, and IEEE 802.11 wireless LANs can be found in the Security Considerations, Section 7.12.

After EAP authentication is complete, the peer will typically transmit and receive data via the authenticator. It is desirable to provide assurance that the entities transmitting data are the same ones that successfully completed EAP authentication. To accomplish this, it is necessary for the lower layer to provide per-packet integrity, authentication and replay protection, and to bind these per-packet services to the keys derived during EAP authentication. Otherwise, it is possible for subsequent data traffic to be modified, spoofed, or replayed.

Where keying material for the lower layer ciphersuite is itself provided by EAP, ciphersuite negotiation and key activation are controlled by the lower layer. In PPP, ciphersuites are negotiated within ECP so that it is not possible to use keys derived from EAP authentication until the completion of ECP. Therefore, an initial EAP exchange cannot be protected by a PPP ciphersuite, although EAP re-authentication can be protected.

In IEEE 802 media, initial key activation also typically occurs after completion of EAP authentication. Therefore an initial EAP exchange typically cannot be protected by the lower layer ciphersuite, although an EAP re-authentication or pre-authentication exchange can be protected.

4. EAP Packet Format

A summary of the EAP packet format is shown below. The fields are transmitted from left to right.

```
 0                   1                   2                   3
 0 1 2 3 4 5 6 7 8 9 0 1 2 3 4 5 6 7 8 9 0 1 2 3 4 5 6 7 8 9 0 1
+-+-+-+-+-+-+-+-+-+-+-+-+-+-+-+-+-+-+-+-+-+-+-+-+-+-+-+-+-+-+-+-+
|     Code      |  Identifier   |            Length             |
+-+-+-+-+-+-+-+-+-+-+-+-+-+-+-+-+-+-+-+-+-+-+-+-+-+-+-+-+-+-+-+-+
|    Data ...
+-+-+-+-+
```

Code

The Code field is one octet and identifies the Type of EAP packet. EAP Codes are assigned as follows:

1 Request
2 Response
3 Success
4 Failure

Since EAP only defines Codes 1-4, EAP packets with other codes MUST be silently discarded by both authenticators and peers.

Identifier

The Identifier field is one octet and aids in matching Responses with Requests.

Length

The Length field is two octets and indicates the length, in octets, of the EAP packet including the Code, Identifier, Length, and Data fields. Octets outside the range of the Length field should be treated as Data Link Layer padding and MUST be ignored upon reception. A message with the Length field set to a value larger than the number of received octets MUST be silently discarded.

Data

The Data field is zero or more octets. The format of the Data field is determined by the Code field.

4.1. Request and Response

Description

The Request packet (Code field set to 1) is sent by the authenticator to the peer. Each Request has a Type field which serves to indicate what is being requested. Additional Request packets MUST be sent until a valid Response packet is received, an optional retry counter expires, or a lower layer failure indication is received.

Retransmitted Requests MUST be sent with the same Identifier value in order to distinguish them from new Requests. The content of the data field is dependent on the Request Type. The peer MUST send a Response packet in reply to a valid Request packet. Responses MUST only be sent in reply to a valid Request and never be retransmitted on a timer.

If a peer receives a valid duplicate Request for which it has already sent a Response, it MUST resend its original Response without reprocessing the Request. Requests MUST be processed in the order that they are received, and MUST be processed to their completion before inspecting the next Request.

A summary of the Request and Response packet format follows. The fields are transmitted from left to right.

```
 0                   1                   2                   3
 0 1 2 3 4 5 6 7 8 9 0 1 2 3 4 5 6 7 8 9 0 1 2 3 4 5 6 7 8 9 0 1
+-+-+-+-+-+-+-+-+-+-+-+-+-+-+-+-+-+-+-+-+-+-+-+-+-+-+-+-+-+-+-+-+
|     Code      |  Identifier   |            Length             |
+-+-+-+-+-+-+-+-+-+-+-+-+-+-+-+-+-+-+-+-+-+-+-+-+-+-+-+-+-+-+-+-+
|     Type      |  Type-Data ...
+-+-+-+-+-+-+-+-+-+-+-+-+-+-+-
```

Code

1 for Request

2 for Response

Identifier

The Identifier field is one octet. The Identifier field MUST be the same if a Request packet is retransmitted due to a timeout while waiting for a Response. Any new (non-retransmission) Requests MUST modify the Identifier field.

The Identifier field of the Response MUST match that of the currently outstanding Request. An authenticator receiving a Response whose Identifier value does not match that of the currently outstanding Request MUST silently discard the Response.

In order to avoid confusion between new Requests and retransmissions, the Identifier value chosen for each new Request need only be different from the previous Request, but need not be unique within the conversation. One way to achieve this is to start the Identifier at an initial value and increment it for each new Request. Initializing the first Identifier with a random number rather than starting from zero is recommended, since it makes sequence attacks somewhat more difficult.

Since the Identifier space is unique to each session, authenticators are not restricted to only 256 simultaneous authentication conversations. Similarly, with re-authentication, an EAP conversation might continue over a long period of time, and is not limited to only 256 roundtrips.

IMPLEMENTATION NOTE The authenticator is responsible for retransmitting Request messages. If the Request message is obtained from elsewhere (such as from a backend authentication server), then the authenticator will need to save a copy of the Request in order to accomplish this. The peer is responsible for detecting and handling duplicate Request messages before processing them in any way, including passing them on to an outside party. The authenticator is also responsible for discarding Response messages with a non-matching Identifier value before acting on them in any way, including passing them on to the backend authentication server for verification. Since the authenticator can retransmit before receiving a Response from the peer, the authenticator can receive multiple Responses, each with a matching Identifier. Until a new Request is received by the authenticator, the Identifier value is not updated, so that the authenticator forwards Responses to the backend authentication server, one at a time.

Length

The Length field is two octets and indicates the length of the EAP packet including the Code, Identifier, Length, Type, and Type-Data fields. Octets outside the range of the Length field should be treated as Data Link Layer padding and MUST be ignored upon reception. A message with the Length field set to a value larger than the number of received octets MUST be silently discarded.

Type

The Type field is one octet. This field indicates the Type of Request or Response. A single Type MUST be specified for each EAP Request or Response. An initial specification of Types follows in Section 5 of this document.

The Type field of a Response MUST either match that of the Request, or correspond to a legacy or Expanded Nak (see Section 5.3) indicating that a Request Type is unacceptable to the peer. A peer MUST NOT send a Nak (legacy or expanded) in response to a Request, after an initial non-Nak Response has been sent. An EAP server receiving a Response not meeting these requirements MUST silently discard it.

Type-Data

The Type-Data field varies with the Type of Request and the associated Response.

4.2. Success and Failure

The Success packet is sent by the authenticator to the peer after completion of an EAP authentication method (Type 4 or greater) to indicate that the peer has authenticated successfully to the authenticator. The authenticator MUST transmit an EAP packet with the Code field set to 3 (Success). If the authenticator cannot authenticate the peer (unacceptable Responses to one or more Requests), then after unsuccessful completion of the EAP method in progress, the implementation MUST transmit an EAP packet with the Code field set to 4 (Failure). An authenticator MAY wish to issue multiple Requests before sending a Failure response in order to allow for human typing mistakes. Success and Failure packets MUST NOT contain additional data.

Success and Failure packets MUST NOT be sent by an EAP authenticator if the specification of the given method does not explicitly permit the method to finish at that point. A peer EAP implementation receiving a Success or Failure packet where sending one is not explicitly permitted MUST silently discard it. By default, an EAP peer MUST silently discard a "canned" Success packet (a Success packet sent immediately upon connection). This ensures that a rogue authenticator will not be able to bypass mutual authentication by sending a Success packet prior to conclusion of the EAP method conversation.

IMPLEMENTATION NOTE Because the Success and Failure packets are not acknowledged, they are not retransmitted by the authenticator, and may be potentially lost. A peer MUST allow for this circumstance as described in this note. See also Section 3.4 for guidance on the processing of lower layer success and failure indications.

As described in Section 2.1, only a single EAP authentication method is allowed within an EAP conversation. EAP methods may implement result indications. After the authenticator sends a failure result indication to the peer, regardless of the response from the peer, it MUST subsequently send a Failure packet. After the authenticator sends a success result indication to the peer and receives a success result indication from the peer, it MUST subsequently send a Success packet.

On the peer, once the method completes unsuccessfully (that is, either the authenticator sends a failure result indication, or the peer decides that it does not want to continue the conversation, possibly after sending a failure result indication), the peer MUST terminate the conversation and indicate failure to the lower layer. The peer MUST silently discard Success packets and MAY silently discard Failure packets. As a result, loss of a Failure packet need not result in a timeout.

On the peer, after success result indications have been exchanged by both sides, a Failure packet MUST be silently discarded. The peer MAY, in the event that an EAP Success is not received, conclude that the EAP Success packet was lost and that authentication concluded successfully.

If the authenticator has not sent a result indication, and the peer is willing to continue the conversation, the peer waits for a Success or Failure packet once the method completes, and MUST NOT silently discard either of them. In the event that neither a Success nor Failure packet is received, the peer SHOULD terminate the conversation to avoid lengthy timeouts in case the lost packet was an EAP Failure.

If the peer attempts to authenticate to the authenticator and fails to do so, the authenticator MUST send a Failure packet and MUST NOT grant access by sending a Success packet. However, an authenticator MAY omit having the peer authenticate to it in situations where limited access is offered (e.g., guest access). In this case, the authenticator MUST send a Success packet.

Where the peer authenticates successfully to the authenticator, but the authenticator does not send a result indication, the authenticator MAY deny access by sending a Failure packet where the peer is not currently authorized for network access.

A summary of the Success and Failure packet format is shown below. The fields are transmitted from left to right.

```
 0                   1                   2                   3
 0 1 2 3 4 5 6 7 8 9 0 1 2 3 4 5 6 7 8 9 0 1 2 3 4 5 6 7 8 9 0 1
+-+-+-+-+-+-+-+-+-+-+-+-+-+-+-+-+-+-+-+-+-+-+-+-+-+-+-+-+-+-+-+-+
|     Code      |   Identifier  |            Length             |
+-+-+-+-+-+-+-+-+-+-+-+-+-+-+-+-+-+-+-+-+-+-+-+-+-+-+-+-+-+-+-+-+
```

Code

> 3 for Success
>
> 4 for Failure

Identifier

> The Identifier field is one octet and aids in matching replies to Responses. The Identifier field MUST match the Identifier field of the Response packet that it is sent in response to.

Length

> 4

4.3. Retransmission Behavior

Because the authentication process will often involve user input, some care must be taken when deciding upon retransmission strategies and authentication timeouts. By default, where EAP is run over an unreliable lower layer, the EAP retransmission timer SHOULD be dynamically estimated. A maximum of 3-5 retransmissions is suggested.

When run over a reliable lower layer (e.g., EAP over ISAKMP/TCP, as within [PIC]), the authenticator retransmission timer SHOULD be set to an infinite value, so that retransmissions do not occur at the EAP layer. The peer may still maintain a timeout value so as to avoid waiting indefinitely for a Request.

Where the authentication process requires user input, the measured round trip times may be determined by user responsiveness rather than network characteristics, so that dynamic RTO estimation may not be helpful. Instead, the retransmission timer SHOULD be set so as to provide sufficient time for the user to respond, with longer timeouts required in certain cases, such as where Token Cards (see Section 5.6) are involved.

In order to provide the EAP authenticator with guidance as to the appropriate timeout value, a hint can be communicated to the authenticator by the backend authentication server (such as via the RADIUS Session-Timeout attribute).

In order to dynamically estimate the EAP retransmission timer, the algorithms for the estimation of SRTT, RTTVAR, and RTO described in [RFC2988] are RECOMMENDED, including use of Karn's algorithm, with the following potential modifications:

  a In order to avoid synchronization behaviors that can occur with fixed timers among distributed systems, the retransmission timer is calculated with a jitter by using the RTO value and randomly adding a value drawn between -RTOmin/2 and RTOmin/2. Alternative calculations to create jitter MAY be used. These MUST be pseudo-random. For a discussion of pseudo-random number generation, see [RFC1750].

b When EAP is transported over a single link (as opposed to over the Internet), smaller values of RTOinitial, RTOmin, and RTOmax MAY be used. Recommended values are RTOinitial=1 second, RTOmin=200ms, and RTOmax=20 seconds.

c When EAP is transported over a single link (as opposed to over the Internet), estimates MAY be done on a per-authenticator basis, rather than a per-session basis. This enables the retransmission estimate to make the most use of information on link-layer behavior.

d An EAP implementation MAY clear SRTT and RTTVAR after backing off the timer multiple times, as it is likely that the current SRTT and RTTVAR are bogus in this situation. Once SRTT and RTTVAR are cleared, they should be initialized with the next RTT sample taken as described in [RFC2988] equation 2.2.

5. Initial EAP Request/Response Types

This section defines the initial set of EAP Types used in Request/Response exchanges. More Types may be defined in future documents. The Type field is one octet and identifies the structure of an EAP Request or Response packet. The first 3 Types are considered special case Types.

The remaining Types define authentication exchanges. Nak (Type 3) or Expanded Nak (Type 254) are valid only for Response packets, they MUST NOT be sent in a Request.

All EAP implementations MUST support Types 1-4, which are defined in this document, and SHOULD support Type 254. Implementations MAY support other Types defined here or in future RFCs.

1 Identity

2 Notification

3 Nak (Response only)

4 MD5-Challenge

5 One Time Password (OTP)

6 Generic Token Card (GTC)

254 Expanded Types

255 Experimental use

   EAP methods MAY support authentication based on shared secrets. If the shared secret is a passphrase entered by the user, implementations MAY support entering passphrases with non-ASCII characters. In this case, the input should be processed using an appropriate stringprep [RFC3454] profile, and encoded in octets using UTF-8 encoding [RFC2279]. A preliminary version of a possible stringprep profile is described in [SASLPREP].

5.1. Identity

Description

The Identity Type is used to query the identity of the peer. Generally, the authenticator will issue this as the initial Request. An optional displayable message MAY be included to prompt the peer in the case where there is an expectation of interaction with a user. A Response of Type 1 (Identity) SHOULD be sent in Response to a Request with a Type of 1 (Identity).

Some EAP implementations piggy-back various options into the Identity Request after a NUL-character. By default, an EAP implementation SHOULD NOT assume that an Identity Request or Response can be larger than 1020 octets.

It is RECOMMENDED that the Identity Response be used primarily for routing purposes and selecting which EAP method to use. EAP Methods SHOULD include a method-specific mechanism for obtaining the identity, so that they do not have to rely on the Identity Response. Identity Requests and Responses are sent in cleartext, so an attacker may snoop on the identity, or even modify or spoof identity exchanges. To address these threats, it is preferable for an EAP method to include an identity exchange that supports per-packet authentication, integrity and replay protection, and confidentiality. The Identity Response may not be the appropriate identity for the method; it may have been truncated or obfuscated so as to provide privacy, or it may have been decorated for routing purposes. Where the peer is configured to only accept authentication methods supporting protected identity exchanges, the peer MAY provide an abbreviated Identity Response (such as omitting the peer-name portion of the NAI [RFC2486]). For further discussion of identity protection, see Section 7.3.

IMPLEMENTATION NOTE The peer MAY obtain the Identity via user input. It is suggested that the authenticator retry the Identity Request in the case of an invalid Identity or authentication failure to allow for potential typos on the part of the user. It is suggested that the Identity Request be retried a minimum of 3 times before terminating the authentication. The Notification Request MAY be used to indicate an invalid authentication attempt prior to transmitting a new Identity Request (optionally, the failure MAY be indicated within the message of the new Identity Request itself).

Type

1

Type-Data

This field MAY contain a displayable message in the Request, containing UTF-8 encoded ISO 10646 characters [RFC2279]. Where the Request contains a null, only the portion of the field prior to the null is displayed. If the Identity is unknown, the Identity Response field should be zero bytes in length. The Identity Response field MUST NOT be null terminated. In all cases, the length of the Type-Data field is derived from the Length field of the Request/Response packet.

Security Claims (see Section 7.2):

Auth. mechanism:	None
Ciphersuite negotiation:	No
Mutual authentication:	No
Integrity protection:	No
Replay protection:	No
Confidentiality:	No
Key derivation:	No
Key strength:	N/A
Dictionary attack prot.:	N/A
Fast reconnect:	No
Crypt. binding:	N/A
Session independence:	N/A
Fragmentation:	No
Channel binding:	No

5.2. Notification

Description

The Notification Type is optionally used to convey a displayable message from the authenticator to the peer. An authenticator MAY send a Notification Request to the peer at any time when there is no outstanding Request, prior to completion of an EAP authentication method. The peer MUST respond to a Notification Request with a Notification Response unless the EAP authentication method specification prohibits the use of Notification messages. In any case, a Nak Response MUST NOT be sent in response to a Notification Request. Note that the default maximum length of a Notification Request is 1020 octets. By default, this leaves at most 1015 octets for the human readable message.

An EAP method MAY indicate within its specification that Notification messages must not be sent during that method. In this case, the peer MUST silently discard Notification Requests from the point where an initial Request for that Type is answered with a Response of the same Type.

The peer SHOULD display this message to the user or log it if it cannot be displayed. The Notification Type is intended to provide an acknowledged notification of some imperative nature, but it is not an error indication, and therefore does not change the state of the peer. Examples include a password with an expiration time that is about to expire, an OTP sequence integer which is nearing 0, an authentication failure warning, etc. In most circumstances, Notification should not be required.

Type

2

Type-Data

The Type-Data field in the Request contains a displayable message greater than zero octets in length, containing UTF-8 encoded ISO 10646 characters [RFC2279]. The length of the message is determined by the Length field of the Request packet. The message MUST NOT be null terminated. A Response MUST be sent in reply to the Request with a Type field of 2 (Notification). The Type-Data field of the Response is zero octets in length. The Response should be sent immediately (independent of how the message is displayed or logged).

Security Claims (see Section 7.2):

Auth. mechanism:	None
Ciphersuite negotiation:	No
Mutual authentication:	No
Integrity protection:	No
Replay protection:	No
Confidentiality:	No
Key derivation:	No
Key strength:	N/A
Dictionary attack prot.:	N/A
Fast reconnect:	No
Crypt. binding:	N/A
Session independence:	N/A
Fragmentation:	No
Channel binding:	No

5.3. Nak

5.3.1. Legacy Nak

Description

The legacy Nak Type is valid only in Response messages. It is sent in reply to a Request where the desired authentication Type is unacceptable. Authentication Types are numbered 4 and above. The Response contains one or more authentication Types desired by the Peer. Type zero (0) is used to indicate that the sender has no viable alternatives, and therefore the authenticator SHOULD NOT send another Request after receiving a Nak Response containing a zero value.

Since the legacy Nak Type is valid only in Responses and has very limited functionality, it MUST NOT be used as a general purpose error indication, such as for communication of error messages, or negotiation of parameters specific to a particular EAP method.

Code

2 for Response.

Identifier

The Identifier field is one octet and aids in matching Responses with Requests. The Identifier field of a legacy Nak Response MUST match the Identifier field of the Request packet that it is sent in response to.

Length

>=6

Type

3

Type-Data

Where a peer receives a Request for an unacceptable authentication Type (4-253,255), or a peer lacking support for Expanded Types receives a Request for Type 254, a Nak Response (Type 3) MUST be sent. The Type-Data field of the Nak Response (Type 3) MUST contain one or more octets indicating the desired authentication Type(s), one octet per Type, or the value zero (0) to indicate no proposed alternative. A peer supporting Expanded Types that receives a Request for an unacceptable authentication Type (4-253, 255) MAY include the value 254 in the Nak Response (Type 3) to indicate the desire for an Expanded authentication Type. If the authenticator can accommodate this preference, it will respond with an Expanded Type Request (Type 254).

Security Claims (see Section 7.2):

Auth. mechanism:	None
Ciphersuite negotiation:	No
Mutual authentication:	No
Integrity protection:	No
Replay protection:	No
Confidentiality:	No
Key derivation:	No
Key strength:	N/A
Dictionary attack prot.:	N/A
Fast reconnect:	No
Crypt. binding:	N/A
Session independence:	N/A
Fragmentation:	No
Channel binding:	No

5.3.2. Expanded Nak

Description

The Expanded Nak Type is valid only in Response messages. It MUST be sent only in reply to a Request of Type 254 (Expanded Type) where the authentication Type is unacceptable. The Expanded Nak Type uses the Expanded Type format itself, and the Response contains one or more authentication Types desired by the peer, all in Expanded Type format. Type zero (0) is used to indicate that the sender has no viable alternatives. The general format of the Expanded Type is described in Section 5.7.

Since the Expanded Nak Type is valid only in Responses and has very limited functionality, it MUST NOT be used as a general purpose error indication, such as for communication of error messages, or negotiation of parameters specific to a particular EAP method.

Code

2 for Response.

Identifier

The Identifier field is one octet and aids in matching Responses with Requests. The Identifier field of an Expanded Nak Response MUST match the Identifier field of the Request packet that it is sent in response to.

Length

>=20

Type

254

Vendor-Id

0 (IETF)

Vendor-Type

3 (Nak)

Vendor-Data

The Expanded Nak Type is only sent when the Request contains an Expanded Type (254) as defined in Section 5.7. The Vendor-Data field of the Nak Response MUST contain one or more authentication Types (4 or greater), all in expanded format, 8 octets per Type, or the value zero (0), also in Expanded Type format, to indicate no proposed alternative. The desired authentication Types may include a mixture of Vendor-Specific and IETF Types. For example, an Expanded Nak

Response indicating a preference for OTP (Type 5), and an MIT (Vendor-Id=20) Expanded Type of 6 would appear as follows:

```
 0                   1                   2                   3
 0 1 2 3 4 5 6 7 8 9 0 1 2 3 4 5 6 7 8 9 0 1 2 3 4 5 6 7 8 9 0 1
+-+-+-+-+-+-+-+-+-+-+-+-+-+-+-+-+-+-+-+-+-+-+-+-+-+-+-+-+-+-+-+-+
|       2       |   Identifier  |            Length=28          |
+-+-+-+-+-+-+-+-+-+-+-+-+-+-+-+-+-+-+-+-+-+-+-+-+-+-+-+-+-+-+-+-+
|   Type=254    |                   0 (IETF)                    |
+-+-+-+-+-+-+-+-+-+-+-+-+-+-+-+-+-+-+-+-+-+-+-+-+-+-+-+-+-+-+-+-+
|                               3 (Nak)                         |
+-+-+-+-+-+-+-+-+-+-+-+-+-+-+-+-+-+-+-+-+-+-+-+-+-+-+-+-+-+-+-+-+
|   Type=254    |                   0 (IETF)                    |
+-+-+-+-+-+-+-+-+-+-+-+-+-+-+-+-+-+-+-+-+-+-+-+-+-+-+-+-+-+-+-+-+
|                               5 (OTP)                         |
+-+-+-+-+-+-+-+-+-+-+-+-+-+-+-+-+-+-+-+-+-+-+-+-+-+-+-+-+-+-+-+-+
|   Type=254    |                   20 (MIT)                    |
+-+-+-+-+-+-+-+-+-+-+-+-+-+-+-+-+-+-+-+-+-+-+-+-+-+-+-+-+-+-+-+-+
|                               6                               |
+-+-+-+-+-+-+-+-+-+-+-+-+-+-+-+-+-+-+-+-+-+-+-+-+-+-+-+-+-+-+-+-+
```

An Expanded Nak Response indicating a no desired alternative would appear as follows:

```
 0                   1                   2                   3
 0 1 2 3 4 5 6 7 8 9 0 1 2 3 4 5 6 7 8 9 0 1 2 3 4 5 6 7 8 9 0 1
+-+-+-+-+-+-+-+-+-+-+-+-+-+-+-+-+-+-+-+-+-+-+-+-+-+-+-+-+-+-+-+-+
|       2       |   Identifier  |            Length=20          |
+-+-+-+-+-+-+-+-+-+-+-+-+-+-+-+-+-+-+-+-+-+-+-+-+-+-+-+-+-+-+-+-+
|   Type=254    |                   0 (IETF)                    |
+-+-+-+-+-+-+-+-+-+-+-+-+-+-+-+-+-+-+-+-+-+-+-+-+-+-+-+-+-+-+-+-+
|                               3 (Nak)                         |
+-+-+-+-+-+-+-+-+-+-+-+-+-+-+-+-+-+-+-+-+-+-+-+-+-+-+-+-+-+-+-+-+
|   Type=254    |                   0 (IETF)                    |
+-+-+-+-+-+-+-+-+-+-+-+-+-+-+-+-+-+-+-+-+-+-+-+-+-+-+-+-+-+-+-+-+
|                               0 (No alternative)              |
+-+-+-+-+-+-+-+-+-+-+-+-+-+-+-+-+-+-+-+-+-+-+-+-+-+-+-+-+-+-+-+-+
```

Security Claims (see Section 7.2):

Auth. mechanism:	None
Ciphersuite negotiation:	No
Mutual authentication:	No
Integrity protection:	No
Replay protection:	No
Confidentiality:	No
Key derivation:	No
Key strength:	N/A
Dictionary attack prot.:	N/A
Fast reconnect:	No
Crypt. binding:	N/A
Session independence:	N/A
Fragmentation:	No
Channel binding:	No

5.4. MD5-Challenge

Description

The MD5-Challenge Type is analogous to the PPP CHAP protocol [RFC1994] (with MD5 as the specified algorithm). The Request contains a "challenge" message to the peer. A Response MUST be sent in reply to the Request. The Response MAY be either of Type 4 (MD5-Challenge), Nak (Type 3), or Expanded Nak (Type 254). The Nak reply indicates the peer's desired authentication Type(s). EAP peer and EAP server implementations MUST support the MD5-Challenge mechanism. An authenticator that supports only pass-through MUST allow communication with a backend authentication server that is capable of supporting MD5-Challenge, although the EAP authenticator implementation need not support MD5-Challenge itself. However, if the EAP authenticator can be configured to authenticate peers locally (e.g., not operate in pass-through), then the requirement for support of the MD5-Challenge mechanism applies.

Note that the use of the Identifier field in the MD5-Challenge Type is different from that described in [RFC1994]. EAP allows for retransmission of MD5-Challenge Request packets, while [RFC1994] states that both the Identifier and Challenge fields MUST change each time a Challenge (the CHAP equivalent of the MD5-Challenge Request packet) is sent.

NOTE [RFC1994] treats the shared secret as an octet string, and does not specify how it is entered into the system (or if it is handled by the user at all). EAP MD5-Challenge implementations MAY support entering passphrases with non-ASCII characters. See Section 5 for instructions how the input should be processed and encoded into octets.

Type

4

Type-Data

The contents of the Type-Data field is summarized below. For reference on the use of these fields, see the PPP Challenge Handshake Authentication Protocol [RFC1994].

```
 0                   1                   2                   3
 0 1 2 3 4 5 6 7 8 9 0 1 2 3 4 5 6 7 8 9 0 1 2 3 4 5 6 7 8 9 0 1
+-+-+-+-+-+-+-+-+-+-+-+-+-+-+-+-+-+-+-+-+-+-+-+-+-+-+-+-+-+-+-+-+
| value-Size    | value ...
+-+-+-+-+-+-+-+-+-+-+-+-+-+-+-+-+-+-+-+-+-+-+-+-+-+-+-+-+-+-+-+-+
| Name ...
+-+-+-+-+-+-+-+-+-+-+-+-+-+-+
```

Security Claims (see Section 7.2):

Auth. mechanism:	Password or pre-shared key.
Ciphersuite negotiation:	No
Mutual authentication:	No
Integrity protection:	No
Replay protection:	No
Confidentiality:	No
Key derivation:	No
Key strength:	N/A
Dictionary attack prot.:	No
Fast reconnect:	No
Crypt. binding:	N/A
Session independence:	N/A
Fragmentation:	No
Channel binding:	No

5.5. One-Time Password (OTP)

Description

The One-Time Password system is defined in "A One-Time Password System" [RFC2289] and "OTP Extended Responses" [RFC2243]. The Request contains an OTP challenge in the format described in [RFC2289]. A Response MUST be sent in reply to the Request. The Response MUST be of Type 5 (OTP), Nak (Type 3), or Expanded Nak (Type 254). The Nak Response indicates the peer's desired authentication Type(s). The EAP OTP method is intended for use with the One-Time Password system only, and MUST NOT be used to provide support for cleartext passwords.

Type

5

Type-Data

The Type-Data field contains the OTP "challenge" as a displayable message in the Request. In the Response, this field is used for the 6 words from the OTP dictionary [RFC2289]. The messages MUST NOT be null terminated. The length of the field is derived from the Length field of the Request/Reply packet.

> **NOTE** [RFC2289] does not specify how the secret pass-phrase is entered by the user, or how the pass-phrase is converted into octets. EAP OTP implementations MAY support entering passphrases with non-ASCII characters. See Section 5 for instructions on how the input should be processed and encoded into octets.

Security Claims (see Section 7.2):

Auth. mechanism:	One-Time Password
Ciphersuite negotiation:	No
Mutual authentication:	No
Integrity protection:	No
Replay protection:	Yes
Confidentiality:	No
Key derivation:	No
Key strength:	N/A
Dictionary attack prot.:	No
Fast reconnect:	No
Crypt. binding:	N/A
Session independence:	N/A
Fragmentation:	No
Channel binding:	No

5.6. Generic Token Card (GTC)

Description

The Generic Token Card Type is defined for use with various Token Card implementations which require user input. The Request contains a displayable message and the Response contains the Token Card information necessary for authentication. Typically, this would be information read by a user from the Token card device and entered as ASCII text. A Response MUST be sent in reply to the Request. The Response MUST be of Type 6 (GTC), Nak (Type 3), or Expanded Nak (Type 254). The Nak Response indicates the peer's desired authentication Type(s). The EAP GTC method is intended for use with the Token Cards supporting challenge/response authentication and MUST NOT be used to provide support for cleartext passwords in the absence of a protected tunnel with server authentication.

Type

6

Type-Data

The Type-Data field in the Request contains a displayable message greater than zero octets in length. The length of the message is determined by the Length field of the Request packet. The message MUST NOT be null terminated. A Response MUST be sent in reply to the Request with a Type field of 6 (Generic Token Card). The Response contains data from the Token Card required for authentication. The length of the data is determined by the Length field of the Response packet.

EAP GTC implementations MAY support entering a response with non-ASCII characters. See Section 5 for instructions how the input should be processed and encoded into octets.

Security Claims (see Section 7.2):

Auth. mechanism:	Hardware token.
Ciphersuite negotiation:	No
Mutual authentication:	No
Integrity protection:	No
Replay protection:	No
Confidentiality:	No
Key derivation:	No
Key strength:	N/A
Dictionary attack prot.:	No
Fast reconnect:	No
Crypt. binding:	N/A
Session independence:	N/A
Fragmentation:	No
Channel binding:	No

5.7. Expanded Types

Description

Since many of the existing uses of EAP are vendor-specific, the Expanded method Type is available to allow vendors to support their own Expanded Types not suitable for general usage.

The Expanded Type is also used to expand the global Method Type space beyond the original 255 values. A Vendor-Id of 0 maps the original 255 possible Types onto a space of $2^{32}-1$ possible Types. (Type 0 is only used in a Nak Response to indicate no acceptable alternative).

An implementation that supports the Expanded attribute MUST treat EAP Types that are less than 256 equivalently, whether they appear as a single octet or as the 32-bit Vendor-Type within an Expanded Type where Vendor-Id is 0. Peers not equipped to interpret the Expanded Type MUST send a Nak as described in Section 5.3.1, and negotiate a more suitable authentication method.

A summary of the Expanded Type format is shown below. The fields are transmitted from left to right.

```
 0                   1                   2                   3
 0 1 2 3 4 5 6 7 8 9 0 1 2 3 4 5 6 7 8 9 0 1 2 3 4 5 6 7 8 9 0 1
+-+-+-+-+-+-+-+-+-+-+-+-+-+-+-+-+-+-+-+-+-+-+-+-+-+-+-+-+-+-+-+-+
|     Type      |               Vendor-Id                       |
+-+-+-+-+-+-+-+-+-+-+-+-+-+-+-+-+-+-+-+-+-+-+-+-+-+-+-+-+-+-+-+-+
|                          Vendor-Type                          |
+-+-+-+-+-+-+-+-+-+-+-+-+-+-+-+-+-+-+-+-+-+-+-+-+-+-+-+-+-+-+-+-+
|              Vendor data...
+-+-+-+-+-+-+-+-+-+-+-+-+-+-+-+-+-+-+-+-+
```

Type

254 for Expanded Type

Vendor-Id

The Vendor-Id is 3 octets and represents the SMI Network Management Private Enterprise Code of the Vendor in network byte order, as allocated by IANA. A Vendor-Id of zero is reserved for use by the IETF in providing an expanded global EAP Type space.

Vendor-Type

The Vendor-Type field is four octets and represents the vendor-specific method Type.

If the Vendor-Id is zero, the Vendor-Type field is an extension and superset of the existing namespace for EAP Types. The first 256 Types are reserved for compatibility with single-octet EAP Types that have already been assigned or may be assigned in the future. Thus, EAP Types from 0 through 255 are semantically identical, whether they appear as single octet EAP Types or as Vendor-Types when Vendor-Id is zero. There is one exception to this rule: Expanded Nak and Legacy Nak packets share the same Type, but must be treated differently because they have a different format.

Vendor-Data

The Vendor-Data field is defined by the vendor. Where a Vendor-Id of zero is present, the Vendor-Data field will be used for transporting the contents of EAP methods of Types defined by the IETF.

5.8. Experimental

Description

The Experimental Type has no fixed format or content. It is intended for use when experimenting with new EAP Types. This Type is intended for experimental and testing purposes. No guarantee is made for interoperability between peers using this Type, as outlined in [RFC3692].

Type

255

Type-Data

Undefined

6. IANA Considerations

This section provides guidance to the Internet Assigned Numbers Authority (IANA) regarding registration of values related to the EAP protocol, in accordance with BCP 26, [RFC2434].

There are two name spaces in EAP that require registration: Packet Codes and method Types.

EAP is not intended as a general-purpose protocol, and allocations SHOULD NOT be made for purposes unrelated to authentication.

The following terms are used here with the meanings defined in BCP 26: "name space", "assigned value", "registration".

The following policies are used here with the meanings defined in BCP 26: "Private Use", "First Come First Served", "Expert Review", "Specification Required", "IETF Consensus", "Standards Action".

For registration requests where a Designated Expert should be consulted, the responsible IESG area director should appoint the Designated Expert. The intention is that any allocation will be accompanied by a published RFC. But in order to allow for the allocation of values prior to the RFC being approved for publication, the Designated Expert can approve allocations once it seems clear that an RFC will be published. The Designated expert will post a request to the EAP WG mailing list (or a successor designated by the Area Director) for comment and review, including an Internet-Draft. Before a period of 30 days has passed, the Designated Expert will either approve or deny the registration request and publish a notice of the decision to the EAP WG mailing list or its successor, as well as informing IANA. A denial notice must be justified by an explanation, and in the cases where it is possible, concrete suggestions on how the request can be modified so as to become acceptable should be provided.

6.1. Packet Codes

Packet Codes have a range from 1 to 255, of which 1-4 have been allocated. Because a new Packet Code has considerable impact on interoperability, a new Packet Code requires Standards Action, and should be allocated starting at 5.

6.2. Method Types

The original EAP method Type space has a range from 1 to 255, and is the scarcest resource in EAP, and thus must be allocated with care. Method Types 1-45 have been allocated, with 20 available for re-use. Method Types 20 and 46-191 may be allocated on the advice of a Designated Expert, with Specification Required.

Allocation of blocks of method Types (more than one for a given purpose) should require IETF Consensus. EAP Type Values 192-253 are reserved and allocation requires Standards Action.

Method Type 254 is allocated for the Expanded Type. Where the Vendor-Id field is non-zero, the Expanded Type is used for functions specific only to one vendor's implementation of EAP, where no interoperability is deemed useful. When used with a Vendor-Id of zero, method Type 254 can also be used to provide for an expanded IETF method Type space. Method Type values 256-4294967295 may be allocated after Type values 1-191 have been allocated, on the advice of a Designated Expert, with Specification Required.

Method Type 255 is allocated for Experimental use, such as testing of new EAP methods before a permanent Type is allocated.

7. Security Considerations

This section defines a generic threat model as well as the EAP method security claims mitigating those threats.

It is expected that the generic threat model and corresponding security claims will used to define EAP method requirements for use in specific environments. An example of such a requirements analysis is provided in [IEEE-802.11i-req]. A security claims section is required in EAP method specifications, so that EAP methods can be evaluated against the requirements.

7.1. Threat Model

EAP was developed for use with PPP [RFC1661] and was later adapted for use in wired IEEE 802 networks [IEEE-802] in [IEEE-802.1X]. Subsequently, EAP has been proposed for use on wireless LAN networks and over the Internet. In all these situations, it is possible for an attacker to gain access to links over which EAP packets are transmitted. For example, attacks on telephone infrastructure are documented in [DECEPTION].

An attacker with access to the link may carry out a number of attacks, including:

1. An attacker may try to discover user identities by snooping authentication traffic.

2. An attacker may try to modify or spoof EAP packets.

3. An attacker may launch denial of service attacks by spoofing lower layer indications or Success/Failure packets, by replaying EAP packets, or by generating packets with overlapping Identifiers.

4. An attacker may attempt to recover the pass-phrase by mounting an offline dictionary attack.

5. An attacker may attempt to convince the peer to connect to an untrusted network by mounting a man-in-the-middle attack.

6. An attacker may attempt to disrupt the EAP negotiation in order cause a weak authentication method to be selected.

7. An attacker may attempt to recover keys by taking advantage of weak key derivation techniques used within EAP methods.

8. An attacker may attempt to take advantage of weak ciphersuites subsequently used after the EAP conversation is complete.

9. An attacker may attempt to perform downgrading attacks on lower layer ciphersuite negotiation in order to ensure that a weaker ciphersuite is used subsequently to EAP authentication.

10. An attacker acting as an authenticator may provide incorrect information to the EAP peer and/or server via out-of-band mechanisms (such as via a AAA or lower layer protocol). This includes impersonating another authenticator, or providing inconsistent information to the peer and EAP server.

Depending on the lower layer, these attacks may be carried out without requiring physical proximity. Where EAP is used over wireless networks, EAP packets may be forwarded by authenticators (e.g., pre-authentication) so that the attacker need not be within the coverage area of an authenticator in order to carry out an attack on it or its peers. Where EAP is used over the Internet, attacks may be carried out at an even greater distance.

7.2. Security Claims

In order to clearly articulate the security provided by an EAP method, EAP method specifications MUST include a Security Claims section, including the following declarations:

a. Mechanism. This is a statement of the authentication technology: certificates, pre-shared keys, passwords, token cards, etc.

b. Security claims. This is a statement of the claimed security properties of the method, using terms defined in Section 7.2.1: mutual authentication, integrity protection, replay protection, confidentiality, key derivation, dictionary attack resistance, fast reconnect, cryptographic binding. The Security Claims section of an EAP method specification SHOULD provide justification for the claims that are made. This can be accomplished by including a proof in an Appendix, or including a reference to a proof.

c. Key strength. If the method derives keys, then the effective key strength MUST be estimated. This estimate is meant for potential users of the method to determine if the keys produced are strong enough for the intended application.

The effective key strength SHOULD be stated as a number of bits, defined as follows: If the effective key strength is N bits, the best currently known methods to recover the key (with non-negligible probability) require, on average, an effort comparable to $2^{(N-1)}$ operations of a typical block cipher. The statement SHOULD be accompanied by a short rationale, explaining how this number was derived. This explanation SHOULD include the parameters required to achieve the stated key strength based on current knowledge of the algorithms.

NOTE Although it is difficult to define what "comparable effort" and "typical block cipher" exactly mean, reasonable approximations are sufficient here. Refer to e.g. [SILVERMAN] for more discussion.

The key strength depends on the methods used to derive the keys. For instance, if keys are derived from a shared secret (such as a password or a long-term secret), and possibly some public information such as nonces, the effective key strength is limited by the strength of the long-term secret (assuming that the derivation procedure is computationally simple). To take another example, when using public key algorithms, the strength of the symmetric key depends on the strength of the public keys used.

d. Description of key hierarchy. EAP methods deriving keys MUST either provide a reference to a key hierarchy specification, or describe how Master Session Keys (MSKs) and Extended Master Session Keys (EMSKs) are to be derived.

e. Indication of vulnerabilities. In addition to the security claims that are made, the specification MUST indicate which of the security claims detailed in Section 7.2.1 are NOT being made.

7.2.1. Security Claims Terminology for EAP Methods

These terms are used to describe the security properties of EAP methods:

Protected ciphersuite negotiation: This refers to the ability of an EAP method to negotiate the ciphersuite used to protect the EAP conversation, as well as to integrity protect the negotiation. It does not refer to the ability to negotiate the ciphersuite used to protect data.

Mutual authentication: This refers to an EAP method in which, within an interlocked exchange, the authenticator authenticates the peer and the peer authenticates the authenticator. Two independent one-way methods, running in opposite directions do not provide mutual authentication as defined here.

Integrity protection: This refers to providing data origin authentication and protection against unauthorized modification of information for EAP packets (including EAP Requests and Responses). When making this claim, a method specification MUST describe the EAP packets and fields within the EAP packet that are protected.

Replay protection: This refers to protection against replay of an EAP method or its messages, including success and failure result indications.

Confidentiality: This refers to encryption of EAP messages, including EAP Requests and Responses, and success and failure result indications. A method making this claim MUST support identity protection (see Section 7.3).

Key derivation This refers to the ability of the EAP method to derive exportable keying material, such as the Master Session Key (MSK), and Extended Master Session Key (EMSK). The MSK is used only for further key derivation, not directly for protection of the EAP conversation or subsequent data. Use of the EMSK is reserved.

Key strength: If the effective key strength is N bits, the best currently known methods to recover the key (with non-negligible probability) require, on average, an effort comparable to $2^{(N-1)}$ operations of a typical block cipher.

Dictionary attack resistance: Where password authentication is used, passwords are commonly selected from a small set (as compared to a set of N-bit keys), which raises a concern about dictionary attacks. A method may be said to provide protection against dictionary attacks if, when it uses a password as a secret, the method does not allow an offline attack that has a work factor based on the number of passwords in an attacker's dictionary.

Fast reconnect: The ability, in the case where a security association has been previously established, to create a new or refreshed security association more efficiently or in a smaller number of round-trips.

Cryptographic binding: The demonstration of the EAP peer to the EAP server that a single entity has acted as the EAP peer for all methods executed within a tunnel method. Binding MAY also imply that the EAP server demonstrates to the peer that a single entity has acted as the EAP server for all methods executed within a tunnel method. If executed correctly, binding serves to mitigate man-in-the-middle vulnerabilities.

Session independence: The demonstration that passive attacks (such as capture of the EAP conversation) or active attacks (including compromise of the MSK or EMSK) does not enable compromise of subsequent or prior MSKs or EMSKs.

Fragmentation: This refers to whether an EAP method supports fragmentation and reassembly. As noted in Section 3.1, EAP methods should support fragmentation and reassembly if EAP packets can exceed the minimum MTU of 1020 octets.

Channel binding: The communication within an EAP method of integrity-protected channel properties such as endpoint identifiers which can be compared to values communicated via out of band mechanisms (such as via a AAA or lower layer protocol).

> **NOTE** This list of security claims is not exhaustive. Additional properties, such as additional denial-of-service protection, may be relevant as well.

7.3. Identity Protection

An Identity exchange is optional within the EAP conversation. Therefore, it is possible to omit the Identity exchange entirely, or to use a method-specific identity exchange once a protected channel has been established.

However, where roaming is supported as described in [RFC2607], it may be necessary to locate the appropriate backend authentication server before the authentication conversation can proceed. The realm portion of the Network Access Identifier (NAI) [RFC2486] is typically included within the EAP-Response/Identity in order to enable the authentication exchange to be routed to the appropriate backend authentication server. Therefore, while the peer-name portion of the NAI may be omitted in the EAP-Response/Identity where proxies or relays are present, the realm portion may be required.

It is possible for the identity in the identity response to be different from the identity authenticated by the EAP method. This may be intentional in the case of identity privacy. An EAP method SHOULD use the authenticated identity when making access control decisions.

7.4. Man-in-the-Middle Attacks

Where EAP is tunneled within another protocol that omits peer authentication, there exists a potential vulnerability to a man-in-the-middle attack. For details, see [BINDING] and [MITM].

As noted in Section 2.1, EAP does not permit untunneled sequences of authentication methods. Were a sequence of EAP authentication methods to be permitted, the peer might not have proof that a single entity has acted as the authenticator for all EAP methods within the sequence. For example, an authenticator might terminate one EAP method, then forward the next method in the sequence to another party without the peer's knowledge or consent. Similarly, the authenticator might not have proof that a single entity has acted as the peer for all EAP methods within the sequence.

Tunneling EAP within another protocol enables an attack by a rogue EAP authenticator tunneling EAP to a legitimate server. Where the tunneling protocol is used for key establishment but does not require peer authentication, an attacker convincing a legitimate peer to connect to it will be able to tunnel EAP packets to a legitimate server, successfully authenticating and obtaining the key. This allows the attacker to successfully establish itself as a man-in-the-middle, gaining access to the network, as well as the ability to decrypt data traffic between the legitimate peer and server.

This attack may be mitigated by the following measures:

a. Requiring mutual authentication within EAP tunneling mechanisms.

b. Requiring cryptographic binding between the EAP tunneling protocol and the tunneled EAP methods. Where cryptographic binding is supported, a mechanism is also needed to protect against downgrade attacks that would bypass it. For further details on cryptographic binding, see [BINDING].

c. Limiting the EAP methods authorized for use without protection, based on peer and authenticator policy.

d. Avoiding the use of tunnels when a single, strong method is available.

7.5. Packet Modification Attacks

While EAP methods may support per-packet data origin authentication, integrity, and replay protection, support is not provided within the EAP layer.

Since the Identifier is only a single octet, it is easy to guess, allowing an attacker to successfully inject or replay EAP packets. An attacker may also modify EAP headers (Code, Identifier, Length, Type) within EAP packets where the header is unprotected. This could cause packets to be inappropriately discarded or misinterpreted.

To protect EAP packets against modification, spoofing, or replay, methods supporting protected ciphersuite negotiation, mutual authentication, and key derivation, as well as integrity and replay protection, are recommended. See Section 7.2.1 for definitions of these security claims.

Method-specific MICs may be used to provide protection. If a per-packet MIC is employed within an EAP method, then peers, authentication servers, and authenticators not operating in pass-through mode MUST validate the MIC. MIC validation failures SHOULD be logged. Whether a MIC validation failure is considered a fatal error or not is determined by the EAP method specification.

It is RECOMMENDED that methods providing integrity protection of EAP packets include coverage of all the EAP header fields, including the Code, Identifier, Length, Type, and Type-Data fields.

Since EAP messages of Types Identity, Notification, and Nak do not include their own MIC, it may be desirable for the EAP method MIC to cover information contained within these messages, as well as the header of each EAP message.

To provide protection, EAP also may be encapsulated within a protected channel created by protocols such as ISAKMP [RFC2408], as is done in [IKEv2] or within TLS [RFC2246]. However, as noted in Section 7.4, EAP tunneling may result in a man-in-the-middle vulnerability.

Existing EAP methods define message integrity checks (MICs) that cover more than one EAP packet. For example, EAP-TLS [RFC2716] defines a MIC over a TLS record that could be split into multiple fragments; within the FINISHED message, the MIC is computed over previous messages. Where the MIC covers more than one EAP packet, a MIC validation failure is typically considered a fatal error.

Within EAP-TLS [RFC2716], a MIC validation failure is treated as a fatal error, since that is what is specified in TLS [RFC2246]. However, it is also possible to develop EAP methods that support per-packet MICs, and respond to verification failures by silently discarding the offending packet.

In this document, descriptions of EAP message handling assume that per-packet MIC validation, where it occurs, is effectively performed as though it occurs before sending any responses or changing the state of the host which received the packet.

7.6. Dictionary Attacks

Password authentication algorithms such as EAP-MD5, MS-CHAPv1 [RFC2433], and Kerberos V [RFC1510] are known to be vulnerable to dictionary attacks. MS-CHAPv1 vulnerabilities are documented in [PPTPv1]; MS-CHAPv2 vulnerabilities are documented in [PPTPv2]; Kerberos vulnerabilities are described in [KRBATTACK], [KRBLIM], and [KERB4WEAK].

In order to protect against dictionary attacks, authentication methods resistant to dictionary attacks (as defined in Section 7.2.1) are recommended.

If an authentication algorithm is used that is known to be vulnerable to dictionary attacks, then the conversation may be tunneled within a protected channel in order to provide additional protection. However, as noted in Section 7.4, EAP tunneling may result in a man-in-the-middle vulnerability, and therefore dictionary attack resistant methods are preferred.

7.7. Connection to an Untrusted Network

With EAP methods supporting one-way authentication, such as EAP-MD5, the peer does not authenticate the authenticator, making the peer vulnerable to attack by a rogue authenticator. Methods supporting mutual authentication (as defined in Section 7.2.1) address this vulnerability.

In EAP there is no requirement that authentication be full duplex or that the same protocol be used in both directions. It is perfectly acceptable for different protocols to be used in each direction. This will, of course, depend on the specific protocols negotiated. However, in general, completing a single unitary mutual authentication is preferable to two one-way authentications, one in each direction. This is because separate authentications that are not bound cryptographically so as to demonstrate they are part of the same session are subject to man-in-the-middle attacks, as discussed in Section 7.4.

7.8. Negotiation Attacks

In a negotiation attack, the attacker attempts to convince the peer and authenticator to negotiate a less secure EAP method. EAP does not provide protection for Nak Response packets, although it is possible for a method to include coverage of Nak Responses within a method-specific MIC.

Within or associated with each authenticator, it is not anticipated that a particular named peer will support a choice of methods. This would make the peer vulnerable to attacks that negotiate the least secure method from among a set. Instead, for each named peer, there SHOULD be an indication of exactly one method used to authenticate that peer name. If a peer needs to make use of different authentication methods under different circumstances, then distinct identities SHOULD be employed, each of which identifies exactly one authentication method.

7.9. Implementation Idiosyncrasies

The interaction of EAP with lower layers such as PPP and IEEE 802 are highly implementation dependent.

For example, upon failure of authentication, some PPP implementations do not terminate the link, instead limiting traffic in Network-Layer Protocols to a filtered subset, which in turn allows the peer the opportunity to update secrets or send mail to the network administrator indicating a problem. Similarly, while an authentication failure will result in denied access to the controlled port in [IEEE-802.1X], limited traffic may be permitted on the uncontrolled port.

In EAP there is no provision for retries of failed authentication. However, in PPP the LCP state machine can renegotiate the authentication protocol at any time, thus allowing a new attempt. Similarly, in IEEE 802.1X the Supplicant or Authenticator can re-authenticate at any time. It is recommended that any counters used for authentication failure not be reset until after successful authentication, or subsequent termination of the failed link.

7.10. Key Derivation

It is possible for the peer and EAP server to mutually authenticate and derive keys. In order to provide keying material for use in a subsequently negotiated ciphersuite, an EAP method supporting key derivation MUST export a Master Session Key (MSK) of at least 64 octets, and an Extended Master Session Key (EMSK) of at least 64 octets. EAP Methods deriving keys MUST provide for mutual authentication between the EAP peer and the EAP Server.

The MSK and EMSK MUST NOT be used directly to protect data; however, they are of sufficient size to enable derivation of a AAA-Key subsequently used to derive Transient Session Keys (TSKs) for use with the selected ciphersuite. Each ciphersuite is responsible for specifying how to derive the TSKs from the AAA-Key.

The AAA-Key is derived from the keying material exported by the EAP method (MSK and EMSK). This derivation occurs on the AAA server. In many existing protocols that use EAP, the AAA-Key and MSK are equivalent, but more complicated mechanisms are possible (see [KEYFRAME] for details).

EAP methods SHOULD ensure the freshness of the MSK and EMSK, even in cases where one party may not have a high quality random number generator. A RECOMMENDED method is for each party to provide a nonce of at least 128 bits, used in the derivation of the MSK and EMSK.

EAP methods export the MSK and EMSK, but not Transient Session Keys so as to allow EAP methods to be ciphersuite and media independent. Keying material exported by EAP methods MUST be independent of the ciphersuite negotiated to protect data.

Depending on the lower layer, EAP methods may run before or after ciphersuite negotiation, so that the selected ciphersuite may not be known to the EAP method. By providing keying material usable with any ciphersuite, EAP methods can used with a wide range of ciphersuites and media.

In order to preserve algorithm independence, EAP methods deriving keys SHOULD support (and document) the protected negotiation of the ciphersuite used to protect the EAP conversation between the peer and server. This is distinct from the ciphersuite negotiated between the peer and authenticator, used to protect data.

The strength of Transient Session Keys (TSKs) used to protect data is ultimately dependent on the strength of keys generated by the EAP method. If an EAP method cannot produce keying material of sufficient strength, then the TSKs may be subject to a brute force attack. In order to enable deployments requiring strong keys, EAP methods supporting key derivation SHOULD be capable of generating an MSK and EMSK, each with an effective key strength of at least 128 bits.

Methods supporting key derivation MUST demonstrate cryptographic separation between the MSK and EMSK branches of the EAP key hierarchy. Without violating a fundamental cryptographic assumption (such as the non-invertibility of a one-way function), an attacker recovering the MSK or EMSK MUST NOT be able to recover the other quantity with a level of effort less than brute force.

Non-overlapping substrings of the MSK MUST be cryptographically separate from each other, as defined in Section 7.2.1. That is, knowledge of one substring MUST NOT help in recovering some other substring without breaking some hard cryptographic assumption. This is required because some existing ciphersuites form TSKs by simply splitting the AAA-Key to pieces of appropriate length. Likewise, non-overlapping substrings of the EMSK MUST be cryptographically separate from each other, and from substrings of the MSK.

The EMSK is reserved for future use and MUST remain on the EAP peer and EAP server where it is derived; it MUST NOT be transported to, or shared with, additional parties, or used to derive any other keys. (This restriction will be relaxed in a future document that specifies how the EMSK can be used.)

Since EAP does not provide for explicit key lifetime negotiation, EAP peers, authenticators, and authentication servers MUST be prepared for situations in which one of the parties discards the key state, which remains valid on another party.

This specification does not provide detailed guidance on how EAP methods derive the MSK and EMSK, how the AAA-Key is derived from the MSK and/or EMSK, or how the TSKs are derived from the AAA-Key.

The development and validation of key derivation algorithms is difficult, and as a result, EAP methods SHOULD re-use well established and analyzed mechanisms for key derivation (such as those specified in IKE [RFC2409] or TLS [RFC2246]), rather than inventing new ones. EAP methods SHOULD also utilize well established and analyzed mechanisms for MSK and EMSK derivation. Further details on EAP Key Derivation are provided within [KEYFRAME].

7.11. Weak Ciphersuites

If after the initial EAP authentication, data packets are sent without per-packet authentication, integrity, and replay protection, an attacker with access to the media can inject packets, "flip bits" within existing packets, replay packets, or even hijack the session completely. Without per-packet confidentiality, it is possible to snoop data packets.

To protect against data modification, spoofing, or snooping, it is recommended that EAP methods supporting mutual authentication and key derivation (as defined by Section 7.2.1) be used, along with lower layers providing per-packet confidentiality, authentication, integrity, and replay protection.

Additionally, if the lower layer performs ciphersuite negotiation, it should be understood that EAP does not provide by itself integrity protection of that negotiation. Therefore, in order to avoid downgrading attacks which would lead to weaker ciphersuites being used, clients implementing lower layer ciphersuite negotiation SHOULD protect against negotiation downgrading.

This can be done by enabling users to configure which ciphersuites are acceptable as a matter of security policy, or the ciphersuite negotiation MAY be authenticated using keying material derived from the EAP authentication and a MIC algorithm agreed upon in advance by lower-layer peers.

7.12. Link Layer

There are reliability and security issues with link layer indications in PPP, IEEE 802 LANs, and IEEE 802.11 wireless LANs:

a. PPP. In PPP, link layer indications such as LCP-Terminate (a link failure indication) and NCP (a link success indication) are not authenticated or integrity protected. They can therefore be spoofed by an attacker with access to the link.

b. IEEE 802. IEEE 802.1X EAPOL-Start and EAPOL-Logoff frames are not authenticated or integrity protected. They can therefore be spoofed by an attacker with access to the link.

c. IEEE 802.11. In IEEE 802.11, link layer indications include Disassociate and Deauthenticate frames (link failure indications), and the first message of the 4-way handshake (link success indication). These messages are not authenticated or integrity protected, and although they are not forwardable, they are spoofable by an attacker within range.

In IEEE 802.11, IEEE 802.1X data frames may be sent as Class 3 unicast data frames, and are therefore forwardable. This implies that while EAPOL-Start and EAPOL-Logoff messages may be authenticated and integrity protected, they can be spoofed by an authenticated attacker far from the target when "pre-authentication" is enabled.

In IEEE 802.11, a "link down" indication is an unreliable indication of link failure, since wireless signal strength can come and go and may be influenced by radio frequency interference generated by an attacker. To avoid unnecessary resets, it is advisable to damp these indications, rather than passing them directly to the EAP. Since EAP supports retransmission, it is robust against transient connectivity losses.

7.13. Separation of Authenticator and Backend Authentication Server

It is possible for the EAP peer and EAP server to mutually authenticate and derive a AAA-Key for a ciphersuite used to protect subsequent data traffic. This does not present an issue on the peer, since the peer and EAP client reside on the same machine; all that is required is for the client to derive the AAA-Key from the MSK and EMSK exported by the EAP method, and to subsequently pass a Transient Session Key (TSK) to the ciphersuite module.

However, in the case where the authenticator and authentication server reside on different machines, there are several implications for security.

a. Authentication will occur between the peer and the authentication server, not between the peer and the authenticator. This means that it is not possible for the peer to validate the identity of the authenticator that it is speaking to, using EAP alone.

b. As discussed in [RFC3579], the authenticator is dependent on the AAA protocol in order to know the outcome of an authentication conversation, and does not look at the encapsulated EAP packet (if one is present) to determine the outcome. In practice, this implies that the AAA protocol spoken between the authenticator and authentication server MUST support per-packet authentication, integrity, and replay protection.

c. After completion of the EAP conversation, where lower layer security services such as per-packet confidentiality, authentication, integrity, and replay protection will be enabled, a secure association protocol SHOULD be run between the peer and authenticator in order to provide mutual authentication between the peer and authenticator, guarantee liveness of transient session keys, provide protected ciphersuite and capabilities negotiation for subsequent data, and synchronize key usage.

d. A AAA-Key derived from the MSK and/or EMSK negotiated between the peer and authentication server MAY be transmitted to the authenticator. Therefore, a mechanism needs to be provided to transmit the AAA-Key from the authentication server to the authenticator that needs it. The specification of the AAA-key derivation, transport, and wrapping mechanisms is outside the scope of this document. Further details on AAA-Key Derivation are provided within [KEYFRAME].

7.14. Cleartext Passwords

This specification does not define a mechanism for cleartext password authentication. The omission is intentional. Use of cleartext passwords would allow the password to be captured by an attacker with access to a link over which EAP packets are transmitted.

Since protocols encapsulating EAP, such as RADIUS [RFC3579], may not provide confidentiality, EAP packets may be subsequently encapsulated for transport over the Internet where they may be captured by an attacker.

As a result, cleartext passwords cannot be securely used within EAP, except where encapsulated within a protected tunnel with server authentication. Some of the same risks apply to EAP methods without dictionary attack resistance, as defined in Section 7.2.1. For details, see Section 7.6.

7.15. Channel Binding

It is possible for a compromised or poorly implemented EAP authenticator to communicate incorrect information to the EAP peer and/or server. This may enable an authenticator to impersonate another authenticator or communicate incorrect information via out-of-band mechanisms (such as via a AAA or lower layer protocol).

Where EAP is used in pass-through mode, the EAP peer typically does not verify the identity of the pass-through authenticator, it only verifies that the pass-through authenticator is trusted by the EAP server. This creates a potential security vulnerability.

Section 4.3.7 of [RFC3579] describes how an EAP pass-through authenticator acting as a AAA client can be detected if it attempts to impersonate another authenticator (such by sending incorrect NAS-Identifier [RFC2865], NAS-IP-Address [RFC2865] or NAS-IPv6-Address [RFC3162] attributes via the AAA protocol). However, it is possible for a pass-through authenticator acting as a AAA client to provide correct information to the AAA server while communicating misleading information to the EAP peer via a lower layer protocol.

For example, it is possible for a compromised authenticator to utilize another authenticator's Called-Station-Id or NAS-Identifier in communicating with the EAP peer via a lower layer protocol, or for a pass-through authenticator acting as a AAA client to provide an incorrect peer Calling-Station-Id [RFC2865][RFC3580] to the AAA server via the AAA protocol.

In order to address this vulnerability, EAP methods may support a protected exchange of channel properties such as endpoint identifiers, including (but not limited to): Called-Station-Id [RFC2865][RFC3580], Calling-Station-Id [RFC2865][RFC3580], NAS-Identifier [RFC2865], NAS-IP-Address [RFC2865], and NAS-IPv6-Address [RFC3162].

Using such a protected exchange, it is possible to match the channel properties provided by the authenticator via out-of-band mechanisms against those exchanged within the EAP method. Where discrepancies are found, these SHOULD be logged; additional actions MAY also be taken, such as denying access.

7.16. Protected Result Indications

Within EAP, Success and Failure packets are neither acknowledged nor integrity protected. Result indications improve resilience to loss of Success and Failure packets when EAP is run over lower layers which do not support retransmission or synchronization of the authentication state. In media such as IEEE 802.11, which provides for retransmission, as well as synchronization of authentication state via the 4-way handshake defined in [IEEE-802.11i], additional resilience is typically of marginal benefit.

Depending on the method and circumstances, result indications can be spoofable by an attacker. A method is said to provide protected result indications if it supports result indications, as well as the "integrity protection" and "replay protection" claims. A method supporting protected result indications MUST indicate which result indications are protected, and which are not.

Protected result indications are not required to protect against rogue authenticators. Within a mutually authenticating method, requiring that the server authenticate to the peer before the peer will accept a Success packet prevents an attacker from acting as a rogue authenticator.

However, it is possible for an attacker to forge a Success packet after the server has authenticated to the peer, but before the peer has authenticated to the server. If the peer were to accept the forged Success packet and attempt to access the network when it had not yet successfully authenticated to the server, a denial of service attack could be mounted against the peer. After such an attack, if the lower layer supports failure indications, the authenticator can synchronize state with the peer by providing a lower layer failure indication. See Section 7.12 for details.

If a server were to authenticate the peer and send a Success packet prior to determining whether the peer has authenticated the authenticator, an idle timeout can occur if the authenticator is not authenticated by the peer. Where supported by the lower layer, an authenticator sensing the absence of the peer can free resources.

In a method supporting result indications, a peer that has authenticated the server does not consider the authentication successful until it receives an indication that the server successfully authenticated it. Similarly, a server that has successfully authenticated the peer does not consider the authentication successful until it receives an indication that the peer has authenticated the server.

In order to avoid synchronization problems, prior to sending a success result indication, it is desirable for the sender to verify that sufficient authorization exists for granting access, though, as discussed below, this is not always possible.

While result indications may enable synchronization of the authentication result between the peer and server, this does not guarantee that the peer and authenticator will be synchronized in terms of their authorization or that timeouts will not occur. For example, the EAP server may not be aware of an authorization decision made by a AAA proxy; the AAA server may check authorization only after authentication has completed successfully, to discover that authorization cannot be granted, or the AAA server may grant access but the authenticator may be unable to provide it due to a temporary lack of resources. In these situations, synchronization may only be achieved via lower layer result indications.

Success indications may be explicit or implicit. For example, where a method supports error messages, an implicit success indication may be defined as the reception of a specific message without a preceding error message. Failures are typically indicated explicitly. As described in Section 4.2, a peer silently discards a Failure packet received at a point where the method does not explicitly permit this to be sent. For example, a method providing its own error messages might require the peer to receive an error message prior to accepting a Failure packet.

Per-packet authentication, integrity, and replay protection of result indications protects against spoofing. Since protected result indications require use of a key for per-packet authentication and integrity protection, methods supporting protected result indications MUST also support the "key derivation", "mutual authentication", "integrity protection", and "replay protection" claims.

Protected result indications address some denial-of-service vulnerabilities due to spoofing of Success and Failure packets, though not all. EAP methods can typically provide protected result indications only in some circumstances. For example, errors can occur prior to key derivation, and so it may not be possible to protect all failure indications. It is also possible that result indications may not be supported in both directions or that synchronization may not be achieved in all modes of operation.

For example, within EAP-TLS [RFC2716], in the client authentication handshake, the server authenticates the peer, but does not receive a protected indication of whether the peer has authenticated it. In contrast, the peer authenticates the server and is aware of whether the server has authenticated it. In the session resumption handshake, the peer authenticates the server, but does not receive a protected indication of whether the server has authenticated it. In this mode, the server authenticates the peer and is aware of whether the peer has authenticated it.

8. Acknowledgements

This protocol derives much of its inspiration from Dave Carrel's AHA document, as well as the PPP CHAP protocol [RFC1994]. Valuable feedback was provided by Yoshihiro Ohba of Toshiba America Research, Jari Arkko of Ericsson, Sachin Seth of Microsoft, Glen Zorn of Cisco Systems, Jesse Walker of Intel, Bill Arbaugh, Nick Petroni and Bryan Payne of the University of Maryland, Steve Bellovin of AT&T Research, Paul Funk of Funk Software, Pasi Eronen of Nokia, Joseph Salowey of Cisco, Paul Congdon of HP, and members of the EAP working group.

The use of Security Claims sections for EAP methods, as required by Section 7.2 and specified for each EAP method described in this document, was inspired by Glen Zorn through [EAP-EVAL].

9. References

9.1. Normative References

[RFC1661]	Simpson, W., "The Point-to-Point Protocol (PPP)", STD 51, RFC 1661, July 1994.
[RFC1994]	Simpson, W., "PPP Challenge Handshake Authentication Protocol (CHAP)", RFC 1994, August 1996.
[RFC2119]	Bradner, S., "Key words for use in RFCs to Indicate Requirement Levels", BCP 14, RFC 2119, March 1997.
[RFC2243]	Metz, C., "OTP Extended Responses", RFC 2243, November 1997.
[RFC2279]	Yergeau, F., "UTF-8, a transformation format of ISO 10646", RFC 2279, January 1998.
[RFC2289]	Haller, N., Metz, C., Nesser, P. and M. Straw, "A One-Time Password System", RFC 2289, February 1998.
[RFC2434]	Narten, T. and H. Alvestrand, "Guidelines for Writing an IANA Considerations Section in RFCs", BCP 26, RFC 2434, October 1998.
[RFC2988]	Paxson, V. and M. Allman, "Computing TCP's Retransmission Timer", RFC 2988, November 2000.
[IEEE-802]	Institute of Electrical and Electronics Engineers, "Local and Metropolitan Area Networks: Overview and Architecture", IEEE Standard 802, 1990.

[IEEE-802.1X]   Institute of Electrical and Electronics Engineers, "Local and Metropolitan Area Networks: Port-Based Network Access Control", IEEE Standard 802.1X, September 2001.

9.2. Informative References

[RFC793]   Postel, J., "Transmission Control Protocol", STD 7, RFC 793, September 1981.

[RFC1510]   Kohl, J. and B. Neuman, "The Kerberos Network Authentication Service (V5)", RFC 1510, September 1993.

[RFC1750]   Eastlake, D., Crocker, S. and J. Schiller, "Randomness Recommendations for Security", RFC 1750, December 1994.

[RFC2246]   Dierks, T., Allen, C., Treese, W., Karlton, P., Freier, A. and P.
Kocher,
    "The TLS Protocol Version 1.0", RFC 2246, January 1999.

[RFC2284]   Blunk, L. and J. Vollbrecht, "PPP Extensible Authentication
Protocol
    (EAP)", RFC 2284, March 1998.

[RFC2486]   Aboba, B. and M. Beadles, "The Network Access Identifier", RFC 2486, January 1999.

[RFC2408]   Maughan, D., Schneider, M. and M. Schertler, "Internet Security Association and Key Management Protocol (ISAKMP)", RFC 2408, November 1998.

[RFC2409]   Harkins, D. and D. Carrel, "The Internet Key Exchange (IKE)", RFC 2409, November 1998.

[RFC2433]   Zorn, G. and S. Cobb, "Microsoft PPP CHAP Extensions", RFC 2433, October 1998.

[RFC2607]   Aboba, B. and J. Vollbrecht, "Proxy Chaining and Policy Implementation in Roaming", RFC 2607, June 1999.

[RFC2661]   Townsley, W., Valencia, A., Rubens, A., Pall, G., Zorn, G. and B. Palter, "Layer Two Tunneling Protocol "L2TP"", RFC 2661, August 1999.

[RFC2716]   Aboba, B. and D. Simon, "PPP EAP TLS Authentication Protocol", RFC 2716, October 1999.

[RFC2865]   Rigney, C., Willens, S., Rubens, A. and W. Simpson, "Remote Authentication Dial In User Service (RADIUS)", RFC 2865, June 2000.

[RFC2960]   Stewart, R., Xie, Q., Morneault, K., Sharp, C., Schwarzbauer, H., Taylor, T., Rytina, I., Kalla, M., Zhang, L. and V. Paxson, "Stream Control Transmission Protocol", RFC 2960, October 2000.

[RFC3162]   Aboba, B., Zorn, G. and D. Mitton, "RADIUS and IPv6", RFC 3162, August 2001.

[RFC3454]   Hoffman, P. and M. Blanchet, "Preparation of Internationalized Strings ("stringprep")", RFC 3454, December 2002.

[RFC3579]   Aboba, B. and P. Calhoun, "RADIUS (Remote Authentication Dial In User Service) Support For Extensible Authentication Protocol (EAP)", RFC 3579, September 2003.

[RFC3580]   Congdon, P., Aboba, B., Smith, A., Zorn, G. and J. Roese, "IEEE 802.1X Remote Authentication Dial In User Service (RADIUS) Usage Guidelines", RFC 3580, September 2003.

[RFC3692]   Narten, T., "Assigning Experimental and Testing Numbers Considered Useful", BCP 82, RFC 3692, January 2004.

[DECEPTION]   Slatalla, M. and J. Quittner, "Masters of Deception", Harper-Collins, New York, 1995.

[KRBATTACK]   Wu, T., "A Real-World Analysis of Kerberos Password Security", Proceedings of the 1999 ISOC Network and Distributed System Security Symposium, http://www.isoc.org/isoc/conferences/ndss/99/proceedings/papers/wu.pdf.

[KRBLIM]   Bellovin, S. and M. Merrit, "Limitations of the Kerberos authentication system", Proceedings of the 1991 Winter USENIX Conference, pp. 253-267, 1991.

[KERB4WEAK]   Dole, B., Lodin, S. and E. Spafford, "Misplaced trust: Kerberos 4 session keys", Proceedings of the Internet Society Network and Distributed System Security Symposium, pp. 60-70, March 1997.

[PIC]   Aboba, B., Krawczyk, H. and Y. Sheffer, "PIC, A Pre-IKE Credential Provisioning Protocol", Work in Progress, October 2002.

[IKEv2]   Kaufman, C., "Internet Key Exchange (IKEv2) Protocol", Work in Progress, January 2004.

[PPTPv1]   Schneier, B. and Mudge, "Cryptanalysis of Microsoft's Point-to-Point Tunneling Protocol", Proceedings of the 5th ACM Conference on Communications and Computer Security, ACM Press, November 1998.

[IEEE-802.11]   Institute of Electrical and Electronics Engineers, "Wireless LAN Medium Access Control (MAC) and Physical Layer (PHY) Specifications", IEEE Standard 802.11, 1999.

[SILVERMAN]   Silverman, Robert D., "A Cost-Based Security Analysis of Symmetric and Asymmetric Key Lengths", RSA Laboratories Bulletin 13, April 2000 (Revised November 2001), http://www.rsasecurity.com/rsalabs/bulletins/bulletin13.html.

[KEYFRAME]   Aboba, B., "EAP Key Management Framework", Work in Progress, October 2003.

[SASLPREP]   Zeilenga, K., "SASLprep: Stringprep profile for user names and passwords", Work in Progress, March 2004.

[IEEE-802.11i]   Institute of Electrical and Electronics Engineers, "Unapproved Draft Supplement to Standard for Telecommunications and Information Exchange Between Systems - LAN/MAN Specific Requirements - Part 11: Wireless LAN Medium Access Control (MAC) and Physical Layer (PHY) Specifications:

                  Specification for Enhanced Security", IEEE Draft 802.11i (work in progress), 2003.

[DIAM-EAP]   Eronen, P., Hiller, T. and G. Zorn, "Diameter Extensible Authentication Protocol (EAP) Application", Work in Progress, February 2004.

[EAP-EVAL]   Zorn, G., "Specifying Security Claims for EAP Authentication Types", Work in Progress, October 2002.

[BINDING]   Puthenkulam, J., "The Compound Authentication Binding Problem", Work in Progress, October 2003.

[MITM]   Asokan, N., Niemi, V. and K. Nyberg, "Man-in-the-Middle in Tunneled Authentication Protocols", IACR ePrint Archive Report 2002/163, October 2002, <http://eprint.iacr.org/2002/163>.

[IEEE-802.11i-req] Stanley, D., "EAP Method Requirements for Wireless LANs", Work in Progress, February 2004.

[PPTPv2]   Schneier, B. and Mudge, "Cryptanalysis of Microsoft's PPTP Authentication Extensions (MS-CHAPv2)", CQRE 99, Springer-Verlag, 1999, pp. 192-203.

Appendix A. Changes from RFC 2284

This section lists the major changes between [RFC2284] and this document. Minor changes, including style, grammar, spelling, and editorial changes are not mentioned here.

- The Terminology section (Section 1.2) has been expanded, defining more concepts and giving more exact definitions.

- The concepts of Mutual Authentication, Key Derivation, and Result Indications are introduced and discussed throughout the document where appropriate.

- In Section 2, it is explicitly specified that more than one exchange of Request and Response packets may occur as part of the EAP authentication exchange. How this may be used and how it may not be used is specified in detail in Section 2.1.

- Also in Section 2, some requirements have been made explicit for the authenticator when acting in pass-through mode.

- An EAP multiplexing model (Section 2.2) has been added to illustrate a typical implementation of EAP. There is no requirement that an implementation conform to this model, as long as the on-the-wire behavior is consistent with it.

- As EAP is now in use with a variety of lower layers, not just PPP for which it was first designed, Section 3 on lower layer behavior has been added.

- In the description of the EAP Request and Response interaction (Section 4.1), both the behavior on receiving duplicate requests, and when packets should be silently discarded has been more exactly specified. The implementation notes in this section have been substantially expanded.

- In Section 4.2, it has been clarified that Success and Failure packets must not contain additional data, and the implementation note has been expanded. A subsection giving requirements on processing of success and failure packets has been added.

- Section 5 on EAP Request/Response Types lists two new Type values: the Expanded Type (Section 5.7), which is used to expand the Type value number space, and the Experimental Type. In the Expanded Type number space, the new Expanded Nak (Section 5.3.2) Type has been added. Clarifications have been made in the description of most of the existing Types. Security claims summaries have been added for authentication methods.

- In Sections 5, 5.1, and 5.2, a requirement has been added such that fields with displayable messages should contain UTF-8 encoded ISO 10646 characters.

- It is now required in Section 5.1 that if the Type-Data field of an Identity Request contains a NUL-character, only the part before the null is displayed. RFC 2284 prohibits the null termination of the Type-Data field of Identity messages. This rule has been relaxed for Identity Request messages and the Identity Request Type-Data field may now be null terminated.

- In Section 5.5, support for OTP Extended Responses [RFC2243] has been added to EAP OTP.

- An IANA Considerations section (Section 6) has been added, giving registration policies for the numbering spaces defined for EAP.

- The Security Considerations (Section 7) have been greatly expanded, giving a much more comprehensive coverage of possible threats and other security considerations.

- In Section 7.5, text has been added on method-specific behavior, providing guidance on how EAP method-specific integrity checks should be processed. Where possible, it is desirable for a method-specific MIC to be computed over the entire EAP packet, including the EAP layer header (Code, Identifier, Length) and EAP method layer header (Type, Type-Data).

- In Section 7.14 the security risks involved in use of cleartext passwords with EAP are described.

- In Section 7.15 text has been added relating to detection of rogue NAS behavior.

Authors' Addresses

Bernard Aboba
  Microsoft Corporation
  One Microsoft Way
  Redmond, WA 98052
  USA

  Phone: +1 425 706 6605
  Fax: +1 425 936 6605
  EMail: bernarda@microsoft.com

Larry J. Blunk
  Merit Network, Inc
  4251 Plymouth Rd., Suite 2000
  Ann Arbor, MI 48105-2785
  USA

  Phone: +1 734-647-9563
  Fax: +1 734-647-3185
  EMail: ljb@merit.edu

John R. Vollbrecht

   Vollbrecht Consulting LLC

   9682 Alice Hill Drive

   Dexter, MI 48130

   USA

   EMail: jrv@umich.edu

James Carlson

   Sun Microsystems, Inc

   1 Network Drive

   Burlington, MA 01803-2757

   USA

   Phone: +1 781 442 2084

   Fax: +1 781 442 1677

   EMail: james.d.carlson@sun.com

Henrik Levkowetz

   ipUnplugged AB

   Arenavagen 33

   Stockholm S-121 28

   SWEDEN

   Phone: +46 708 32 16 08

   EMail: henrik@levkowetz.com

Full Copyright Statement

Intellectual Property

The IETF takes no position regarding the validity or scope of any Intellectual Property Rights or other rights that might be claimed to pertain to the implementation or use of the technology described in this document or the extent to which any license under such rights might or might not be available; nor does it represent that it has made any independent effort to identify any such rights. Information on the procedures with respect to rights in RFC documents can be found in BCP 78 and BCP 79.

Copies of IPR disclosures made to the IETF Secretariat and any assurances of licenses to be made available, or the result of an attempt made to obtain a general license or permission for the use of such proprietary rights by implementers or users of this specification can be obtained from the IETF on-line IPR repository at http://www.ietf.org/ipr.

The IETF invites any interested party to bring to its attention any copyrights, patents or patent applications, or other proprietary rights that may cover technology that may be required to implement this standard. Please address the information to the IETF at ietf-ipr@ietf.org.

Acknowledgement

Funding for the RFC Editor function is currently provided by the Internet Society.

GLOSSARY

802.3

A standard published by the IEEE that defines the signal characteristics and operation of a wired local area network. Defines the use of CSMA for providing multiple access to the network, which is similar to what's implemented in 802.11 wireless LANs.

802.11

A standard published by the IEEE that defines the radio characteristics and operation of a medium-range radio frequency local area network. Specifies the use of CSMA as the primary method for sharing access to a common air medium.

802.11a

A specific Physical Layer of the 802.11 standard that defines operation in the 5 GHz frequency band with data rates up to 54 Mbps; not directly compatible with 802.11b or 802.11g networks.

802.11b

A specific Physical Layer of the 802.11 standard that defines operation in the 2.4 GHz frequency band with data rates up to 11 Mbps; directly compatible with 802.11g networks.

802.11g

A specific Physical Layer of the 802.11 standard that defines operation in the 2.4 GHz frequency band with data rates up to 54 Mbps; backwardly compatible with 802.11b networks.

802.11n

A specific Physical Layer of the 802.11 standard that defines operation in the 2.4 GHz and 5 GHz frequency bands with data rates up to 100 Mbps; backwardly compatible with 802.11b and 802.11g networks.

802.15

A standard published by the IEEE that defines the radio characteristics and operation of wireless personal area networks; based on the Bluetooth specification.

802.16

A standard published by the IEEE that defines the radio characteristics and operation of wireless metropolitan area networks.

Access point

A hardware device that creates a radio cell that provides signal coverage for wireless client devices whereby the client devices can associate with the access point. This enables the wireless client devices to send and receive data over the wireless network. An enterprise or city often has dozens, hundreds, or even thousands of access points installed at various locations so that the radio cells of adjacent access points overlap slightly. The multiple overlapping radio cells create continuous signal coverage so that wireless client devices can roam from an area covered by one access point to an area covered by a different access point. An access point translates between wireless network protocols and wired network protocols.

Active scanning

A roaming function for 802.11-based clients that broadcasts probe request frames to search for other access points. Access points that receive the probe requests send probe response frames so that the client can determine which access points to associate with based on the signal strength of the probe responses.

Ad hoc channel

RF channel set in a wireless client device for purposes of connecting to ad hoc networks. The ad hoc channel set in the wireless clients must match in order to connect to the same ad hoc network.

Ad hoc mode

A configuration of a wireless network that allows communications directly from one client device to another without the need for the signals to travel through an access point. Ad hoc mode applies to both wireless PANs and wireless LANs.

Air medium

The air between two wireless devices; radio waves or infrared light travels through the air medium. Radio waves, generally in the 2.4 GHz or higher frequencies, are the most common signaling for wireless networks. Most of the 802 standards, such as 802.11a, 802.11b, 802.11g, 802.11n, 802.15, and 802.16, utilize radio waves. There is an infrared version of 802.11, but there are very few, if any, implementations.

Antenna

A physical device that converts electrical signals to radio or light waves (and vice versa) for propagation through the air medium. Antennas may be omni-directional (which distributes radio waves in all directions) or directional (which focus the radio waves more in one direction than others).

Association

A process whereby an 802.11 station (client device) becomes a part of the wireless LAN. After association, the client device can proceed with authentication processes and access network services.

Authentication

The process of verifying the identity of a person or thing, such as a computing device.

Authentication server

A physical device that stores authentication information, such as usernames and passwords, and verifies the identity of a particular device needing to be authenticated. The authentication server requests the credentials from the supplicant. The supplicant then offers the credentials to the authentication server. Nearly all authentication servers implement RADIUS. In an enterprise system, the authentication server is likely a separate component attached to the network. Typically, multiple authentication servers are present to improve availability and performance. Each authenticator points to a primary authentication server, with possibly several others listed as secondary servers that can be called upon if the primary authentication server is unresponsive. In some cases, the authentication server may be embedded in the authenticators.

Authenticator

A physical device that works at Layer 2 and acts as a security gate between the supplicants and the protected network. Each port of the authenticator remains closed until the authentication system verifies the credentials of the supplicant and deems that the supplicant is authorized to access the protected network. Once the system authenticates the supplicant, the authenticator opens a port so that the supplicant can access the protected network. When the supplicant and authentication server converse, all communications flows through the authenticator. The authenticator may be a wired switch or a wireless access point, depending on the implementation, that implements 802.1X port-based authentication protocols.

Auto configuration

An 802.1X port requires that supplicants perform some sort of authentication. Initially, a port set to auto is in an unauthorized state, letting only EAP traffic enter the protected network to reach the authentication server. After the authentication process takes place, and the supplicant is authorized to enter the protected network, the port switches to an authorized state for that particular supplicant. If the state of the link connected to the port goes down, then the port set to auto generally switches to an unauthorized state.

Automatic data rate

A feature for wireless client devices and access points to automatically adjust their data rate. This allows the radio to decrease its transmission data rate when excessive retransmissions are occurring or the received signal levels are too low. By lowering the data rate, wireless communications can operate over a longer range or in the midst of RF interference. In most cases, the data rate on the client radio should be set to Auto or Best Rate, depending on the name the manufacturer gives to the automatic data rate feature. This is the most effective setting if the client roams throughout the network and experiences varying signal levels. For stationary applications, a fixed data rate may be best. For example, you may want to choose the highest fixed data rate if it's desirable to limit the effective range of the network for security purposes.

Beacon

An 802.11 frame that wireless access points periodically broadcast. The beacon also carries information about the network, such as the SSID and data rate capability. Beacons enable wireless adapters to identify the presence of the router. If more than one access point is part of the same network, then the wireless adapters use the signal strength of the received beacons to determine which one to associate with.

Beacon period

The time between beacons sent by a wireless access point. By default, the beacon period is 100 milliseconds. In most cases, you don't need to change the beacon interval. Sometimes the beacon interval is adjusted to extend battery life in the wireless client devices. If you increase the beacon interval to one or two seconds, then the wireless adapters sleep longer and conserve more battery power, but the longer beacon interval can cause throughput performance to decrease. Longer beacon intervals may also negatively affect roaming. Because beacons are occurring less often, a user roaming through a facility may cause the applicable client radio to not identify access points soon enough to accommodate roaming before losing connection with a particular access point.

Bluetooth

A specification published by the Bluetooth Special Interest Group that defines the radio characteristics and operation of a short-range, low-power radio frequency network. Many devices today support Bluetooth, which is part of the IEEE 802.15 standard.

Bridge

A device that interconnects two networks at Layer 2. A bridge forwards data packets to another network based on the MAC address found in the packet header. Bridges play a key role in the deployment of wireless MANs.

Client adapter

A physical device installed in a client device that provides an interface to the network. A client adapter may be wireless (based on 802.11/Wi-Fi standards) or wired (based on 802.3/Ethernet standards).

Client card

See *client adapter*.

Client device

A physical device that a user can utilize to interface with the network and make use of applications. Typical users of a network are most familiar with PCs, laptops, and printers, but IP phones, cameras, game machines, and audio equipment are also becoming increasingly common client devices for networks.

Client radio

A wireless client adapter that may be integrated inside a client device or installed into the PC Card interface.

CompactFlash (CF)

SanDisk Corporation first introduced CF in 1994, but wireless LAN radio cards were not available in CF form factors until recently. A CF card is very small, weighing half an ounce, and is less than half the thickness and one quarter the volume of PC Card radio cards. The CF cards also draw very little power, which enables batteries to last longer than devices using PC Cards. Some PDAs come with direct CF interfaces, which results in a very lightweight and compact wireless PDA.

Coverage hole

An area of a facility where signals of the wireless network are not strong enough to support reliable connections to the network. After installing a wireless LAN, changes within the facility may alter RF signal propagation and disrupt 802.1X port-based authentication system protocols.

CSMA (carrier sense multiple access)

A process that allows multiple 802.11 stations to share a common air medium. Stations attempt to transmit data only when no other station is transmitting. Otherwise, collisions will occur, and the station must retransmit the data.

Data Link Layer

Establishes and maintains link-level connections between network devices, such as the link between an Ethernet card and an Ethernet switch. The IEEE 802 standards, such as 802.3 and 802.11, implement Data Link Layer functions.

Data rate

The number of bits in a frame sent per second between two network components. This should not be confused with throughput, which is the total number of bits sent over a given period of time (which could include multiple frames and the quiet time between the frames).

Descriptor Type field

A field that is one octet in length and represents the type of Key Descriptor being carried by the corresponding EAPOL-Key packet.

DHCP (Dynamic Host Configuration Protocol)

A protocol that automatically assigns unique IP addresses within a specified range to network devices.

Digital certificate

An electronic message that contains the credentials of a particular user. Digital certificates are used as a means for authenticating users or their computer devices without requiring users to input usernames and passwords.

Downlink

The flow of control and data signals between a wireless access point and a client radio, in the direction from the access point to the client radio.

EAP-Failure packet

Sent by the authenticator to the supplicant if the result of the authentication process indicates that the supplicant is not authorized to access the protected network. This packet doesn't contain an EAP Data field.

EAP-FAST (Flexible Authentication via Secure Tunneling)

An EAP-Method type ("43") developed by Cisco as a replacement for LEAP. In fact, some of the Cisco access points and client radio cards readily support EAP-FAST. EAP-FAST provides mutual authentication through the use of a Protected Access Credential (PAC) instead of digital certificates. An administrator can distribute the PACs manually or automatically via the authentication server. The advantage of EAP-FAST is that an enterprise doesn't need to deploy any digital certificates.

EAP-Method Data field

Contains information corresponding to the particular EAP-Method type and applicable protocol exchanges. For example, the EAP-Method Data field may be carrying credentials, such as a digital certificate, from the supplicant to the authentication server.

EAP-Method encapsulation

EAP-Method data is sent between the supplicant and the authenticator in EAP packets. An authenticator, for example, communicates EAP-Method data via an EAP Request packet. When traveling between the authenticator and the authentication server, EAP-Method data is sent in RADIUS packets. RADIUS Access-Request packets carry EAP-Method data from the authenticator to the authentication server, and RADIUS Access-Accept packets carry EAP-Method data from the authentication server to the authenticator. Together, EAPOL and RADIUS packets effectively transport EAP-Method data among the supplicant, authenticator, and authentication server.

EAP-Method Expanded NAK

Represented by a decimal "254" in the Type field of an EAP-Method packet. As the name implies, the Expanded NAK expands the capability of the Legacy NAK and conforms to the general Expanded Type packet structure. Similar to the Legacy NAK, the Expanded NAK allows the supplicant, for example, to propose an authentication method to the authentication server, but the Expanded NAK is much more flexible. The Expanded NAK enables port-based authentication systems to have a much larger possible number of EAP-Method types, well beyond the limits of the eight-octet limit (maximum 255) of the EAP-Method Type field. An Expanded NAK is sent in an EAP Response packet only after receiving an Expanded NAK in an EAP Request packet.

EAP-Method Experimental type

Represented by a decimal "255" in the Type field of an EAP-Method packet. The Experimental type has no standardized format or content. Anyone is free to structure the packets as they wish to allow for experimentation.

EAP-Method Generic Token Card (GTC) type

Represented a decimal "6" in the Type field of an EAP-Method packet. As with MD5-Challenge and OTP, GTC is one of the original authentication processes defined by EAP. GTC provides only one-way authentication, which allows supplicants to authenticate themselves with an authentication server. With GTC, an authentication request from the authenticator contains a displayable message, and the authentication response from the supplicant includes token card data read from a token card device that's needed for authentication. When receiving a GTC authentication request, the supplicant can respond with a Legacy NAK or Expanded NAK instead of the GTC response.

EAP-Method Identity packet

Represented by a decimal "1" in the Type field of an EAP-Method packet. EAP-Method Identity packets may be used before or during an authentication process. For example, with specific EAP-Methods that implement mutual authentication, the EAP-Method Identity packets generally convey information regarding the credentials of the supplicant or the authentication server. In other cases, the EAP-Method Identity packets only convey the credentials of the supplicant.

EAP-Method Legacy NAK type

Represented by a decimal "3" in the Type field of an EAP-Method packet. A supplicant, for example, sends a Legacy NAK packet when the supplicant is unable to support an authentication type (EAP-Method) that the authentication server proposes. The Legacy NAK packet identifies one or more EAP-Method types that the supplicant can support. If the Legacy NAK identifies EAP-Method type "0," this indicates that the authenticator has no viable alternatives and the authenticator should not send any more requests. The Legacy NAK type is very limited in allowing the supplicant to request a different authentication method because the Legacy NAK can only be sent in EAP Response packets.

EAP-Method MD5-Challenge type

Represented by a decimal "4" in the Type field of an EAP-Method packet. MD5-Challenge is one of the original authentication processes defined by EAP. MD5 provides only one-way authentication, which allows supplicants to authenticate themselves with an authentication server through the use of a user password. When a user initially enters his or her password to establish an account on the authentication server, the authentication server stores the hash of the password instead of the password itself to avoid storing the password in unencrypted form. The hash is a 128-bit fingerprint often called a *message digest*. Later, whenever the user logs into the system, the supplicant computes the hash of the password that the user inputs when logging into the system and sends the hash value to the authentication server for verification. The authentication server verifies the password by performing an MD5 hash of it.

EAP-Method Notification type

Represented by a decimal "2" in the Type field of an EAP-Method packet. The Notification packets may be used before or during an authentication process. The reception of a Notification packet causes the receiving entity to send a Notification packet in response. For example, an authentication server may send a Notification to the supplicant to provide status of authentication. A Notification packet, for instance, could alert the supplicant that the user must reenter his or her password because the password didn't match what's stored in the authentication server. The supplicant would then respond with the credentials.

EAP-Methods (Primary)

End-to-end, logical communications mechanism between a supplicant and an authenticator server in a port-based authentication system. Sometimes an EAP-Method is called an "EAP Authentication type" or just simply "EAP type." An EAP-Method actually implements the authentication process, whereas other protocols, such as EAPOL and RADIUS, merely transport the EAP-Method data.

EAP-Packet

Sometimes referred to as a Type "0" EAPOL packet or EAPOL data packet, meaning that the packet is carrying an EAP packet. This requires the destination, whether it's the supplicant or the authenticator, to merely strip off the EAPOL header and process the EAP packet. Thus, Type "0" EAPOL packets merely pass through EAP packets, which are generally carrying EAP-Method data. After link initiation, the most common EAPOL packets are EAP-Packet entities.

EAP Request packet

The authenticator communicates with the supplicant using EAP-Request packets. For example, the authenticator issues EAP-Request packets to deliver EAP-Method data traveling from the authentication server to the supplicant. Alternately, the supplicant may send an EAP-Request packet to demand the identity of the supplicant, depending on the EAP-Method in use.

EAP Response packet

The supplicant issues an EAP Response packet to communicate with the supplicant, such as when sending EAP-Method data or credentials requested by the supplicant.

EAP-Success packet

Based on the outcome of the EAP-Method procedures, the authenticator sends an EAP-Success packet to the supplicant if the authentication server informs the authenticator that the supplicant is authorized to access the protected network. This packet doesn't contain an EAP Data field.

EAP-Method One-Time Password (OTP) type

Represented by a decimal "5" in the Type field of an EAP-Method packet. OTP is one of the original authentication processes defined by EAP. OTP provides only one-way authentication, which allows supplicants to authenticate themselves with an authentication server. When receiving an OTP authentication request, the supplicant responds with an OTP response, Legacy NAK, or Expanded NAK.

EAP-Method Type field

A field containing an eight-octet value that identifies a specific EAP-Method. There are many EAP-Methods, some of which are originally defined by the EAP specification (RFC 3748) and many others that are optional and proprietary. The value of the EAP-Method Type field indicates what the EAP packet carries.

EAP-SIM (Subscriber Identity Module) type

Offers mutual authentication for SIM cards installed in GSM cellular telephones. EAP-SIM allows the card to authenticate with a GSM authentication server and vice versa. Smart phones with EAP-SIM can also authenticate with Wi-Fi hotspots when roaming from a GSM network to the hotspot.

EAP-TLS (EAP with Transport Layer Security) type

Represented by a decimal "13" in the Type field of an EAP-Method packet. EAP-TLS provides mutual authentication whereby both the supplicant and the authentication server prove their identities to each other. EAP-TLS makes use of public key cryptography for authentication purposes, which could involve smart cards or digital certificates. EAP-TLS has the broadest support in supplicants and authentication servers. For example, Cisco, FreeRADIUS, Funk, Interlink, Meetinghouse, Microsoft, and Radiator have RADIUS server support for EAP-TLS. Communications between the supplicant and the authentication server is via an encrypted TLS tunnel, which makes EAP-TLS very secure. EAP-TLS is best for enterprises that have digital certificates already deployed and utilize Microsoft Windows-based supplicants, especially those equipped with Windows XP, Windows 2000, and Windows Vista. If your clients are already equipped with Windows, then you're in a good position to implement EAP-TLS.

EAP-TTLS (Tunneled Transport Layer Security) type

Represented by a decimal "21" in the Type field of an EAP-Method packet. EAP-TTLS was developed by Funk Software and Certicom, as an extension of EAP-TLS. Similar to EAP-TLS, EAP-TTLS is a certificate-based, mutual authentication system, but it requires only server-side certificates by connecting the supplicant to the authentication server via TLS through a secure tunnel. Users authenticate themselves with a password, rather than a certificate. This greatly reduces the complexity of the port-based authentication system because there's no need to install and manage certificates on the client devices. Funk Software is the primary supporter of EAP-TTLS. In order to utilize EAP-TTLS, you must usually install third-party 802.1X supplicant software.

EAP Code field

A field that identifies the type of EAP packet.

EAP Data field

The data field of an EAP packet depends on the packet type. For instance, EAP Request and EAP Response packets have Data fields. In some cases, the EAP Data field may not include any data.

EAP Identifier field

This field makes it possible to match EAP Response packets to the applicable EAP Request packets.

EAP Length field

Two octets long and identifies the number of octets comprising the EAP packet. The EAP Length field value includes the EAP Code, Identifier, Length, and Data fields, which represents the length of the entire EAP packet. Thus, the EAP Length field value is the same as the EAPOL length field value.

EAP types

Define the structure of the EAP Request and EAP Response packets. The EAP type controls what the EAP packet carries. Types 1, 2, and 3 are special case types, and the remaining types are for authentication exchanges.

EAPOL (EAP-over-LAN)

Defined in the 802.1X standard to adapt EAP communications for operation over LANs. In order to do this, EAPOL provides additional header fields to EAP packets and creates some specialized EAP packet types. In addition, EAPOL transports EAP packets as data in the packet body of EAPOL packets. EAPOL is the primary communications protocol between a supplicant and an authenticator in a port-based authentication system. The EAPOL protocol operates at Layer 2 to prevent a supplicant from connecting to the network before authenticating. This is done by exploiting access controls offered by IEEE 802.1D, which defines MAC bridges and is required by all 802 LANs. The protocol ensures that EAPOL packets are the first ones sent on the link.

EAPOL-Encapsulated-ASF-Alert packet

A packet useful when the supplicant must send information to the protected side of the network before authentication is complete. For example, the supplicant may need to send a status message to a server. The contents of the EAPOL-Encapsulated-ASF-Alert are generally proprietary.

EAPOL encapsulation

Takes place in order to support the communications between the supplicant and the authenticator. EAPOL is the overall port-based authentication entity that requires transportation by a link protocol.

EAPOL-Key packet

A packet that can be sent by either the supplicant or the authenticator. The EAPOL-Key packet is optional. If the 802.1X implementation requires the transport of keys between the supplicant and the authenticator, the Packet Body of an EAPOL-Key packet contains a Key Descriptor with the format illustrated in Figure 3-8 in Chapter 3.

EAPOL-Logoff packet

A packet that the supplicant sends to the authenticator to gracefully return the authenticated port to an unauthorized state. This could occur when the user decides to log off from a particular system residing on the protected side of the network. The use of EAPOL-Logoff packets is ideal because it makes efficient use of authenticator resources.

EAPOL-Start packet

The normal authentication process begins when the link state changes from down to up. The authenticator generally initiates the authentication process when this transition from down to up occurs, such as when a user on an Ethernet network first boots up the computer. If the link is already up and the supplicant needs to authenticate, then the supplicant must initiate the authentication process by sending an EAPOL-Start packet to grab the attention of the authenticator. The authenticator then knows to initiate the authentication process.

EAPOL Length field

A field that is two octets in length and defines the length of the Packet Body field within an EAPOL packet.

EAPOL Type field

A field that is one octet in length and identifies the type of EAPOL packet being sent.

EAPOL Version field

Identifies the version of the EAPOL protocol that the sender of the EAPOL packet supports.

Encryption

The scrambling of data bits according to a key prior to sending the data over a network. WEP and WPA are examples of encryption used by wireless LANs.

Ethernet

Depicts 802.3 wired local area networks. Ethernet is a common type of network that companies use to interconnect PCs and servers. Ethernet provides the distribution system of most wireless LANs.

Expanded EAP-Method type

Represented by a decimal "254" in the Type field of an EAP-Method packet. The EAP-Method Expanded NAK is an Expanded EAP-Method type. The Expanded NAK allows port-based authentication systems to have a much larger possible number of EAP-Method types, well beyond the eight-octet limit (maximum 255) of the EAP-Method Type field. In general, the Expanded types are intended for vendors in order to support their own EAP-Methods, which are not suitable for general usage.

Forced-authorized

If a port on an authenticator is set to forced-authorized, the authenticator will forward all traffic coming to that port. Thus, the port is forced to authorize all supplicants. This is usually the default configuration.

Forced-unauthorized

Configuration of an authenticator port that disables the forwarding of traffic from all supplicants through that port. The switch or access point set to forced-unauthorized ignores all authentication requests. This could be done to manually guard a particular port from all client devices. It locks down the port from potential attack.

Fragmentation

A process that breaks 802.11 data frames into smaller frames that are sent separately over the wireless network. This can be effective when counteracting the damaging affects of RF interference. If interference hits a full-sized (unfragmented) data frame, then the access point must retransmit the entire frame, which takes time and adds considerable overhead to the network. With fragmentation, errors will likely occur in one of the fragments, which don't take nearly as long to retransmit.

Frequency

The number of times per second that a signal repeats itself. Often measured in hertz (Hz), which is the number of cycles occurring each second. Frequencies of wireless LANs, for example, are within the 2.4 GHz and 5 GHz bands.

H.323

An umbrella specification defined by the International Telecommunications Union Standardized Sector that includes a group of protocols for sending voice and video over IP-based networks.

Hacker

A person who has the desire and ability to steal information that resides on a network. Hackers often try to break into corporate systems for fun in order to exploit the vulnerabilities of wireless networks.

Hotspot

The location of a public wireless LAN. Hotspots are found within areas where people congregate with computer devices, such as at airports, hotels, convention centers, and coffee shops.

Hub

A physical device that implements the IEEE 802.3 standard and operates as a single collision domain. When a device connected to a port on a hub connects a device connected to a different port on the same hub, the devices connected to the other ports on the hub can't communicate with the hub and form other connections. All devices interfacing with the ports on a hub, except the two already connected with each other, are blocked. As a result, most enterprises use switches instead of hubs.

IEEE (Institute of Electrical and Electronics Engineers)

A standards development organization responsible for creating and maintaining most standards applying to computer networks. IEEE 802 standards play a big role in 802.1X port-based authentication systems. 802.1X is certainly part of the 802 standards. 802.3 and 802.11 are also very important, as they carry the authentication traffic.

Industry Standard Architecture (ISA)

The most common bus interface in desktop PCs. ISA has been around since the early 1980s for use in the IBM PC/XT and PC/AT. Because of this, the proliferation of the ISA has been significant. Despite its lack of speed (2 Mbps), nearly all PCs manufactured until several years ago had at least one ISA bus. However, the ISA bus has failed to keep pace with the rest of the computer industry, and other higher speed alternatives are now available. ISA doesn't impose too much of a performance impact on 802.11b wireless LANs, but it's not advisable to purchase new ISA cards, as they may become obsolete.

Infrastructure wireless LAN

Uses access points and is by far the most common. With infrastructure wireless LANs, you set the channel of the network in the access point, and the client radio automatically tunes to that channel before associating with the access point. The client radio is configured for operation over an infrastructure by default, so you don't have to configure the channel for the client radio.

Interoperability

A condition whereby computer devices are able to successfully interface with a wireless network.

IP (Internet Protocol)

A protocol that routes packets between computer devices attached to a network. The IP protocol places a header field in front of each packet. This field contains the source and destination IP address of the packet.

IP address

A value that represents the address corresponding to a connection of a network device to the network. For example, every wireless network NIC will have an IP address. Each NIC must have an IP address associated with it if the user will be making use of TCP/IP applications, such as sending and receiving e-mail, browsing the web, or interfacing with a corporate application server.

IPSec (IP Security)

A protocol that supports the secure exchange of packets at the Network Layer of a network. IPSec is commonly implemented in VPNs and encrypts data packets across the entire network (often referred to as *end-to-end encryption*).

Juniper Networks' Odyssey Access Client (OAC)

Provides enterprise-class 802.1X access client software, which is compatible with Juniper Networks' Odyssey Access Server (retired in May 2007) or Steel-Belted Radius. A specialized version of OAC is FIPS 140-2 Level 1 Validated, which meets security requirements of government agencies. Juniper Networks now recommends interfacing OAC with only Steel-Belted Radius or Juniper's Infranet Controller. The Juniper OAC is a good choice for high-end security.

LDAP (Lightweight Directory Access Protocol)

A protocol that enables accessing information directories.

LEAP (Lightweight Extensible Authentication Protocol) type

EAP-Method type "17" was developed by Cisco for wireless LANs. LEAP provides encryption through dynamically generated WEP (Wired Equivalent Privacy) keys and makes use of strong user passwords for authenticating supplicants. LEAP is available for most Cisco devices and some vendor devices that license the use of LEAP. It's possible to crack LEAP, however, with a tool called ASLEAP, although you might find some authentication systems using LEAP. For new implementations, strongly consider a different protocol. If you want to stay with the Cisco line, then consider EAP-FAST.

Local area network (LAN)

Connects computer devices that span the size of a building or college campus. An enterprise facility or hospital will likely have a LAN that connects PCs and corporate servers. A warehouse clerk, for example, may use a PC connected to a LAN to find the status of received goods or to set up a shipping transaction. A LAN will also generally connect to the Internet, enabling users of the LAN to browse websites and send e-mail to other users who are not connected to the LAN.

Medium

The space or thing in which communications signals propagate. With wireless networks, the medium is air.

Medium access

A process whereby multiple computer devices share a common medium. The most common medium access method for wireless networks is CSMA.

Mesh network

A network that makes use of mesh nodes to create signal coverage over a large area where it's not feasible to install a wired network connection to each access point. Many municipalities are installing Wi-Fi mesh networks to provide wireless connectivity for mobile Wi-Fi-equipped client devices. For example, a city may deploy a mesh network to support wireless public safety applications or wireless work order processing. In addition, a municipal Wi-Fi network can provide public Internet access throughout the city.

Mesh node

Similar to a wireless access point, the mesh node offers a Wi-Fi interface to client devices based on the 802.11 protocol. However, mesh nodes don't require a cable to connect to a switch. Instead, each mesh node is capable of receiving packets from a wireless client device and forwarding the packets to another mesh node. The mesh nodes implement a routing mechanism that moves packets toward a mesh node that has a link back to a central connection point. Some of the mesh nodes are also gateways, which generally use a point-to-point radio link (called *backhaul*) that connects the gateway to the central point. For client devices connecting to a mesh node (not a gateway), a data packet hops from one mesh node to another until the packet arrives at a gateway, which then sends the packet directly to the central point.

Metropolitan area network (MAN)

Provides network connectivity over the area of an entire city or metropolitan city area. For cities such as Houston and Los Angeles, a MAN can span hundreds of square miles. In other places, such as smaller cities, a MAN may only cover a few square miles.

Mini-PCI

A small version of a standard desktop PCI card. It has all the same features and functionality of a normal PCI card, but is about one quarter the size. Mini-PCI cards are integrated within laptops as an option to buyers, with antennas that are often integrated out of view within the monitor's case or even next to the LCD screen. A strong advantage of this form of radio NIC is that it frees up the PC Card slot for other devices. In addition, manufacturers can provide Mini-PCI based wireless connectivity at lower costs.

NAT (Network Address Translation)

A protocol that maps official IP addresses to private addresses that may be in use on their internal networks. For example, a broadband Internet service provider may offer a home user only one official IP address. NAT, along with DHCP, enables the homeowner to have multiple PCs and laptops sharing the single official IP address.

Network interface card (NIC)

Also referred to as client cards or network adapters, network interface cards interface the client device (and other network devices) to the network. For example, you can interface a laptop to a wireless network by installing an 802.11 PC Card in the laptop. The NIC is the actual network connection, addressable by a MAC address. Also known as a *radio card* or a *client card*.

Network Layer

Provides routing throughout the network for data packets going from one network entity to another. The Internet Protocol (IP) is an example of a Network Layer Protocol.

Open System Interconnection (OSI)

A logical network reference model whereby each layer of the model represents specific functions. A network may not implement all of the possible functions, but the model covers most of them. Each layer of the model does work for the layer above it and doesn't care what happened at lower layers. In fact, each layer is unaware that lower layers are doing anything. In some cases, standards, such as IEEE 802.3 and IEEE 802.11, will subdivide layers of the OSI model into multiple sublayers.

Open1X

An open-source project for Linux platforms for implementing 802.1X solutions. Open1X supports both authenticators and supplicants. It is an alternative solution for implementing 802.1X on Linux platforms. Refer to `http://open1x.sourceforge.net` for an update on Open1X.

Optical fiber cabling

Consists of strands of glass that conduct light efficiently from one end to the other. The advantages of optical fiber over metallic wiring include the following: fiber supports much higher data rates (up to tetra bits per second), it doesn't emit electromagnetic fields, and it operates over relatively long ranges. Thus, optical fiber systems are more secure and capable of supporting higher speed delivery of information. In addition, optical fiber is practical for providing high-speed connections between buildings throughout cities. An issue with optical fiber, though, is that it is relatively expensive to install for each client device inside a company. In some cases, however, especially where client devices are beyond the 300-foot range from a wiring closet, optical fiber may be the only way to connect the clients.

PC Card

Developed in the early 1990s by the Personal Computer Memory Card International Association (PCMCIA), the PC Card is a credit-card-size peripheral device that can provide extended memory, modems, connectivity to external devices, and, of course, wireless LAN capabilities to laptops. They are the most widely available cards for portable devices, such as laptops. In fact, they are now more prevalent than ISA or PCI cards because of their use in a growing number of laptops.

PC Card Converter

A physical device that enables you to share a PC Card with your desktop PC. This enables a user to purchase one card for use in both types of computers. For example, you can take the PC Card along on a business trip or home from work and use the same card when back in your office using a PC.

PCI card

Peripheral Component Interconnect (PCI) bus is the most popular bus interface for PCs today and boasts a throughput rate of 264 Mbps. Intel originally developed and released PCI in 1993, and it satisfies the needs of most recent generations of PCs for multimedia, graphics, and networking cards.

PEAP (Protected Extensible Authentication Protocol) type

EAP-Method type "25," which is similar to EAP-TTLS and developed by Microsoft, Cisco, and RSA Security. As with EAP-TTLS, PEAP doesn't require certificates on the client devices. It offers secure transport of authentication data, which could include legacy passwords. PEAP accomplishes this by using tunneling between PEAP clients and an authentication server. The advantage of PEAP is that it is free.

Personal area network (PAN)

Connects computer devices within a relatively small area, such as in the immediate vicinity of a person's body. A PAN may require wires for connecting the devices, or connectivity may be wireless.

Physical Layer

Defines the electrical and mechanical specifications of the interface between network devices. For example, IEEE 802.11g is a Physical Layer standard that specifies the use of radio waves at 2.4 GHz.

Port-based authentication

A collection of EAPOL, EAP, EAP-Methods, and RADIUS that implement a system controlling access to a network.

Power-save mode

An 802.11 function (when enabled) that allows wireless client radios to enter a sleep mode, which draws less current and extends battery life.

Preamble

Found at the beginning of an 802.11 frame, the preamble synchronizes the receiver with the frame. In the access point, you can set the radio preamble to long or short. The short preamble improves performance. Most vendor client radios and access points support short preambles, but some older client radios only support long preambles. Therefore, setting the preamble to long ensures compatibility when using older devices. Research each client radio that you plan to use on the network to determine whether you need to support long preambles. If there is no requirement for long preambles, then configure the access point for short preamble.

Protection mechanisms

The 802.11 standard includes the optional use of protection mechanisms for when an 802.11g network accepts associations from 802.11b client radios. This is necessary to reduce collisions between 802.11g and 802.11b radios when transmitting data. Generally, the CTS-to-self setting is best because it minimizes overhead on the network, which improves the performance of a mixed 802.11b/g network. With CTS-to-self, a client radio will transmit a CTS (clear-to-send) frame to itself with a value in the duration field of the 802.11 frame header that informs other stations to hold off transmitting for a period of time long enough for the sending station to transmit its data. This function only requires the transmission of one overhead frame (the CTS frame), whereas the RTS/CTS function requires the transmission of two overhead frames (RTS and CTS).

Public wireless LAN

A type of wireless LAN, often referred to as a hotspot, that anyone with a properly configured computer device can access.

Quiet period

The amount of time before making another authentication attempt after an unsuccessful authentication.

RADIUS

The primary communications mechanism between an authenticator and an authentication server in a port-based authentication system. Sometimes the authentication server that implements RADIUS is called a "RADIUS server." The RADIUS protocols between the authenticator and the authentication server transport the EAP-Method data in encrypted format. The 802.1X standard and EAP specification do not require RADIUS as the authentication server, but RADIUS is by far the most common. The authenticator sends EAP-Method data to the authentication server via RADIUS Access-Request frames, and the authentication server sends EAP-Method data to the authenticator in Access-Challenge packets.

RADIUS Access-Accept packet

Sent from the RADIUS server to the authenticator in response to a RADIUS Access-Request. For example, the Access-Accept packet may carry an acceptance or configuration information for a particular supplicant. The Identifier field value of the Access-Accept packet must match the Identifier value in the corresponding Access-Request packet.

RADIUS Access-Challenge packet

Sent from the RADIUS server to the authenticator in response to an Access-Request packet. The Identifier field value of the Access-Challenge must match the Identifier value in the corresponding Access-Request packet. The Attributes field of an Access-Challenge packet may have one or more of the following attributes: State, Reply-Message, Vendor-Specific, Idle-Timeout, Session-Timeout, and Proxy-State.

RADIUS Access-Reject packet

Sent from the RADIUS server to the authenticator in response to a RADIUS Access-Request. The Access-Reject packet is sent when any of the attributes in the Access-Request are not acceptable. The Identifier field value of the Access-Accept must match the Identifier value in the corresponding Access-Request packet. The Attributes field of an Access-Reject packet may include one or more Reply-Message attributes with a text message, which the authenticator can display to the user.

RADIUS Access-Request packet

Sent from the authenticator to the RADIUS server to carry data pertinent to the EAP-Method in use. For example, the Access-Request packet could include the supplicant's credentials. All authentication implementations must issue an Access-Request packet when authenticating the supplicant. The Access-Request generally contains the User-Name attribute and the NAS-IP-Address attribute (or a NAS-Identifier attribute).

RADIUS Accounting-Request packet

Sent from the authenticator to the RADIUS server to request accounting information.

RADIUS Accounting-Response packet

Sent from the RADIUS server to the authenticator in response to the Accounting-Response packet, it must match the Identifier value in the corresponding Accounting-Request.

RADIUS attributes

Contained within a RADIUS packet and communicated between the authenticator and the RADIUS server. More than 100 attributes are defined in a combination of RFC 2865 and vendor documentation.

RADIUS Attributes field

A variable-length field that contains specific data elements being communicated between the authenticator and the authentication server.

RADIUS Authenticator field

A field that is 16 octets in length and contains a value that varies according to the RADIUS packet type being sent.

RADIUS Code field

A field that is one octet in length and identifies the type of RADIUS packet.

RADIUS EAP-Message attribute

The primary attribute for 802.1X because it encapsulates the EAP-Method data between the authenticator and the authentication server. The EAP-Message attribute actually contains the EAP-Method packet. All other RADIUS attributes in 802.1X port-based authentication implementations are peripheral to the EAP-Message attribute.

RADIUS Identifier field

A field that is one octet in length. Similar to the EAP protocol, the Identifier field of a RADIUS packet makes it possible to match RADIUS Access-Challenge packets with Access-Request packets.

RADIUS Idle-Timeout attribute

Establishes the maximum number of seconds the supplicant can be in an idle state before being disconnected from the network. This attribute is sent from the RADIUS server to the authenticator only in RADIUS Access-Accept or Access-Challenge packets. The length of the Idle-Timeout attribute is always six octets. The value field is four octets and contains a 32-bit unsigned integer, which represents the maximum number of seconds the applicable supplicant can be idle.

RADIUS Length field

A field that is two octets long and identifies the number of octets comprising the RADIUS packet. The maximum length of the RADIUS packet is 4,096 octets. The RADIUS Length field value includes the EAP Code, Identifier, Length, Authenticator, and Attribute fields.

RADIUS Message-Authenticator attribute

May be used by the RADIUS server in any RADIUS Access-Request packet to authenticate RADIUS Access-Requests. In addition, the Message-Authenticator attribute may check the integrity of Access-Requests to prevent spoofing. When supporting EAP-Message attributes, all Access-Request, Access-Accept, Access-Reject or Access-Challenge packets must include the Message-Authenticator attribute.

RADIUS NAS-IP-Address attribute

Indicates the IP address of the authenticator that is requesting authentication of the suppliant. The NAS-IP-Address attribute is only used in RADIUS Access-Request packets. Either the NAS-IP-Address attribute or the NAS-Identifier attribute must be present in an Access-Request packet. This attribute is always six octets in length, and four octets are allocated to the Address field.

RADIUS NAS-Port attribute

Includes the physical port number (not TCP or UDP port) of the authenticator requesting authentication of the suppliant. The NAS-Port attribute is only used in RADIUS Access-Request packets. This attribute is always six octets in length, four of which are allocated to the Port Number field.

RADIUS Password-Retry attribute

Can be included in a RADIUS Access-Reject packet to indicate the number of authentication attempts a user may perform before being disconnected. This attribute is always six octets in length. The Value field is four octets and includes an integer specifying the number of password retry attempts that the user can perform.

RADIUS Service-Type attribute

Identifies the type of service the supplicant is requesting or the RADIUS server is granting. The Service-Type attribute is used in both Access-Request and Access-Accept packets. This attribute is always six octets in length, and the Value field is four octets. The authenticator treats any service types granted by the RADIUS server that aren't supported as Access-Reject packets.

RADIUS Session-Timeout attribute

Establishes the maximum number of seconds the supplicant will have service. This attribute is sent from the RADIUS server to the authenticator only in RADIUS Access-Accept or Access-Challenge packets. The length of the Session-Timeout attribute is always six octets. The Value field is four octets and contains a 32-bit unsigned integer, which represents the maximum number of seconds the applicable supplicant can have service.

RADIUS Termination-Action attribute

Indicates the action that the authenticator should take when the specified service is completed. The Termination-Action attribute is only used in Access-Accept packets. The Value field is four octets in length and can either be "0" (for Default) or "1" (for Radius Request). If the Value Field is "Radius Request" then the authenticator may send a new Access-Request to the RADIUS server after the service is terminated.

RADIUS User-Name attribute

Identifies the name of the user being authenticated and is sent from the authenticator to the RADIUS server in a RADIUS Access-Request packet. This is a very common attribute. The username is one or more octets in length.

RADIUS Vendor-Specific attribute

Allows vendors to implement proprietary attributes not suitable for general use. The inclusion of additional attributes, however, doesn't interfere with the operation of the RADIUS protocol. If a RADIUS server receives a RADIUS packet containing a Vendor-Specific attribute that it doesn't understand, then the RADIUS server discards the attribute and likely sends an applicable message to the authenticator.

Re-authentication Period Value

The amount of time that passes before the supplicants must re-authenticate.

Request Authenticator

In RADIUS Access-Request packets, the content of the Authenticator field is the Request Authenticator. This value is a random number and should be unpredictable and unique. The shared secret configured in the authenticator and the authentication server is combined with the Request Authenticator and put through a one-way, MD5 hash to create the digest value (16 octets in length) that is XOR'd with the user's password. The RADIUS Access-Request packet carries this result in the User-Password attribute. The Request Authenticator value changes whenever the Identifier field changes.

Response Authenticator

The Response Authenticator resides in the Authenticator field of RADIUS Access-Accept, Access-Reject, and Access-Challenge packets. The Response Authenticator is a one-way, MD5 hash calculated over the entire length of the corresponding RADIUS Access-Request packet and the shared secret.

Retry timeout value

Amount of time that the authenticator will wait before resending a packet if no response is heard from the supplicant or authentication server. Most port-based authentication systems have a separate retry timeout value for the supplicants and authentication servers. When implementing a wireless system, it may be beneficial to allocate a higher retry timeout value due to potential delays over the wireless network.

RF (radio frequency) channel

The specific frequency to which a client radio or access point is set for operation. In most cases, the access point is set to a static RF channel. The client radio in the user devices scans all channels for available access points and then tunes to the RF channel of the access point as part of the connection process with the access point. The 802.11 standard defines up to 14 different RF channels for access points operating in the 2.4 GHz band. In the U.S., the FCC allows operation in only the first 11 channels. Other countries may use more or fewer channels, depending on their regulations. The RF channels of access points overlap significantly, leaving only channels 1, 6, and 11 that don't overlap.

RF interference

Signals that may impede the operation of a wireless network. RF interference occupies the air medium, which delays users from sending/receiving data and causes collisions and resulting retransmissions. This causes delays on the network, which may impact the operation of an 802.1X port-based authentication system. In some cases, you might need to adjust 802.1X system configuration parameters, such as timeouts, in order to compensate for RF interference, as well as other impairments. The combination of high noise levels and high retry rates generally indicates that RF interference is affecting your wireless LAN. If the noise level is above -85dBm in the band where your users are operating, then RF interference has the potential to cause poor performance.

RF signal

A signal that is designed to propagate through the air medium.

RF site survey

A process that determines the locations of access points that provide required signal coverage.

Rogue access point

An access point that is unauthorized and has configuration settings that may enable someone to gain access to network resources.

Router

A physical device that routes packets through a network infrastructure based on the IP address carried within each packet. The IP address corresponds to the addressing that many applications respond to. As packets flow into one particular port, the router determines which outbound port to use to move the packet closest to the intended destination. A routing protocol keeps track of which outbound ports provide optimum routing, maintaining this data in a routing table.

SecureW2

An open-source EAP-TTLS client for Microsoft Windows platforms. If the Windows Authentication Client doesn't fulfill your requirements, then consider using SecureW2 to create a custom 802.1X/EAP solution. Refer to www.securew2.com to download SecureW2 software and documentation.

Server

A device that hosts application software and databases for users to access on the network. For example, an enterprise may have a warehouse management system that warehouse clerks and managers can access in order to perform inventories, check stock levels, and execute shipping of warehouse items. An authentication server runs RADIUS in order to process client devices that are authenticating with the network. A server is a centralized and shared component of the network.

Session Initiation Protocol (SIP)

Developed by the Internet Engineering Task Force (RFC 2543), SIP defines a protocol based on Internet specifications, such as Hypertext Markup Language and Simple Mail Transfer Protocol, for sending voice over IP-based networks.

SSID (service set identifier)

Provides a name that wireless clients use when identifying a particular wireless LAN. The SSID can consist of up to 32 alphanumeric, case-sensitive characters, and it's configured in each access point. The SSID is displayed when a wireless network is found. In order to associate with an access point, the client radio must be configured with the SSID of the access point. Windows performs this configuration on the client radio automatically when the user chooses to connect to a particular wireless LAN (SSID), displayed in the Windows wireless configuration utility.

Signal-to-noise ratio (SNR)

A value, measured in dB, that reflects the signal power (in dBm) minus the noise power (in dBm).

Snooper

Someone who casually, and usually inadvertently, interfaces with a wireless network.

Supplicant

A client that needs to be authenticated to the network before being allowed access to it. In order to be considered a valid supplicant, a typical client device, such as a laptop or IP phone, must implement 802.1X and a specific EAP-Method. Windows XP, for example, comes with 802.1X built in with a variety of EAP-Methods, such as EAP-TLS. The actual communications between the supplicant and the authenticator is accomplished via EAPOL, which is defined by 802.1X. EAPOL delivers (encapsulates) the EAP and EAP-Method frames as data. See Chapter 6.

Switch

A physical device that implements what's referred to as *switched-Ethernet* connects a device on one port directly with another device on a different port. This connection doesn't preclude devices connected to other ports from communicating with the switch and forming connections with other devices. After the connection between two devices is made inside the switch, other devices can contend for connections. A switch offers much faster performance than a hub. In general, switches are relatively simple devices. They forward nearly all data, including multicast packets, throughout the network based on the Medium Access Control (MAC) address that each packet is carrying. The MAC address is the actual physical address to which the network devices respond, similar to the number and street address of your home or office.

TCP (Transmission Control Protocol)

A protocol that establishes and maintains connections between computer devices attached to a network. TCP is used in conjunction with IP, which is commonly referred to as TCP/IP.

Terminal emulation

A mechanism that enables users to interface over a network to applications running on a centralized computer. VT-220, 3270, and 5250 are types of terminal emulation.

Transceiver

A device that both transmits and receives information. The transceiver resides in a radio NIC.

Transmit power

The signal level emitted by a client radio or wireless access point. Usually, it's advantageous to set the transmit power of the client radio to the highest value, which maximizes the uplink range between the client and the access point. If there's a need to support high capacity with the wireless LAN, then lower transmit power settings may be beneficial to decrease the cell size of the network, which improves capacity.

Transport Layer

Establishes and maintains end-to-end connections between network entities. Transmission Control Protocol (TCP) is an example of a Transport Layer protocol.

Uplink

The flow of control and data signals between a wireless access point and a client radio, in the direction from the client radio to the access point.

User-Password attribute

Identifies the password of the user being authenticated. It is sent from the authenticator to the RADIUS server in a RADIUS Access-Request packet. The user password is one or more octets in length, and is hidden prior to transmission in the Access-Request packet. The password is first padded with nulls to a multiple of 16 octets. A one-way, MD5 hash is then calculated over the shared secret and Request Authenticator. The result of this calculation is XOR'ed with the first 16 octets of the password and placed at the beginning of the User-Password attribute Value field.

VLAN (virtual LAN)

A logical collection of network devices that communicate with each other over the same physical network, but where network devices on one VLAN can't communicate with network devices on a another VLAN (unless provisions are made to connect the different VLANs).

VoIP (voice-over-IP)

A technology for sending voice signals over an IP-based network.

VPN (virtual private network)

Special software on the client device that controls access to remote applications and secures the connection from end to end using encryption.

WEP (Wired Equivalent Privacy)

A part of the 802.11 standard that defines encryption between devices connected to a wireless local area network.

Wide area networks (WANs)

A type of computer network that covers very large areas, including the entire globe. Companies with offices spread throughout a country or the entire world can make use of a WAN to interconnect the individual networks in offices. The Internet is actually a WAN that many companies depend on every day for supporting e-mail, file transfer, and access to remote applications. In some cases, a company may create a private WAN. For example, a retail company may link all of its stores to a central data center. Every night, each of the stores can upload sales data and download changes, such as price updates. WANs make use of long-haul leased terrestrial or satellite links.

Wi-Fi

A brand name given to wireless LANs that comply with standards as defined and published by the Wi-Fi Alliance. Wi-Fi standards are based on the 802.11 standard.

Wi-Fi Protected Access (WPA)

A security protocol defined by the Wi-Fi Alliance that enables computer devices to periodically obtain a new encryption key. WPA version 1 implements TKIP and WEP, whereas WPA version 2 implements the full 802.11i standard (which includes AES).

WiMAX

A relatively new specification issued by the WiMAX Forum for providing wireless network connectivity within metropolitan areas. WiMAX is based on the IEEE 802.16 standard. The most current version of the standard, IEEE 802.16-2005, addresses both fixed and mobile wireless connectivity. Many of the WiMAX deployments to date use the licensed frequency spectrum. For example, Sprint Nextel is in the process of deploying mobile WiMAX in many major U.S. cities. Some cities deploying Wi-Fi mesh networks use fixed WiMAX for connecting mesh nodes (gateways) to central points in the system. Eventually, WiMAX may replace Wi-Fi as the technology of choice for wireless MANs as more and more client devices become equipped with WiMAX.

Windows Authentication Client

A supplicant built into Microsoft Windows Vista, Windows XP, and Windows Server 2003 for 802.1X authentication using the Extensible Authentication Protocol (EAP). The Microsoft 802.1X Authentication Client uses 802.1X to authenticate Wi-Fi and Ethernet connections by using either EAP-TLS or PEAP. Windows XP Service Pack 1 also supports PEAP-TLS and PEAP-MS-CHAP v2. For native support, the Windows Authentication Client is preferred if you plan to use Windows operating systems on client devices.

Wireless LAN

A type of computer network that satisfies wireless networking needs within the area of a building or large campus. 802.11 and Wi-Fi are popular standards defining wireless LANs.

Wireless MAN

A type of computer network that satisfies wireless networking needs within the area of a city. Wireless MANs make use of 802.16 and proprietary standards.

Wireless mode

The specific wireless standard (or set of standards) that a wireless adapter or access point implements. Many of the client radio manufacturers have implemented multiple-mode radios whereby the radio can interface with a combination of 802.11a, 802.11b, and 80211g networks. If the client radio supports multiple modes, then there will likely be a configuration setting for identifying the combination of network types with which the client radio will interface.

Wireless WAN

A network that satisfies wireless networking needs over a large geographical area, such as a country or the entire world. Satellites offer a means for extending radio signals over a wireless WAN.

WISP (wireless Internet service provider)

A company that offers wireless connection services to the Internet for homes and offices. WISPs often provide wireless access in public wireless LAN hotspots.

wpa_supplicant

A free software implementation of the IEEE 802.11i (WPA2) supplicant for Linux, BSD, and Microsoft Windows.

Index

Index